Reading Portrait Photographs in Proust, Kafka and Woolf

Reading Portrait Photographs in Proust, Kafka and Woolf

Modernism, Media, and Emotion

Marit Grøtta

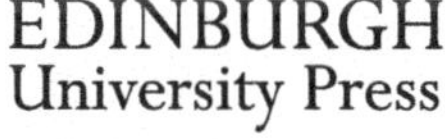

EDINBURGH
University Press

Edinburgh University Press is one of the leading university presses in the UK. We publish academic books and journals in our selected subject areas across the humanities and social sciences, combining cutting-edge scholarship with high editorial and production values to produce academic works of lasting importance. For more information visit our website: edinburghuniversitypress.com

Edinburgh University Press Ltd
13 Infirmary Street
Edinburgh EH1 1LT

First published in hardback by Edinburgh University Press 2024

Typeset in 11/13 Adobe Sabon by
IDSUK (DataConnection) Ltd, and
printed and bound by CPI Group (UK) Ltd,
Croydon, CR0 4YY

A CIP record for this book is available from the British Library

ISBN 978 1 3995 2698 2 (hardback)
ISBN 978 1 3995 2699 9 (paperback)
ISBN 978 1 3995 2700 2 (webready PDF)
ISBN 978 1 3995 2701 9 (epub)

Contents

Figures

Acknowledgments

This book is the outcome of a longstanding fascination with portrait photographs and the ways they are depicted in works of literature. I would like to express my gratitude to all those who have taken an interest in the project as it developed and offered advice, support, and inspiration.

I thank my students for their active participation in my seminars "Faces, Portraits, and Photographs" and "Reading Images," which I taught at the University of Oslo during this period. They made me realize the extent to which the topics of faces and photographs speak to our contemporary lives.

I thank Jean-Michel Rabaté, Kaja Silverman, and Eduardo Cadava for stimulating discussions on photography during my research stay at the University of Pennsylvania in fall 2018. I remain indebted to their insights into the world of photographs. My warmest thanks also to John Durham Peters for inviting me to give a guest lecture on the book's topic at Yale University in fall 2018 and for inspiring dialogues and insightful thoughts.

Next up, I wish to thank photographer and professor Jeannette Christensen at the Oslo National Academy of the Arts for inviting me to engage with her photographic work "Woman interrupted," which gave me aesthetic input and food for thought.

My heartful thanks to Christian Refsum, Tone Selboe, and Kristin Gjesdal for reading and commenting on the manuscript and bringing valuable insights to the project. Further, I thank my research group Temporal Experiments at the University of Oslo for inspiring and constructive exchanges over the years and for allowing me to present the Proust chapter in a workshop during winter 2022. I am also grateful to my colleagues at the Section of Comparative Literature for creating working environments marked by enthusiasm and solidarity, to the Department of Literature Area Studies and European Languages at the University of Oslo for generous support over the years, and to Unifor for funding my research stay at the University of Pennsylvania in 2018.

Not least, I thank the anonymous readers at Edinburgh University Press for their valuable comments and advice and the editors Jackie Jones and Elizabeth Fraser for their generous support and guidance.

The first section of the chapter on Woolf was published as an article in *Journal of Modern Literature* in 2022 under the title "Showing Seeing: The Study of Faces and Portrait Photographs in Virginia Woolf's Early Novels." The first section of the Proust chapter was published as an article in the Norwegian journal *Agora: Journal for metafysisk spekulasjon* in 2016 under the title "Fotografi og følelser: Proust, portrettfotografier og lengselen etter å nå utover seg selv" [Photography and feelings: Proust, portrait photographs and the longing to reach beyond oneself]. I am grateful to the editors for permission to reuse this material.

Introduction: Reading Faces in the Age of Portrait Photography

With the spread of portrait photographs in the modernist period, face studies became more important than ever. Portrait photographs allowed for the reading of faces without the presence of the sitter, inviting close attention to sitters' gazes, gestures, and ways of presenting themselves to the camera. The beholders could feel their enigmatic attraction: a human face taken out of its everyday context; a gaze that seemed to look through the viewer, infinitely out of reach. An almost ghostlike presence, transported by light. Every analog photograph has a history of pairs of eyes looking at it, investing it with emotion: sympathy, love, jealousy, dismay. Such photographs are touched, held, kissed, and tossed away; they are provided with frames or put into albums. They also have a history of fading and decay; over time, they become shaded, tainted, or folded, dissolving between someone's hands or slowly fading in a drawer.

During the decades before and after 1900, the portrait photograph started to appear as a literary motif. Marcel Proust, Franz Kafka, and Virginia Woolf stand out as particularly important in this respect. All of them had personal experiences with portrait photographs and were passionate about the medium. In their work, they reflected upon the phenomenon, depicting how their characters collect, behold, and cherish portrait photographs. Yet they also recognized the disturbing aspects of portrait photographs and paid attention to the difficulty of reading faces, the problem of the unreturned gaze, and the challenge of living with ghostlike doubles. Not least, they employed literature to reflect upon portrait photographs as a medium and the uncertain status of the human face.

This study seeks to explore the role of portrait photographs in the writings of Proust, Kafka, and Woolf and discusses new ways of seeing and understanding the human face in the modernist period. My chief interest lies in the attraction of portrait photographs and their emotional and relational implications. The book offers a comparative study of the motif of contemplating portrait photographs in three modernist writers and discusses the characters' ambivalent responses to the medium. I understand this ambivalence in terms of a historical tension and see the modernists as depicting a new visual era marked by the increased circulation of photographs.

In modernist studies, the fact that modernist literature emerged in a period that witnessed the spread of photographs and film has been acknowledged for some time. However, the role of portrait photographs has received less attention. Indeed, portraits may seem like an untimely topic, associated with realist regimes of representation and nineteenth-century conceptions of subjectivity. With analog portrait photographs, however, a whole series of questions that literally complicate the picture come to the fore: the question of mediation, the interplay of absence and presence, and the imprint of time and death. Early in the twentieth century, the spread of this medium contributed to shaping the contact between individuals and in many respects transformed human relations and the perception of the human face. This affected not only intimate relations such as love relations, family relations, and friendship, but also the perception of strangers, and, more generally, the relation between the private and the public spheres. It should therefore come as no surprise that perceptive writers such as Proust, Kafka, and Woolf took an interest in the phenomenon and explored it in their writings. In my view, this largely neglected topic offers an exciting approach to modernist literature, as it allows us to reconsider central issues related to modernist writing, the new visual culture, and the possibilities for contact, communication, and sympathy early in the twentieth century.

A key question in this regard is how we today should understand the role of the media in the modernist period. Traditionally, modernism has been described in terms of a crisis of communication and community, resulting in isolation and fragmentation. But it would perhaps be more accurate to describe this as a period in which the concepts of communication and connectedness were transformed. The new media played a major role in this undertaking. At the turn of the twentieth century, photographs (as well as telephones) allowed people to connect across time and space and inspired a desire for connectedness and a new notion of "telepresence." Everyday practices related to portrait photography started to profoundly influence social life, such as having one's photograph taken, exchanging photographs, collecting photographs in albums, displaying photographs in interiors, and using photographs as meditation objects. As they started to take over for face-to-face relations, they created feelings of presence, identification, and empathy and engendered affective relations to the medium, but they also caused frustration, dismay, and indifference. My aim is to examine how Proust, Kafka, and Woolf engaged with this situation.

Exploring the attraction of portrait photographs, we should acknowledge that they are not at all simple forms of representation, but rather a seemingly magical blend of flesh and light, of paper and chemistry. They are technical pictures appropriating the traditional genre of portraiture to depict a face and a person. Hence, my examination will not deal with portrait photographs in a narrow sense, but rather the constellation of *photography*, *portraiture*, and *faces*. Faces are in themselves media; we communicate through our faces, through silent miens and discreet gestures, using more than forty facial muscles in what Erving Goffman has called "face work."[1] We respond emotionally to faces; they create sympathy or antipathy, reassure us or trouble us, leave us indifferent or appeal to us, causing interest and desire. On a daily basis, we engage in the reading of faces, and presumably both nurture and nature (both our training and our instincts) play a part in this undertaking. Indeed, this silent communication is part of our most intimate practices. This is also why the human face is one of the most basic motifs in art; the genre of portraiture has a long tradition of depicting and revealing faces, in different aesthetic and cultural regimes. When portrait photographs started to replace painted portraits during the mid-nineteenth century, however, a new series of questions emerged. Photographs seemed to privilege the surface, mechanically reproducing a person's external appearances, and at the same time they caused a fascination that is hard to capture. In my view, the complex relation between faces, portraiture, and photography is key to understand the role of portrait photographs at the turn of the century.

Adding the medium of literature to this constellation makes it even more complex, at least at a theoretical level. Yet the writings of Proust, Kafka, and Woolf allow us to consider the role of portrait photographs within the context of a (literary) life world and thus make it more tangible. Depicting how their characters collect, contemplate, and cherish portrait photographs, these writers explore ambivalent responses to the medium and highlight its fragile status.

1. Goffman, "Face-Work."

In this manner, they foreground the characters' emotional investment in portrait photographs and show how they contribute to forg-
ing and shaping intersubjective bonds. By highlighting the role of
portrait photographs in the early twentieth century, Proust, Kafka,
and Woolf offer profound reflections on the early phase of technical
images and on life with mediated faces.

Today portrait photographs may seem a thing of the past. We have
more modern "face technologies" such as Facebook, Instagram, and
Snapchat, digital platforms that preclude the touching and handling
of images. We also have "machine vision" that does the reading of
faces for us. Indeed, we live in "face societies" marked by an inflation
of faces that matter little to us, be they anonymous faces, media faces,
or celebrity faces. Yet today's negligence of faces is in fact a strong
argument for a renewed consideration on the status of the human face
and the impact of current face technologies. In my view, we still have
much to learn from the era of analog photographs, when mediated
faces first started to make an impact on everyday human relations.
The spread of portrait photographs represented a major break in the
cultural history of the human face, with repercussions that are very
much present in our own time.

In this book, I hope to show that Proust, Kafka, and Woolf may
enable us to better understand the uncertain status of the human face
in modernity (the age of portrait photography) and, subsequently,
to better grapple with the question of the human face today (the age
of Facebook and face recognition technology). More specifically, the
aim of this study is fourfold: it seeks to understand the emotional
and relational role of portrait photographs in the writings of Proust,
Kafka, and Woolf; to come to terms with the uncertain status of the
human face in the modernist period; to comprehend how the spread
of portrait photographs transformed the relation between the private
and the public spheres; and to deepen our understanding of the relation between old and new face technologies.

While I build on previous research, I seek to make a novel argument regarding the contemplation of portrait photographs in Proust,
Kafka, and Woolf. Offering a comparative examination, I focus on
the beholders' emotional engagement with portrait photographs and
their ambivalent responses to such pictures, which often negotiate
between absorption and detachment, between gratification and frustration. My contention is that the writings of Proust, Kafka, and
Woolf uncover the emotional and relational implications of portrait
photographs and suggest how the modernist generation tried to come
to terms with technical images and mediated faces.

Beside these common features, I address the specificity of Proust's, Kafka's, and Woolf's approaches to portrait photographs. I argue that Proust is ultimately interested in the *truth* of portrait photographs; that Kafka's concern is the *power* of portrait photographs, and that Woolf addresses the question of *sympathy* in relation to portrait photographs. Moreover, I suggest that Proust's, Kafka's, and Woolf's ambivalent views on the medium should be related to specific societal changes in their day. Proust's concern with the truth of photographs is marked by the dynamic relation between the private and the public in the age of the illustrated press; Kafka's concern with the power of photographs is marked by the dynamic relation between identity and anonymity in the age of biopolitics; Woolf's concern with sympathy and portrait photographs is marked by the dynamic relation between the familiar and the foreign in the age of globalization.

Looking into these societal contexts, I aim to shed light on a larger issue that seems somewhat ungraspable: how human relations changed in the age of portrait photography. The writings of Proust, Kafka, and Woolf reveal how a set of societal boundaries inherited from the nineteenth century (the private/the public, anonymity/identity, familiar/foreign) started to transmute with the spread of portrait photographs, roughly during the decades before and the decade after 1900. If we can begin to understand the modernist media paradigm, we may also draw a line to our digital media culture, realizing how the modernists' ways of living with technical images and mediated faces both resemble and differs from our mediated lives today.

In the following sections, I outline the historical and theoretical perspectives that are used in this book. I first address the topics of reading *faces*, *portraits*, and *photographs*. Next, I turn to the question of how *literature* looks at portrait photographs, and present, in more detail, my argument regarding the modernist engagement with them.

The Difficulty of Reading Faces

Where does the discourse pertaining to the reading of faces come from? The idea that it is possible to gain knowledge of a person's inner states from their outer countenance reaches back to antiquity, but it first reached prominence through Johann Caspar Lavater's physiognomic studies in the 1770s.[2] Lavater's work inspired a widespread

---

2. Important forerunners were Giambattista della Porta in the sixteenth century and Charles Le Brun in the seventeenth century

practice of reading faces and influenced literature, art, and scientific thought far into the nineteenth century. In *Physiognomic Fragments for Furthering the Knowledge and Love of Man*, published between 1775 and 1778, he developed a quasi-scientific way of reading the human face. In some respects, his approach anticipated the positivist sciences, but it had a strong theological foundation. Lavater believed in the connection between mind and body and searched for the influences of the spirit upon the facial features. He saw the face as a presentation of moral truth revealing the sitter's distance from or closeness to the divine ideal.[3] Further, the impact of Emanuel Swedenborg is particularly interesting; following him, Lavater saw human physiognomy as a form of wordless speech. For Swedenborg, the divine *Ursprache* was physiognomic and transparent, conveying a person's inner thoughts immediately, but after the Fall, man's physiognomy was transformed and his countenance became non-transparent, thus necessitating the invention of word-speech.[4]

However, this study of physiognomic features and moral character depended upon adequate representations of faces, and to that end, an apparatus for the making of silhouettes was put to use. It consisted of a chair and a semitransparent screen placed at the sitter's side that allowed the drawer to see the contours of the head rather than all the details.[5] Hence the silhouettes craze in Lavater's day. This early form of "face technology," facilitating the reading of profiles, can be seen as a pre-photographic technology. Yet traditional portrait paintings were also important for Lavater. Responding to his own question "What is portrait painting?" he asserted that it communicates the image of an individual and thereby depicts something that cannot be conveyed by words. While nature itself is in permanent transformation, portraits allow for time to be brought to a standstill: "It is to me indisputable that better knowledge of man may be obtained from portraits than from nature, she being thus uncertain, thus fugitive."[6] He further compares the countenance to the rather profane theater: "The countenance is the theatre

3. His object of study was the hard parts of the face, that is, the skull and the bones, or rather the shape of the nose and the curve of the front. Awkward as this may sound today, it should be acknowledged that his views included an idea of the growth of character; he considered the bones as moderately malleable and assumed that neither the skull of a man nor his character would be fixed before middle age.

4. Stemmler, "Physiognomical Portraits," 153–5.

5. Stoichita, "Johann Caspar Lavater's 'Essays on Physiognomy,'" 30–1.

6. Lavater, *Essays on Physiognomy*, 172.

on which the soul exhibits itself; here must its emanations be studied and caught."[7]

After Lavater, physiognomic thought influenced portrait painting for a long period, and it also had a strong impact on the depiction of characters in literary fiction from Goethe to Dickens.[8] In the nineteenth century, physiognomic ideas persisted, but were increasingly oriented toward the study of social types and connected with social and political ideas. The craze of *physiologies* in France in the 1840s was an offspring of physiognomic ideas; this literary genre described the different types one could encounter in a Parisian crowd and facilitated the readability of the city.[9] However, physiognomic thought was based on problematic premises, and this contributed to its decline. It inspired phrenology, a quasi-scientific method that claimed to determine an individual's race, character, and intelligence on the basis of skull size and shape. When physiognomic ideas started to become associated with racist ideologies, they were discredited in many circles. Still, such ideas continued to influence fascist and racist ideologies and was used to discriminate and exclude specific groups also in the twentieth century.[10]

It is against this background that the modernists' attempt at reading faces should be seen. For this generation of writers and artists, the face had become a problem—an enigma that could not easily be deciphered. Significant in this respect was the growing interest in the depths of the subject, and the emergence of new and clinical ways of studying individuals. Psychology would become a major field for the study of faces in the twentieth century, and art and literature delved deeply into the problem of the human face.[11] In the modernist period, the reading of faces had become a highly uncertain enterprise, and the genre of portraiture reflected this new situation.

Redefining Portraiture

The inauguration of the National Portrait Gallery in London in 1856 testified to the cult of "great men" that dominated in the nineteenth

---

7. Lavater, *Essays on Physiognomy*, 171.
8. Tytler, *Physiognomy*; Pearl, *About Faces*.
9. Stierle, *La Capitale des signes*; Prendergast, *Paris and the Nineteenth Century*; Pearl, *About Faces*.
10. For an examination of the relation between physiognomy and racial theories, see Gray, *About Face*.
11. The work of Paul Ekman has been important in the field of psychology; see, for instance, Ekman, *Emotions Revealed*.

century, when physiognomic ideas still informed the discourse surrounding portraiture. The modernists took issue with this conception of portraiture, as well as the bourgeois ideals and the realist regime of representation that underpinned them. After Freud, the face was no longer seen as a mirror of the soul. On the one hand, the modernist period represents the decline of portrait painting; there was no longer a strong interest in depicting people according to bourgeois standards, and new currents such as impressionism, cubism, and abstraction undermined the former conventions of portrait paintings. On the other hand, the art of portraiture was reinvented in this period; a new way of depicting faces took form that challenged or blocked the "inner life" associated with portrait painting. In the paintings of Édouard Manet, Paul Cézanne, Pablo Picasso, Vanessa Bell, and Chaim Soutine, for example, the beholder was confronted with faces that were variously blank, blurred, disfigured, erased, or grotesque. A case in point is Manet's *In the Conservatory* from 1878–79, portraying a woman whose face is blank and utterly inaccessible for her male companion. The blank face does not offer itself for reading, and it does not express an inner state; the eyes have ceased to be a window of the soul. As Jonathan Crary has argued, the "disengagement of perception" from a model of interiority is important in Manet's work. His faces are marked by "casual amorphousness" and no longer disclose interiority and self-reflection.[12] These works show how a "crisis of the face" emerged in modernist portraiture.

In theories of portraiture, the relation between inner life and outer appearances is described in different ways. G. W. F. Hegel saw the genre of portraiture as reflecting an ideal midway between spirit and exteriority, stressing that a portrait should not be too concerned with external similarity but convey a person's "spiritual personality." Rather than losing himself in naturalistic details, the painter should use his imagination to paint a total picture of a person's inner spirit. When this was achieved, the portrait would be truer than the corresponding face; it would give a "conception of spiritual vitality unlike what a face actually confronting us gives."[13] This means that the portrait for Hegel has a revelatory function; it reveals a person's spirit to the beholder and in that manner gives a *true* picture of a person.

The relation between exteriority and interiority (or the mind–body problem) is also at the heart of contemporary philosopher Cynthia Freeland's *Portraits and Persons*. She asserts that a portrait

12. Crary, *Suspensions of Perception*, 83; 92.
13. Hegel, *Aesthetics 2*, 866.

must show three things: a recognizable, physical body, signs of inner life, and an awareness of the depicting process from both subject and artist.[14] Her definition nicely captures several aspects of that which makes a portrait interesting to look at; not merely a person's outer countenance, but also how it depicts a person's self-awareness and inner life. Yet it may seem particularly suited to describe traditional portraits, and one may ask to what degree it is underpinned by Hegelian and physiognomic ideals rather than modernist views of portraiture. To understand the ways in which a portrait communicates, we may need to complicate the basic model for thinking about the genre, and to this purpose, Jean-Luc Nancy's perspectives in *Portrait* are helpful.[15]

Nancy's thinking is premised upon the critique of the metaphysics of presence sustaining Western conceptions of subjectivity. In keeping with this, he reflects on portraiture in terms of an ontology of the subject and stresses the convergence between the history of the portraiture and the history of the subject. He helpfully proposes that the subject is never fully present and makes itself known through a play of absence and presence (the sacred is the model for this mode). Accordingly, portraiture does not simply seek to give presence to someone absent, but to provide access to absence and to a process through which a self-relation is established. In this regard, the gaze plays a major role in the portrait. For Nancy, the gaze is a departure from the subject and an opening toward the world and the beholder; it is through this opening that the subject becomes subject. In looking, the subject is itself at stake, and it is this troublesome self-relation that is depicted in the portrait. Nancy sees the beholder as implicated in this endeavor. Because the look of the sitter is doubled by the "look" of the portrait as such (the total construction of the painter), the portrait engages the beholder in an exchange of looks, opening up the possibility of an encounter. Refusing the interiority model, Nancy insists that this all takes place on a surface level and describes the portrait in terms of exposure. Thus Nancy abandons the understanding of portraiture in terms of representation and identity in favor of the notion of portraiture as presentation (of an absence) and otherness (as the premise of subjectivity). This way of thinking is in my view well suited for the modernist paradigm.

In *Face and Mask: A Double History*, art historian Hans Belting is equally skeptical toward the idea of the face as a guarantee of

14. Freeland, *Portraits and Persons.*
15. Nancy, *Portrait.*

"presence" and subjectivity.[16] His overall perspective for thinking about faces is the cultural history of masks, which he sees as testifying to an inherent split in the history of faces. With the advent of portrait photography, this split became decisive, he asserts, because the face and its representation no longer belong to a shared situation. With the era of technological reproducibility, the representation thus takes on a life on its own. This perspective allows us to recognize how the advent of portrait photographs represented a break in the cultural history of the face while also reinforcing more traditional problems pertaining to ways of representing and perceiving the face.

These considerations make it apparent that the genre of portraiture puts into play a number of philosophical questions: not only the relation between interiority and exteriority (mind and body), but also the ontology of the subject, the infinity of the human face, the dialogic gaze, and the ways in which art makes these questions tangible. Not least, they demonstrate the complexity of our efforts to read the face of a portrait photograph.

Faces, Gazes, and Visual Technology

The advent of photography created new conditions for thinking about portraiture. The new technology made the sitter's face shine forth with an uncanny presence, as if the medium of light had been harnessed to make teleportation possible. Yet photographic technology also turned the art of portraiture into a mechanical process, replacing the synthetic work of the painter with a procedure involving chemistry, technology, and light. For the first time, the human face could now be reproduced and circulated at a low cost. Moreover, they had a format that allowed them to be held between two hands, which created a new intimacy between the sitter and the beholder.

In the history of photography, however, the role of portrait photographs in private life has been downgraded, perhaps because the spread of photographs in public life seemed more consequential.[17] Yet

16. Belting, *Face and Mask*.
17. For a discussion of how the role of photographs in private life has been neglected in the history of photography, see Sandbye, "Looking at the Family Photo Album." For a study of photographic practices as part of an ideology cultivating family relations and intimacy, see Hirsch, *Family Frames*. Other important contributions to the study of photography in the private sphere are Bourdieu, *Photography*; Langford, *Suspended Conversations*; Batchen, *Forget Me Not*.

with the "affective turn" in the humanities, we should be able to see the role of portrait photographs in a new light.[18] As Mark Goble has argued, the modernists showed a remarkable love of and affection for the new media (telephones, telegraphs, and phonographs) in their writings.[19] Similarly, in the medium of portrait photography, the modernists found a form of communication that was not about the transmission of messages, but about quiet forms of sharing, taking part, or being in touch—as in a secular prayer, one might say.[20]

One of the most lucid comments on the emotional aspects of photography was published by Walter Benjamin in 1931, and some of his perspectives deserve to be recapitulated in this context. In "Little History of Photography," Benjamin looked back at the rise and fall of portrait photography, seeing it as paralleling the rise and fall of the bourgeoisie. He discusses the transition from the first, "naïve" decades after 1839 to the period that saw its industrialization and commercialization (1860/1870 onward). Benjamin stresses how the first generation of sitters were marked by a certain integrity and naivety; having not yet learned how to pose, they confidently look into the camera. He notes that the "human countenance had a silence about it in which the gaze rested" and that they were "shyly drawing back into their private space."[21] Because of the long exposure time, they would slowly grow into the picture, which would gain a synthetic quality and thus resemble paintings rather than snapshots. This is why he claimed that these portraits still had "an aura about them." In his 1936 artwork essay, Benjamin makes this point explicit: "In the fleeting expression of a human face, the aura beckons from early photography for the last time."[22] This aura would disappear as soon as photographic technology became more perfected, and the sitters learned how to control their appearances. Also interesting are Benjamin's reflections on the sitter's feeling of alienation before the camera (in his 1940 essay on Baudelaire): "What was inevitably felt to be inhuman [. . .] in daguerreotypy was

18. Writers such as Eve K. Sedgwick, Silvan Tomkins, Sianne Ngai, Roland Barthes, and Deleuze and Guattari have contributed to the "affective turn" in the humanities.
19. Goble, *Beautiful Circuits*, 19.
20. As John Durham Peters explains, the word "communication" has several significations, and one of them is about partaking, that is, "belonging to a social body via an expressive act that requires no response or recognition." For a discussion of this broad definition of communication, see Peters, *Speaking into the Air*, 7.
21. Benjamin, "Little History of Photography," 279; 286.
22. Benjamin, "The Work of Art," 27.

the (prolonged) looking into the camera, since the camera records our likeness without returning our gaze. Inherent in the gaze, however, is the expectation that it will be returned by that on which it is bestowed."[23] Stressing this expectation to have one's gaze returned, Benjamin makes the "unreturned gaze" emblematic of the modern experience as such. In this manner, he links up with Georg Simmel's claims about the prevalence of the blasé face in the modern cities, but he specifically addresses the new media context.[24]

This way of connecting faces, gazes, visual technology, and literature is in my view tremendously fruitful, and I fully subscribe to Benjamin's claim about Baudelaire's pioneering role.[25] In the following chapters, however, I wish to show that experiences with portrait photographs were more fully described in the generation of writers that followed Baudelaire and who were, in fact, closer to Benjamin's own time. In the writings of Proust, Kafka, and Woolf, we find scenes involving photographs and faces as well as remarkably nuanced depictions of what it was like to live in the age of photography. A study of these writings may allow us to complicate the ideas of the waning of the aura, the unreturned gaze, and the experience of beholding a portrait photograph at the beginning of the century. It may also allow us to discuss various aspects of the photographic culture that emerged early in the twentieth century, when the "industrialization" of photography had made its mark.

In addition to Benjamin, Roland Barthes's influential *Camera Lucida* (1980) is a key reference for discussions of the contemplation of photographs, and his attention to his mother's childhood photograph, together with a tacit influence from Proust, links his perspectives to the modernist period.[26] Offering a phenomenological approach, he describes ways of being affected by photographs, and, just like Benjamin, he pays close attention to how the sitters present themselves to the camera. When he describes what he finds moving in the childhood photograph of his mother, he points to her "naïve attitude" and "sovereign innocence." Referring to other photographs of her, he observes that she "'lent' herself to the photograph" and acted

23. Benjamin, "On Some Motifs in Baudelaire," 204.
24. Simmel, "The Metropolis and Modern Life."
25. I discuss Baudelaire's engagement with various nineteenth-century media, including photography, in my previous book, Grøtta, *Baudelaire's Media Aesthetics: The Gaze of the* Flâneur *and 19th-century Media*.
26. Also important is his plan for a seminar on Proust and photography at the Collège de France, which I will discuss in the Proust chapter; see Barthes, "Proust and Photography."

"*with discretion*," not struggling with her image and not supposing herself.[27] This trustful way of placing oneself in front of the camera seems to differ from the paradox of the "photographic look," which Barthes describes later. This is a look that is directed toward the lens but holds something back and thus appears to see without seeing: "It is because the look, eliding the vision, seems held back by something interior. [. . .] In fact, he is looking at nothing; he *retains* within himself his love and his fear: that is the Look."[28] The attraction of the photograph thus stems from a paradox: the look of the sitter is exposed but, at the same time, withdraws. Barthes here describes how a sitter must balance the demands of the camera with one's own integrity and how a photograph involves both "showing and hiding."

The photograph's ability to capture something secretive and semi-invisible and to expose it was key to the first vogue of theoretical reflections on photography and film. The new visual media were seen as bringing about a new vision and as inculcating an increased visual awareness. Portrait photographs reproduced faces with a new accuracy, capturing significant details such as gazes, gestures, and micro-expressions. Film close-ups zoomed in on the human face and revealed micro-movements as they unfolded over sequences in time. These media invited face studies and allowed the face to shine forth with a new valence. Whereas László Moholy-Nagy in 1925 claimed that photography allowed us to see the world with entirely different eyes, Benjamin a few years later described how the medium made the "optical unconscious" visible to us.[29] Moreover, Béla Balázs was concerned with how silent film made man visible *again*. In *Visible Man* (1924), he saw the film medium as countering the abstract and conceptual culture of print and promoting bodily expressiveness and visual sensitivity. Techniques such as the close-up and prolonged attention to gestures allowed for a close study of a person's intimate face and body language, revealing a world of micro-physiognomy that could not be seen with the naked eye. For Balázs, the expressivity of the facial close-up articulated a psychic disposition and connected the body and the mind, the outer and the inner states.[30]

---

27. Barthes describes her attitude in the following manner: "The distinctness of her face, the naïve attitude of her hands, the place she had docilely taken without either showing or hiding herself, and finally her expression [. . .] all this constituted the figure of a sovereign *innocence*." Barthes, *Camera Lucida*, 69.
28. Barthes, *Camera Lucida*, 113.
29. Moholy-Nagy, *Malerei, Fotografie, Film*; Benjamin, "Little History of Photography." See also Gunning's essay on film and physiognomy, "In Your Face".
30. Steimatsky, *The Face on Film*, 32.

The close-up thus represented the "lyrical essence" of film and transcended ordinary forms of communication.[31]

An important feature of photography and film theories in this period was to see mediation as a form of revelation and mediated images as lessons in seeing, inducing visual literacy and making people conscious of the world surrounding them. In this manner, photography and film theory would engage in ontological questions and would have a say in what we perceive to be real. Film historian Tom Gunning describes this as early cinema's "gnostic mission."[32] Photography and film would make human beings visible, enhance human expressivity, and give lessons in facial and gestural communication. My claim is that Proust's, Kafka's, and Woolf's fascination with portrait photography is in various ways related to this experience of a new visibility and a heightened affective state. These writers were not committed to the writing of theory but offered important insights about the new media situation in a literary form.

Literature Looks at Portrait Photographs

After these introductory perspectives on faces, portraits, and photographs, let us now consider how they might be relevant for modernist writings. As I will show, Proust, Kafka, and Woolf all use the contemplation of portrait photographs as a leitmotif and thus tease out the emotional and relational implications of the new medium. Yet they address the topic of portrait photographs in subtle ways rather than through grand gestures.

Examining this motif we should acknowledge that the literary attention to faces and photographs is part of an endeavor to find a new epistemological founding for literary characters.[33] If we look at

31. Balázs, *Early Film Theory*, 37
32. Gunning, "In Your Face." In a similar vein, Noël Carroll takes early film theory to be exploring the philosophical and ontological aspects of film and considers this a major drive behind the renewed interest in these theories. See Carroll, "Béla Balázs." Kaja Silverman has pursued a related approach with respect to photography, proposing to rethink the history of photography in terms of analogy and revelation, seeing photography not as a technology but rather as a mode in which the world reveals itself to us. See Silverman, *Miracle of Analogy*. Recent tendencies in media theory thus take their inspiration from early theories on film and photography, acknowledging their pioneering work.
33. Already in the nineteenth century, portrait photographs were used by novelists to carve out new ideas about the subject, to some degree anticipating twentieth-century (post-Freud) conceptions of the self. See Rugg, *Picturing Ourselves*; Blackwood, *The Portrait's Subject*.

the nineteenth-century novel, for instance Balzac and Dickens, we find that the depiction of characters and human faces was influenced by physiognomic thought and a belief that it was possible to read people's inner feeling through their outer features. As the physiognomic paradigm collapsed, along with the simplistic signification model that it relied upon, the modernists offered character descriptions that subverted the idea that it was possible to reach an interior through the exterior.[34] Sensitive to new ideas about the subject circulating in their day, they problematized the very idea of a "self" and explored new ways of depicting characters.[35] In modernist novels, we read about blank faces, unreadable faces, and faces that express emotions in complex ways. Moreover, we find scenes in which the characters study faces in photographs, trying to figure out the "enigma" of the other, remaining intrigued, captivated, or confused, by the picture. Such scenes not only depict a character's difficulty in reading a face in a photograph; they also depict how a character is affected by the picture. They thus suggest that the picture has the power to create hesitation, instability and affect in the beholder.

Furthermore, we should see this engagement with faces and photographs as part of a widespread tendency in modernist literature: an increased interest in visual phenomena and visuality as such. In a situation when "the interior" (the psyche) is considered unreliable and language is seen as deceitful, vision appears to represent an alternative mode, seemingly closer to truth. Drawing on the visual and gestural language of photography and film, Proust, Kafka, and Woolf often prioritize visual descriptions over narrative development.[36] They offer *ekphrastic* depictions of portrait photographs, literary *close-ups* of faces, and, not the least, they use the technique of *showing seeing*, that is, literary scenes that foreground the visual

34. Yet the understanding of physiognomy could be complex; sometimes a mocking tone marked a distance to physiognomic ideas or served to ascribe such ideas to specific characters. See Pearl, *About Faces*; Pawlikowska, *Anti-Portraits*.
35. Virginia Woolf's renowned essay "Modern Fiction" testifies to this endeavor. On modernist characters (especially Woolf) and the lack of a "self," see Deleuze and Guattari, *What is Philosophy?* and Rabaté, *The Pathos of Distance*. For an overall discussion of the notion of "character," see Anderson, Felski, and Moi, *Character*, and especially Anderson's discussion of Woolf.
36. W. J. T. Mitchell's work on ekphrasis is illuminating as to the ways in which visual and literary elements interact. See Mitchell, *Picture Theory*. Louise Hornby's *Still Modernism* contributes more specifically to our understanding of the role of photography and film in modernist literature, in particular with respect to the dynamic between photographic stillness and filmatic movement. See Hornby, *Still Modernism*.

activity of the characters.[37] Using these techniques, they show how their characters study other people's ways of appearing, paying close attention to the play of faces, gazes, and gestures. By way of photographs and detailed visual descriptions, they convey an idea of silence and speechlessness, even if this is conveyed through language. Thus, Proust, Kafka, and Woolf foreground the silent expressiveness of faces, highlighting the relation between the visible and the invisible, the said and the unsaid.

Now, the modernists' ways of creating literary characters have been widely explored in modernist studies, and so has the visual language of modernist novels. Moreover, the modernists' interest in photographs has been documented and discussed from a number of perspectives, especially in relation to Proust.[38] In this book, I build on the existing body of research, but I offer a specific argument regarding the contemplation of portrait photographs, and I present a redescription of a series of tensions marking the period. My contention is that Proust, Kafka, and Woolf explore the emotional and relational implications of portrait photographs, attentive to the sitters' gazes, gestures, and ways of presenting themselves. In their writings, the reading of portrait photographs is thus embedded in emotional issues and a wish to connect with the person in the photograph. More specifically, I argue that their writings on portrait photographs are characterized by five (interrelated) features.

First, these writers describe *the attraction of portrait photographs* and show how such pictures invite prolonged attention. Portrait photographs act on the beholder and elicit an array of emotions in the characters. As a consequence, the beholder engages physically with the portrait photographs, touching them, kissing them, and caring for them. Exploring the relation between the portrait photographs and the beholder, Proust, Kafka, and Woolf suggest that such pictures are active, not passive, and they affect the beholder in profound ways.

Second, Proust, Kafka, and Woolf depict responses to portrait photographs that are marked by *emotional ambivalence*. On the

---

37. Mitchell uses the term "showing seeing" to name a pedagogical exercise in visual studies; a version of the show-and-tell exercise in which the object of the performance is "the process of seeing itself." Mitchell, "Showing Seeing," 176. The aim of the exercise is to make students pay attention to that which is usually taken for granted in visual processes. Although I use the term "showing seeing" in a difference sense, seeing it as a literary technique, I am indebted to Mitchell's overall project.

38. I engage with previous research in the three main chapters on Proust, Kafka, and Woolf respectively.

one hand, they describe an emotional investment in portrait photographs, a desire for connectedness and feelings of joy and passion. On the other hand, they highlight the difficulty of reading faces, the experience of the unreturned gaze, and feelings of frustration or indifference. This emotional ambivalence, I argue, is related to the uncertain status of such pictures in the modernist period. Moreover, this ambivalence is often highlighted in scenes in which the act of looking passes through several stages.

Third, they depict the *paradoxical* modus operandi of photographic pictures; they both show and hide, reveal and conceal. On the one hand, such photographs make visible a person's pose, gaze, and gestures; on the other hand, they are marked by silence and opacity. Portrait photographs allow the beholder to study a play of absence and presence and a self that is in play, but the sitter still remains an enigma to the beholder.

Fourth, Proust, Kafka, and Woolf depict how the study of portrait photographs serve as *lessons in otherness*. Portrait photographs create an increased awareness of the relation between self and other and demonstrate the impossibility of penetrating the mind of the person in the photograph. This can be understood as a learning process in which the characters (in various ways and to various degrees) learn to live with mediated connections and, moreover, to relate to other human beings as "outsides" (and not simply as "masks" or "projections"). This, in turn, affects the beholder's sense of self and may lead to uncertainty as well as thoughtfulness.

Fifth, they depict how the characters' repeated encounters with portrait photographs serve to develop (various levels of) *visual literacy*. The characters must learn to balance immersion and detachment, or sympathy and indifference. This suggests how visual competence evolved early in the twentieth century, paving the way for more analytical and trained ways of relating to photographs—perhaps at the expense of more sensitive and more complex ways of relating to photographs.

If these are the key features characterizing the modernists' ways of engaging with portrait photographs, there are also significant differences between the three writers; indeed, their reflections on portrait photographs appear as integrated in their overall literary projects. Examining the writings of Proust, Kafka, and Woolf in three consecutive chapters, I attempt both to tease out their common features and to explore their distinctive approach to photographs. I argue that Proust is concerned with the *truth* of photographs, that Kafka explores the *power* of photographs, and that Woolf studies the question of *sympathy* in relation to photographs. In their own way, these writers inquire into the possibilities of photographs at a time when the status of such pictures is changing.

Private and Public Faces

Up to now I have focused mainly on the contemplation of portrait photographs that takes place within the private circle, but in the modernist period photographed faces appeared also in other settings. Of course, Proust, Kafka, and Woolf were highly conscious of the changing environments for portrait photographs and sensitive to the various contexts of the photographs they described, so contextual factors need to be taken into consideration. We may distinguish roughly between four photographic contexts, keeping in mind that photographs travel easily from one context to another, as do the ideas, emotions, affects, and habits pertaining to them. First, as already explained, the exchange of portrait photographs between family members, lovers, friends, and acquaintances was a common social practice marking private and semiprivate life in the decades before and after 1900. Portrait photographs were the "social media" of the modernist period, connecting people and creating affective responses. Alfred Lichtwark testified to this when he claimed in 1907 that "[i]n our age there is no work of art that is looked at so closely as a photograph of oneself, one's closest relatives and friends, one's sweetheart."[39] Portraits were chosen by beholders and arranged in personal albums or collections, where they could be touched and looked at repeatedly by the owner. This photographic practice created feelings of identification, sympathy, and connectedness and brought about a love of the medium.

Second, during the years 1880–1914, photographs also found their ways into magazines and newspapers and thus became a part of public life. Accordingly, new structural conditions for photography were established as the "control of the image" was relocated from individual photographers to large manufacturers and the press.[40] This led to an important change in the viewers' relation to images; photographs in newspaper and magazine images were now selected

---

39. Benjamin, "Little History of Photography," 287. Benjamin's quotation is taken from Lichtwark's introduction to Fritz Matthies-Masuren, *Künstlerische Photographie. Entwicklung und Einfluss in Deutschland*, 16.
40. Marien, *Photography*, 173.

by professionals and had a short lifespan.[41] This changed the sitters' influence over the pictures that were taken of them; their faces could now appear in public contexts beyond their control and circulate widely without their consent. The radical novelty of having one's face published in the public is revealed in the debates over "the right to one's own image" which emerged in Germany early in the twentieth century. The public circulation of photographed faces was by many perceived as a breach of privacy that called for juridical regulation.[42] Certainly, many individuals contributed to the public circulation of faces by having "official" photographs taken of themselves, especially those who aspired to celebrity, but the point is that the distribution of images and the power relations changed drastically.

Third, photographs were in this period increasingly used for identification purposes and clinical studies, with influence from physiognomic ideas. By means of photography, police records documented the face of each suspect, felon, and outlaw, thus mapping the population and facilitating a series of disciplinary mechanisms. Photographs were also used in quasi-scientific projects to document various clinical conditions (such as hysteria), thus objectivizing the subjects and putting them in categories.[43] Not least, portrait photographs were used to map national types, from nineteenth-century photographs from the colonies to German photographic projects during the interwar years.[44] In this manner, photography was used to reduce human beings to narrow identities in order to discriminate and exclude those who fell outside of a specific norm. Influenced by Michel Foucault's work, contemporary scholarship has uncovered the normative and often racist motivations of such practices.[45]

Fourth, we find a cosmopolitan way of thinking about photography, which grew increasingly after the First World War. Claims about the revelatory potential of photography and film often went hand in hand with universalist, cosmopolitan, or global-scale visions,

41. Marien, *Photography*, 241.
42. Andriopoulos, "Terror of Reproduction," 153.
43. However, the documentary value of such photographs can be contested insofar as the photographed person was often playing out certain effects corresponding to the expectations of the photographer (consciously or unconsciously). See, for instance, Prodger, "Photography and the Expression of the Emotion" for an illuminating discussion of Darwin's use of photography.
44. See Stetler, *Stop Reading! Look!* for a discussion of the vogue for portrait photography in the Weimar Republic and various takes on "Germanness."
45. See Finn, *Capturing the Criminal Image*; Hamilton and Hargreaves, *The Beautiful and the Damned.*

where photography and film were seen as world languages that could potentially unite human beings. Such ideas were adopted in a number of cosmopolitan and socialist projects (such as Albert Kahn's photographic archive and August Sander's photography books), as well as a number of international organizations (such as the United Nation and affiliated institutions).[46] Their visions were grounded on the idea that the gaze of the camera offers a non-subjective view of the world, transcends language barriers, and gives access to a shared experience. Photographer August Sander's radio talk "Photography as a World Language" [Photographie als Weltsprache] (1931) testifies to this, as does Balázs's belief in film as an international means of communication capable of serving a coming "people of the world."[47]

The extensive use of photographed faces in commercial, governmental, and cosmopolitan contexts created uncertainty in the viewing situation and incited a learning process in spectators; they would need to further their visual competence and learn to process an abundance of pictures of people they did not know. We may venture to say that the increased circulation of mediated faces triggered a reconfiguration of societal boundaries. The face now transgressed the boundaries of the private world and started to circulate more widely, independent of the sitter. This media change is important because face-to-face encounters are basic to human relations, and the possibility of mediated faces—or "traveling" faces—transforms these relations. In my

46. The League of Nations was loosely associated with the philanthropist Albert Kahn's global photographic project "Archives de la Planète" (1908–31), documenting the ways in which people lived all around the world and aiming to promote internationalism and peace. See Amad, *Counter-Archive*, 102; Bjorli and Jakobsen, *Cosmopolitics of the Camera*. Further, the United Nations has since its inception used photographic campaigns (photographs displayed on exhibition boards) to promote global understanding, from the "Know Your United Nation" campaign in 1947 onward. As Susan Sontag has pointed out, Edward Steichen's photography exhibition *The Family of Man* (1955) can be considered in the same perspective. See Sontag, *On Photography*, 32. Moreover, the link between peace work and photography was made visible in 1974, when the International Photographic Council was created, an organization officially associated with the UN. Its motto was "Peace through Understanding, Understanding through Photography, the Universal Language."

47. Sander, "Photography as a Universal Language"; Carroll, "Béla Balázs," 60. Closer to our day, we find theoretical support for such an approach to photography and film in Vilém Flusser's theories. Flusser argued that the era of individuality had ended with the advent of photography and claimed that the new visual culture broke through the shelf of individuality in order to penetrate "the territory of intersubjectivity." Flusser, *Into Immaterial Culture*.

view, the increased circulation of portrait photographs outside of the boundaries of the private circle is key to understanding the ambivalent views on portrait photographs in Proust, Kafka, and Woolf. Using the motif of portrait photographs, they depict how human relations started to change in a new media age.

Theories of Faces and Photographs

The question that emerges is what theoretical perspectives might be fitting to grasp this photographic complexity, especially with respect to understanding the relational and emotional implications of portrait photographs. I have already pointed to a few theoretical approaches that to my mind are illuminating, but the question deserves a more explicit discussion. In theories of faces and photographs, we may distinguish roughly between, on the one hand, critical approaches and, on the other, phenomenological and affective approaches. These are often perceived as opposites, even if they typically refer to different kinds of photographs and to different photographic contexts. Critical media theories often target pictures used for commercial and scientific (or quasi-scientific) purposes, whereas affective and phenomenological approaches more often address the solitary contemplation of portrait photographs. (Needless to say, these boundaries are not clear-cut.) Even if it seems that critical and phenomenological/affective perspectives clash in debates on photographed faces, however, both may help us understand ambivalences in the beholder, various degrees of visual literacy, and, not least, historical change. Let us take a quick look at some influential theoretical positions (without attempting to cover the whole field):

An important influence is Emmanuel Levinas's writings on the face as the silent appeal of the other, imploring the beholder to acknowledge the difference of the other and inspiring compassion, respect, and sympathy. As the encounter with the other is—in its authentic form—affective and pre-discursive, the face affects us without us being conscious of it, he asserts.[48] However, Levinas maintains that an authentic face cannot be captured in a picture, as pictures (and vision as such) works to reduce alterity, and he thus discards a media perspective. We find similar perspectives in Giorgio Agamben's essay "The Face," which is influenced by Levinas and Martin Heidegger.

48. Levinas, *Totality and Infinity*, 199–200.

Agamben attempts to move beyond ideas of authenticity and interiority, acknowledging that the face is never transparent and must be seen in terms of exteriority. He asserts that the face is the place where human beings are exposed to one another—while at the same time hiding: "The face is at once the irreparable being-exposed of humans and the very opening in which they hide and stay hidden."[49] However, he also points to the ways in which appearance today has become a problem for human beings, who want to "take possession" of their own appearance.[50] Appearance is human beings' condition of existence, he asserts, just like language, and the face is not exposing something specific, but rather exposing its own status as a medium; its own communicability.[51] With Agamben, we can thus see the face as a threshold involving both showing and hiding, and we can see appearance as human beings' troublesome condition of existence.

In this line of thought, gestures play an important role, as they reveal a way of appearing, and to throw light on the role of gestures both in private and social life, Agamben quotes the German critic Max Kommerell (who was Benjamin's contemporary):

> However compelling it may be for an Other, gesture never exists only for him; indeed, only insofar as it also exists for itself can it be compelling for the Other. Even a face that is never witnessed has its mimicry; and it is very much a question as to which gestures leave an imprint on its physical appearance, those through which he makes himself understood with others or, instead, those imposed on him by solitude and inner dialogue. A face often seems to tell us the history of solitary moments.[52]

This means that gestures are not only part of our interaction with others, but also part of our interaction with ourselves and therefore something very private. Still, we carry with us these gestures when we show our faces to others, and in this manner, we make visible features of our private lives—the life of thought and emotion—to others.

When Agamben turns to photography, these reflections on faces and gestures are crucial, as are also Benjamin's pioneering work on

---

49. Agamben, "The Face," 91.
50. Agamben, "The Face," 91.
51. The problem of mediation is thus transposed to being generally; hence, Agamben's interest in *gestures*, *styles*, *modes of being*, and *forms-of-life*. Denouncing essentialist approaches to "life," Agamben argues in favor of a *modal ontology*. See Agamben, *Use of Bodies*.
52. Agamben, "Kommerell," 78.

the medium.[53] Agamben points to an intimate connection between gestures and photography, stressing how gestures are made visible in a photograph as contractions of time, giving weight to a whole life.[54] For Agamben, there is an ethical imperative in photographs of this kind, imploring the beholder to acknowledge and remember the person in the photograph.

Similar aspects are accentuated in Barthes's phenomenological study of photographs, but without Benjamin and Agamben's messianic undertones. Stressing how photographs may capture someone's "air"—that is, their way of being—he points to that which attracts us in a photograph. He compares the contemplation of such photographs with human prayer, observing that one often beholds them in privacy and that this is an altogether intimate affair.[55] For Barthes, such photographs attest to absence—to those who have lived and "that which has been"—and is closely connected to time and death. Depicting the experience of contemplating portrait photographs, he speaks of the feeling of being touched by the "radiation" from a real body, comparing this to the delayed rays from a star.[56] Barthes thus envisions photographic technology as a cosmology in which persons may connect across time and place.[57]

However, other theoretical perspectives invite more skeptical ways of thinking about faces and photographs, and important in this regard is the critique of the "face" as guarantee for humanist values. Countering Levinas's view of the face as a primordial ethical appeal, Gilles Deleuze and Félix Guattari see the face as a historical construction used by the white man to assume superiority and implore all "others" to "assume a face."[58] Seeing "faciality" as a placeholder for key ideas about the Western subject, they call for a defacialization to unleash the forces that are bound up in facialization processes. Yet they assert that this process is extremely difficult and that a dismantling of the face would have to start in the middle of the face itself.

53. See, especially, Benjamin's discussion of Davis Octavius Hill's Newhaven fishwife photographs. Benjamin, "Little History of Photography."
54. Agamben, "Judgment Day," 24. I will come back to this essay in the Proust chapter.
55. Barthes, *Camera Lucida*, 97. See Sarah Sentilles, "The Photograph as Mystery" on Barthes's use of theological language in the book.
56. Barthes, *Camera Lucida*, 80–1.
57. We should not forget Barthes' critical perspective on mediated faces in illustrated magazines. See Barthes, "The Face of Garbo."
58. Deleuze and Guattari, *A Thousand Plateaus*, 167–91.

In this context, they refer to the immense joy and desire with which painters have used the face of Christ, thus suggesting that defacialization has a long tradition in painting. Portrait photographs, however, are a different story for Deleuze and Guattari, although not completely. In keeping with their critique of faciality, they consider portrait photographs as devices that bind up desire. But photographs can also work in the opposite direction and unleash desire through a process of proliferation. Interestingly, they find both processes at work in Kafka's fiction.[59]

Also important is Susan Sontag's critique of the practices of looking that emerge in a photographic culture. With the spread of cameras and photographs, people got used to looking at others from a distant and safe position, she asserts, thus furthering detachment and indifference in the spectator.[60] Sontag also offers a critique of the media's ways of covering war and suffering, and the widespread belief that pictures of people suffering foster empathy. Referring to Woolf's "Three Guineas," she counters the naïve universalism that often underpins "humanitarian" views of photography and claims that specific and conflicting positions must be recognized.[61] However, a different approach to the question of empathy is found in Ulrich Beck's study of the globalization processes after the Second World War, *Cosmopolitan Vision* (2006). Beck asserts that, due to the advent of the visual media, "the spaces of our emotional imagination have expanded in a transnational sense," leading to a globalization of emotions and inducing

59. Deleuze and Guattari, *Kafka*, 4; 61.
60. Sontag, *On Photography*. The widespread tendency to objectivize the other in modern visual culture is also the concern of Laura Mulvey, who has taken issue with "the male gaze" as a visual norm, that is, a gaze that sees women as objects of male desire. Mulvey, "Visual Pleasure and Narrative Cinema." Although her argument mainly pertains to film (and the whole cinematic apparatus), it has influenced discussion on photographic gazes, as well.
61. Sontag, *Regarding the Pain of Others*. Similar questions are addressed by Luc Boltanski, who discusses "distant suffering," that is, our responses to the suffering of others as presented through the media, both photographs (such as slave photographs) and television. Offering philosophical perspectives, he asserts that the bourgeoisie is, in fact, grounded in a "politics of pity," with the aim of establishing a just society. Discussing various modes of the politics of pity, Boltanski addresses the "crisis of pity" he sees a marking our day and envisions a way out of this crisis. Boltanski, *Distant Suffering*. Allan Sekula, too, offers a profound critique of the idea of photography as a universal language; see Sekula, "The Traffic in Photographs."

cosmopolitan empathy.[62] To support his argument, Beck refers briefly to the impact of television images, cinema, and mass media, but he does not mention the medium of photography or the period *before* the Second World War. Yet it could be argued that the globalization of emotions started with the worldwide spread of photographs at the beginning of the twentieth century, that is, the age of Proust, Kafka, and Woolf. And while we may acknowledge, with Beck, that the globalization of images in some contexts may have created "cosmopolitan empathy," we may concede, with Sontag, that such tendencies did not erase the differences in positions, interests, and ways of looking. To some degree, these perspectives are complementary and may help us understand various historical and cultural situations.

These debates demonstrate that the human face—and the mediated face in particular—is fervently disputed today and remind us that it cannot be considered independent of the existent power and media structures. One may even venture to say that the face is up for grabs. But even if it may seem that critical and phenomenological/affective perspectives clash in these debates, we find more complex positions once we look behind the slogans. Both Agamben and Deleuze and Guattari in fact acknowledge the dual forces at play in relation to the face today: Whereas capitalist and imperialist forces (assisted by various face technologies) prey on the human face, reducing it to identity and mask, painting and photography may—at their best—reveal the face to us, unleashing it from the mask. As we will see, Proust, Kafka, and Woolf's writings on faces and portrait photography offer insight into the workings of these dual forces in the early days of the new media. Indeed, my study of these writers has strengthened my belief that it is possible to carve out a space between, on the one hand, critical approaches to faciality and media technology, and, on the other hand, naïve and simplistic beliefs in faces and portraits as the locus of the human, which both risk being reductive. In my view, we need to better understand the face's mode of being and the ways in which portrait photographs communicate. We should acknowledge that faces are fluid and ungraspable, entailing a perpetual play of expressions and activating intricate relations between "presence" and "absence." Further, we should understand how portrait photographs may both enhance the "enigma" of the face and reveal the face to us.

62. Beck, *Cosmopolitan Vision*, 5–8.

Modernism, Media, and Emotion

Exploring the role of portrait photographs in the writings of Proust, Kafka, and Woolf, I wish both to draw attention to the modernists' ways of engaging with such pictures and to throw light on our relation to photographs today. I am discussing works of literature from a specific historical interval: after the invention of portrait photography, but before the dominance of mediated faces in film and on digital media. The works in question are marked by an emotional ambivalence toward portrait photographs, which in my view is indicative of the epistemological conditions marking the early days of analog pictures, that is, a visual culture dominated by photographs and early film—and not yet by film as a mass medium.[63] Reading these works we see how the modernists tried to come to terms with an emergent media paradigm.

In considering various affective responses to analog photographs, we should recall that most theories of emotion and affect see feelings as social, and further, that our capacity to grasp and discuss feelings is liable to historical change. As Raymond Williams has argued, a period may be marked by feelings that one does not yet have a vocabulary for and that are "at the edge of semantic availability."[64] In her book on "ugly feelings," Sianne Ngai refers to Williams, arguing that "ugly" and "uncanonical" feelings are marked by their deeply equivocal status and by emotional illegibility.[65] In my view, these perspectives are helpful to understand the complex affective register marking the media paradigm of the decades before and after 1900. I side Williams in his wish to discern the historical-material aspects of emotions, and I side with Ngai in her wish to study ambiguous emotions and emotional illegibility within specific cultural contexts.[66]

63. The difference between still images and moving images, between portrait photographs and film, is crucial as these media create different ways of relating to images. Theories of affect often take film or digital media as their point of departure, seeing movement as a key factor in the creation of affect.
64. Williams, "Structures of Feeling," 132.
65. Ngai, *Ugly Feelings*, 25. Katja Haustein has used a similar approach to Proust and photography; see Haustein, *Regarding Lost Time*, 54–67. I discuss her work in the chapter on Proust.
66. Ngai, *Ugly Feelings*, 3; 10; 7. Even if the feelings I discuss are not limited to "ugly feelings," in Ngai's sense of the word, such feelings are included in the emotional register I study.

The reading of portrait photographs in modernist literature involves a vast array of emotions; it spans from love, affection, and sympathy to jealousy, frustration and indifference, and emotions sometimes border on affect.[67]

Looking back at the modernist fascination with portrait photographs from today's media-saturated age is a curious undertaking. Today's media platforms, digital networks, and visual literacy are so much more advanced than the corresponding photographic technologies and competences a hundred years ago. Still, some things remain very much the same. Encounters with mediated faces continue to mark our everyday lives: from Facebook and FaceTime to Instagram and Zoom. This means that our relation to faces and various face technologies is still in play, but due to our visual and technological literacy today, we may be less conscious of the role of faces and photographs than the generation to which Proust, Kafka, and Woolf belonged. That is why we should look back to the generation that first started to live with technical images and experienced the attraction and frustration related to mediated faces.

Reading the modernists, we realize how they struggled to comprehend and come to terms with a visual paradigm that we take for granted today. By studying their engagement with portrait photographs, I believe we may also learn something about our own relation to such pictures. Indeed Proust, Kafka, and Woolf may show us that other ways of relating to photographs are possible. We may better understand how technical images and mediated faces affect our everyday lives. We may become more attentive to some of the faces and photographs surrounding us. And we may again marvel over the look in a portrait photograph and the infinity of a face.

67. As for the relation between *emotion* and *affect*, I follow Ngai's way of seeing these as modal differences rather than clear-cut categories. See Ngai, *Ugly Feelings*, 25–7. In critical theory, Deleuze's and Massumi's work on affect have been influential; they see emotions as referring to feelings that are given a meaning, whereas affects refer to feelings that are disconnected from meaningful sequencing. See Massumi, "The Autonomy of Affect"; Deleuze and Guattari, *What is Philosophy?* In the introduction to the *Routledge International Handbook of Emotions and Media*, the editors describe the difference between affect and emotion in the following manner, referring to the work of the psychologists J. A. Russell and L. F. Barrett: "A crucial difference between affects and emotions is that emotions have an object and relate to meaningful events whereas affects and moods are rather free-floating and objectless." Döveling and Konijn, *Routledge International Handbook of Emotions and Media*, 8.

Chapter 1

Truth in Photographs: Marcel Proust

In Marcel Proust's seven-volume novel *In Search of Lost Time* [*À la recherche du temps perdu*], the first-person narrator repeatedly affirms that we do not see things objectively but perceive the world through a subjective filter. In this narrative, leading toward the narrator becoming a writer, portrait photographs come to play an intriguing role. Insofar as photographs are pictures produced outside the narrator's consciousness, bearing a trace of "reality," he must come to terms with their meaning and status, and they perform a singular attraction on him. Especially, portrait photographs of the women he dreams about feeds his desires, as they seem to promise access, contact, and love. As the narrative unfolds, this love of photographs gives insight into the sentimental education of the narrator.

Proust wrote *The Search* at a time when photographs were already spread widely, and the novel is rich in insight about the early days of technical images. The first volume was published in 1913, whereas the story of the whole series spans from the late nineteenth century to the aftermath of the First World War. Just as Benjamin two decades later, Proust could thus look back at the rise of portrait photography and describe the spread of the medium as well as the various responses to it over time. Born in 1871, Proust witnessed the "industrialization" of photography firsthand and saw how private people started to purchase portrait photographs and learned to pose. He also saw how photographs travelled from the private to the public sphere, first with the popularity of celebrity cards and postcards and later with the emergence of the illustrated press. But Proust tells a story that Benjamin did not tell: depicting everyday responses to photographs, he shows what it was like to live with the new regime of technical images. He describes how portrait photographs could *still* seem attractive and enigmatic while also causing frustration and alienation. This is also why Proust's view of photography is somewhat difficult to grasp; he did not express a single, dogmatic statement about the medium but recognized the various types and uses of photographic technology in a period of transition. Using the motif of the portrait photograph, Proust described how people started to learn how to live with technical images around the turn of the century, but also predicted how the rise of the illustrated press would lead to a more superficial and commercial use of photographs.

The role of portrait photographs in Proust's novel is especially interesting because Proust himself had a passion for portrait photographs and collected pictures of persons he loved or admired. As reported by his later admirer, the French-Hungarian photographer Brassaï, Proust kept the pictures in the drawer of his bedside table and implored his visitors to study them.[1] Unfortunately, Proust's original photographic collection is lost, but Paul Nadar's photographs of Proust's circle provide a clue as to the nature of Proust's album and serve as its surrogate.[2] Yet, as Brassaï noted, Proust's engagement with photography was not taken seriously in the early reception of his work but was considered as merely having anecdotic value. After a century of thinking about photography, however, we should be able to recognize that Proust's reflections on photography were pioneering and that several leading twentieth-century critics of photography, such as Kracauer, Benjamin, and Barthes, are heavily indebted to him. We could venture to say that he explored in a literary form a series of issues related to photography that others have later developed theoretically. Proust depicted the key features of the new media technology.

In recent years, a number of researchers have contributed to a discussion of photographic motifs, metaphors, and structures in *The Search*, acknowledging that Proust's engagement with photography was marked by tension. The works of Mieke Bal, Katja Haustein, Sara Danius, Mary Bergstein, Ainé Larkin, and Suzanne Guerlac should be highlighted in this respect.[3] Yet, despite this interest in Proust and photography in general, the role of portrait photographs specifically has in my view been underestimated.[4] In fact, the role of photographs

<hr>

1. Brassaï, *Marcel Proust*. Brassaï was the artist name of the photographer Gyula Halász (1899–1984). The book was published posthumously.
2. Bernard, *Le Monde de Proust*.
3. See Bal, *The Mottled Screen*; Danius, *The Senses of Modernism, Prousts Motor*, and "Proust—Benjamin: Om fotografin"; Yacavone, "Barthes et Proust"; Larkin, *Proust Writing Photography*; Haustein, *Regarding Lost Time*; Bergstein, *In Looking Back One Learns to See*; and Guerlac, *Proust, Photography, and the Time of Life*.

proper is not always at the center of discussion on Proust and photography; many researchers have given prominent place to the use of photographic metaphors and the "aesthetics of photography" in Proust.[5] These distinctions, however, are not always clear-cut, and it is often a question of different approaches and different emphasis.

However, this study focuses specifically on the role of portrait photographs in Proust's novel, and this approach may perhaps allow us to reconsider two widely discussed topics in relation to Proust. First, many researchers have pointed out that Proust uses photographic metaphors to describe the *mechanical* character of voluntary memory,

4.   Important contributions in this respect are Brassaï, who stressed Proust's interest in portrait photographs, Katja Haustein, who has highlighted the importance of images of other persons in Proust's work and explored "the enigma of character", and Mary Bergstein, who considers how portrait photographs serve as a source of daydreaming and as talisman figures in the novel. Further, Áine Larkin has explored scenes involving portrait photographs under the heading "Thematic Appropriations of Photography" in Proust. Most recently, Suzanne Guerlac has discussed scenes involving portrait photographs in her examination of the stories of three of Proust's characters (the grandmother, Albertine, and Odette), while focusing on the experience of lived time. Although my book has a different aim and focus than previous books discussing this topic, my examination sometimes overlaps with theirs. See Brassaï, *Marcel Proust*; Haustein, *Regarding Lost Time*, 38; Bergstein, *In Looking Back One Learn to See*, 22; 104; and Larkin, *Proust Writing Photography*, 10–47, Guerlac, *Proust, Photography, and the Time of Life*.

5.   Mieke Bal's pioneering work on "visual writing" is important; she explores visual representation in the novel generally, focusing on visual "scenes" and representations of paintings, and she shows how an aesthetics of photography informs Proust's writing (especially through a play with close-up and distance view). Bal's argues that "flatness" plays an important role in Proust's poetics and highlights two aspects of flatness; on the one hand, the absence of depth invites the work of the imagination; on the other hand, flatness tends toward the banal. I find this argument illuminating, but Bal's examination leaves little space for studying Marcel's engagement with proper photographs in this perspective. In the conclusion, she states: "The mental photograph is 'truer' than the material one, which is too docile," and she claims that the mental photograph serve "as a springboard" where "the other can be known, time can be fixed, and space can be spread out." Sara Danius and Patrick Mathieu, too, explore the aesthetics of photography in Proust in illuminating ways. A more recent contribution is Suzanne Guerlac's book, which examines the importance of lived time in Proust, arguing that impressions are treated photographically in the novel (she refers to this as "Proust's poetic of (photographic) impressions") and asserting that the novel records the dynamic time of change. See Bal, *The Mottled Screen*, 245; Danius, *The Senses of Modernism*; Mathieu, *Proust, une question de vision*; Guerlac, *Proust, Photography, and the Time of Life*, 183.

which contrasts with the plentiful, sensuous images of involuntary memory. This has been a commonplace in Proust studies and corresponds to a well-established critique of photography in Proust's day, which dismissed the medium as a mechanical art. But can we infer from these metaphors that Proust or the narrator saw photography merely as a mechanical art? In my view, a study of the motif of portrait photographs in the novel allows for a more nuanced understanding of this issue. Second, many researchers have studied how Marcel's *mental* images are often described through photographic metaphors, seeing the *reading, developing,* and *projecting* of such mental images as key to his subjective way of processing the world. Yet what happens when Marcel engages with portrait photographs rather than mental images of others? Are these encounters, too, marked by the primacy of Marcel's imagination, and should we describe them in terms of projection, as is often done? In my view, a study of such scenes allows us to reconsider the projection theory and acknowledge more complex ways of engaging with photographs.

My hypothesis is that Proust is primarily concerned with the truth of photographs, that is, their ability to elicit aesthetic revelation and insight. For Proust, truth is intrinsically linked to the aesthetic sphere and is lost in the pragmatics of everyday life. Hence his trouble with photographic pictures: Insofar as portrait photographs have aesthetic qualities but are still technical images and not art objects, they are marked by an intriguing ambiguity. In *The Search*, they serve as a testing ground for the passionate protagonist, who is notoriously attracted to such pictures. Looking for truth in photographs, he experiences both gratification and disappointment in relation to such pictures, and he discovers that they make possible different ways of seeing.

Further, my overall aim is to examine the emotional and relational role of portrait photographs in *The Search* and the ways in which they create passionate responses. As Eduardo Cadava and Paola Cortés-Rocca have shown, there is a close connection between love and photography in Proust.[6] Moreover, Gilles Deleuze has showed the importance of desire in Proust, stressing that this desire is directed toward the love object in the hope that it will yield absolute truth.[7] Exploring a variety of scenes, I show how portrait photographs are invested with desire, and how the attraction of photographs ultimately

6.   Cadava and Cortés-Rocca, "Notes on Love and Photography."
7.   Deleuze, *Proust and Signs.*

leads to a reflection on truth. Yet this search for truth in photographs is often described as problematic; the beholders struggle to come to terms with the pictures they engage with, and the encounters may lead to delight and discovery as well as frustration and alienation.

I first examine the narrator's passion for portrait photographs and his efforts to obtain pictures of the women he desires and admires. This inclination, I propose, is indicative of a new tendency to entertain an intimate, affective, and tactile relation to photographs, and it demonstrates the importance of photographs in Marcel's sentimental education. Next, I study how the narrator engages in face studies, seeing facial lines and gestures as revealing the truth about a person. I argue that the study of portrait photographs in Proust is associated with a process of subjective "development" and an experience of revelation and truth. In the third section, I look at an opposite tendency in the novel: encounters with portrait photographs that give access to otherness and exteriority. Although such experiences are brief and temporary, I suggest that they contribute to the protagonist's visual education and are crucial to the insights in the novel. In the concluding section, I discuss Proust's search for truth in photographs in light of the emergence of the illustrated press. I consider how the spread of portrait photographs in the mass media reconfigured the relation between the private and public spheres and suggest that this development is key to Proust's ambivalent views on portrait photographs.

Desire for Photographs

A love of portrait photographs permeates Proust's novel.[8] The characters' engagement with portrait photographs is marked by passionate feelings and various forms of physical contact, such as touching, embracing, kissing, and even spitting. Throughout the novel, the narrator attempts to get hold of photographs of people he admires and dreams about: the actress La Berma, his childhood's love object Gilberte, the aristocratic beauty Mme de Guermantes, and Alber-

8. All references are to the following editions and translations, abbreviated as shown: RTP: Marcel Proust, *À la recherche du temps perdu 1–4*, edited by Jean-Yves Tadié. Paris: Gallimard (Bibliothèque de la Pléiade), 1987–9. SLT: Marcel Proust, *In Search of Lost Time 1–4*, edited by William C. Carter. Translated by C. K. Scott Moncrieff and William C. Carter. New Haven: Yale University Press, 2013–21. ISLT: In *Search of Lost Time 5–6*. Translated by C. K. Scott Moncrieff and Terence Kilmartin and revised by D. J. Enright. London: Vintage Books, 1992. (English translations are from two sources because the Yale edition of Proust's *In Search of Lost Time* has not yet been completed.)

tine, the girl he falls in love with as a young man. It is today well known that Proust had the same obsession with photographs and could go to extremes to acquire photographs of those he longed to get *in touch* with; for instance, he tried to procure a photograph of Jeanne Pouquet, the young girl who inspired the character Gilberte in the novel, and even embarrassed himself in his attempt to secure it, but without any success.[9] Proust is thus describing a passion for portrait photographs that he knew intimately, and the novel uncovers how such pictures could create a variety of affective responses in various circumstances.

The first photograph that is subject to scrutiny in the novel depicts a renowned actress named La Berma, and Marcel's view of it is described as highly ambivalent. La Berma is the one Marcel dreams about as a child, and his longing is bound up with his fascination for the theater and his expectation that theater performances can offer a revelation of truth. After having studied theater programs and posters for a long time, he is finally allowed to see La Berma live, but he is somewhat disappointed by her performance and confused by the public's vulgar response to her. As he ponders his views of La Berma, he gets the opportunity to purchase a photograph of her, a so-called celebrity photograph. Even if he understands that this is a picture produced for the masses, he is attracted to it in a peculiar way. The picture permits him to study La Berma's face closely, but it also prompts thoughts about the medium itself:

> On our way home Françoise made me stop at the corner of the rue Royale, before an open-air stall from which she selected for her own New Year's Day presents photographs of Pius IX and Raspail, while for myself I purchased one of Berma. The innumerable admirers fascinated by that artist gave an air almost of poverty to this one face that she had to respond with, unalterable and precarious like the garments of people who do not have a change of clothes, this face on which she must continually expose to view only the tiny dimple over her upper lip, the arch of her eyebrows, and a few other physical peculiarities always the same, which, when it came to it, were at the mercy of a burn or a blow. This face, moreover, could not in itself have seemed to me beautiful, but it gave me the idea, and consequently the desire to kiss it by reason of all the kisses that it must have received, for which, from its page in the album [*du fond de la "carte-album"*], it seemed still to be appealing with that coquettishly tender gaze and that artificially ingenuous smile. (SLT 2, 65–6)

9.   Brassaï, *Marcel Proust*, 77.

En rentrant, Françoise me fit arrêter, au coin de la rue Royale, devant un étalage en plein vent où elle choisit, pour ses propres étrennes, des photographies de Pie IX et de Raspail et où, pour ma part, j'en achetai une de la Berma. Les innombrables admirations qu'excitait l'artiste donnaient quelque chose d'un peu pauvre à ce visage unique qu'elle avait pour y répondre, immuable et précaire comme ce vêtement des personnes qui n'en ont pas de rechange, et où elle ne pouvait exhiber toujours que le petit pli au-dessus de la lèvre supérieure, le relève-ment des sourcils, quelques autres particularités physiques, toujours les mêmes qui, en somme, étaient à la merci d'une brûlure ou d'un choc. Ce visage, d'ailleurs, ne m'eût pas à lui seul semblé beau, mais il me donnait l'idée et par conséquent, l'envie de l'embrasser à cause de tous les baisers qu'il avait dû supporter et que, du fond de la « carte-album », il semblait appeler encore par ce regard coquette-ment tendre et ce sourire artificiellement ingénu. (RTP 1, 478)

This rich passage allows for several comments. First, it demonstrates that public figures such as actresses, politicians, and even the pope now circulate in the public not merely as names, but also *as images*. The new visual media thus allow people to put a face to a well-known name. Actresses were particularly popular motifs, and it is well known

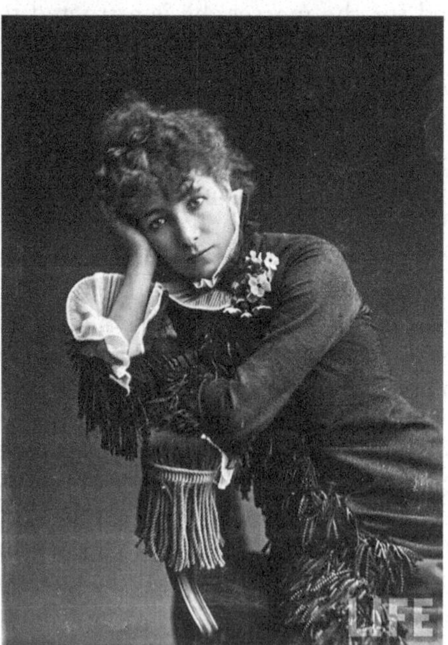

Figure 1.1   Portrait photograph of actress Sarah Bernhardt by Paul Nadar, circa 1878. Available in the public domain via Wikimedia Commons.

that Proust took both Sarah Bernhardt and Réjane as models for La Berma; indeed, pictures of both these women circulated widely in Proust's day.[10] Second, pictures of celebrities could be purchased and brought home by any individual; they could even be put in albums along with family members and contemplated and caressed at will. In this manner, the pictures would cross the boundaries between the public and the private spheres. When the quotation refers to a *carte album* of La Berma, it points to a photographic format whose size was adapted to albums and the craze for collecting photographs (it came on the market a decade or two after the *carte de visite* and was somewhat larger). Proust thus describes a photographic format for which tactile contact was key; a medium created to receive touches and caresses.

Third, we should note that the narrator reflects on the nature of celebrity photographs created for a mass audience. He points out that La Berma must respond to all her admirers with the same face ("this one face" ["ce visage unique"]), and that to have only one face is to be poor. He also comments on her way of presenting herself to the audience: her way of exposing her upper lip and the arch of her eyebrows as well as her "artificially ingenuous smile" [sourire artificiellement ingénu]. This posed picture has nothing of the *aura* that Benjamin later saw in the first generation of portrait photographs. However, earlier in the first volume, Marcel expresses his admiration for theatricality in photographs; he refers to "the theatrical appearance that I admired in photographs of actresses" (SLT 1, 87) ["l'aspect théâtral que j'admirais dans les photographies d'actrices" (RTP 1, 76)]. In view of this, we may assume that he does not look for an *aura* in the picture; rather he studies her way of presenting herself to the camera. Moreover, we may perceive a feeling of compassion in the narrator's description of it—conveyed by the words "poor" [*pauvre*] and "precarious" [*précaire*], as well as the expression "at the mercy of a burn or a blow" ["à la merci d'une brûlure ou d'un choc"]. This shows that the narrator recognizes La Berma's vulnerability in front of the camera and suggests that compassion plays a role in young Marcel's engagement with the photograph.

Marking his distance to himself as a youth, the narrator relates that this image could not in itself have seemed beautiful back then,

10. In her study of celebrity, Sharon Marcus shows how the new media (the popular press and commercial photography) and the emergence of a passionate celebrity culture were instrumental in making Sarah Bernhardt a star of her day. Marcus, *The Drama of Celebrity*.

but that it still aroused vivid emotions in him, and a desire to kiss it. This desire is described as prompted by other men's desire for La Berma, and thus appears to be rooted in some kind of collective desire akin to jealousy. This collective desire seems to be mediated by the picture itself; it stems from the depth of the picture [*du fond de la "carte-album"*]. It is just as if the narrator grants the mass-produced picture some sort of agency; a power that urges young Marcel to kiss it. The *attractive* qualities of this photograph are described further a few pages later, when Marcel is alone in his room at night and studies it once more:

> I lit my candle again, to look once more at her face. At the thought that it was, no doubt, at that very moment being caressed by those men whom I could not prevent from giving to Berma and receiving from her joys superhuman but vague, I felt an emotion more cruel than voluptuous, a longing that was aggravated presently by the sound of a horn, as one hears it on the nights of the Lenten carnival. (SLT 2, 67–8)

> Je rallumai ma bougie éteinte pour regarder encore une fois son visage. À la pensée qu'il était sans doute en ce moment caressé par ces hommes que je ne pouvais empêcher de donner à la Berma, et de recevoir d'elle, des joies surhumaines et vagues, j'éprouvais un émoi plus cruel qu'il n'était voluptueux, une nostalgie que vint aggraver le son du cor, comme on l'entend la nuit de la Mi-Carême. (RTP 1, 480)

Here, too, the attraction is ascribed to some kind of collective desire; young Marcel seems to realize that he is part of a mass audience and that La Berma's face is subject to other men's desires as well. This creates vivid emotions in him—somewhat aggressive feelings of jealousy mixed with severe longing. Interestingly, these emotions are associated with the Lenten carnival, marking that a period of privation (Lent) is halfway through but still not over. It thus seems that the picture cannot fully satisfy Marcel's longing and leaves him in a limbo between desire and fulfilment. The scenes where Marcel studies La Berma's picture shows his desire and jealousy as well as his feeling of disappointment with respect to the picture. However, the retrospective narrator seems capable of coming to terms with this picture and its affective implications. Commenting on young Marcel's desire, he analyzes the logic of the mass-produced picture.

Shortly after this passage, we read about Marcel's desire for Gilberte's photograph, which takes a somewhat different form. She is the rather posh daughter of family friend Charles Swann and his wife Odette, and Marcel meets her regularly. Still, he feels that he is not close enough to her and is painfully aware that he is at the mercy of her caprices. Longing for Gilberte after being separated for a time, he realizes that he has forgotten her face and her features, and he comes to think of her plaits, which have brushed his cheek a number of times. Meditating on those moments, Marcel expresses his desire to possess a photograph not so much of Gilberte as of her plaits, as though he were trying to connect with her through a synesthetic formula:

> But since I never hoped to obtain an actual fragment of those plaits, if at least I had been able to have their photograph, how far more precious than one of a sheet of flowers drawn by Leonardo! To acquire one, I stooped – with friends of the Swanns and even with photographers – to servilities that did not procure for me what I wanted, but tied me for life to a number of extremely boring people. (SLT 2, 84)

> Mais n'espérant point obtenir un morceau vrai de ces nattes, si au moins j'avais pu en posséder la photographie, combien plus précieuse que celle de fleurettes dessinées par le Vinci ! Pour en avoir une, je fis auprès d'amis des Swann et même de photographes, des bassesses qui ne me procurèrent pas ce que je voulais, mais me lièrent pour toujours avec des gens très ennuyeux. (RTP 1, 494)

The desire for a photograph of Gilberte's plaits reveals how photographs are part of a process of substitutions and replacements. This could be seen as a fetishistic inclination; Marcel's desire is directed toward Gilberte's hair rather than the whole person and toward a photograph rather than the braids themselves. Proust thus demonstrates that direct touch is unobtainable and that pictures have started to serve as stand-ins. We may note that the imaginary photograph of the plaits is compared to a picture of small flowers drawn by Leonardo da Vinci, which suggests that the aesthetic form of the plaits plays a role in this fantasy.[11] At the same time, the sensuousness of the experience is assured by the fact that such a photograph can be touched and studied endlessly. Yet it is ironic that Marcel tried hard to obtain a photograph that would merely have served as a

11. Both Mieke Bal and Mary Bergstein have commented on Proust's use of chiaroscuro, and Bergstein especially refers to Leonardo da Vinci's way of using it to stimulate the imagination. See Bal, *The Mottled Screen*, 25–8; Bergstein, *In Looking Back One Learns to See*, 206–17.

substitute, and even embarrassed himself to that end, with no positive outcome. This shows that, even if a photograph is out of reach, the possibility of obtaining it feeds Marcel's dreams.

Another early scene shows how Marcel learns about a debauched way of using of photographs. It involves Mlle Vinteuil, the daughter of a prudish composer, and her female lover, who both enjoy causing a scandal. When young Marcel catches sight of them through a window, they find themselves in an intimate situation, and he unintentionally becomes the witness of their revolt against Mlle Vinteuil's recently deceased father. Mlle Vinteuil has placed her father's photographic portrait in such a way that he overviews the act, and they discuss whether they should spit on his photograph or not: "Oh! There's my father's picture looking at us; I can't think who can have put it there" (SLT 1, 185) ["Oh ! ce portrait de mon père qui nous regarde, je ne sais pas qui a pu le mettre là" (RTP 1, 160)], Mlle Vinteuil exclaims, pretending to be shocked. Taking up the photographs, she dares her lover to spit on it, whereupon her lover replies: "Not dare to spit on it? On *that*?" (SLT 1, 186) ["Je n'oserait pas cracher dessus ? sur *ça* ?" (RTP 1, 161)] The narrator describes this as an act of profanation: "This photograph served them, no doubt, habitually in their ritual profanations" (SLT 1, 185) ["Ce portrait leur servait sans doute habituellement pour des profanations rituelles" (RTP 1, 160)]. This comment underlines to what degree their interaction with the photograph differs from a respectful and loving treatment of family photographs and demonstrates that the portrait is here made the object of affects and harassment. Through this scene Proust demonstrates that photographs engender not merely desire and love but also more ugly feelings of resentment, rage, and revolt. Moreover, by depicting Marcel in a voyeuristic position, he shows how the protagonist learns about such feelings. The scene depicts a ritualistic way of engaging with a portrait photograph; here a photograph serves as a "double" for an absent person, allowing the women to "talk back" to him from a position of power. At the same time, however, the photograph appears to have some kind of agency because it provokes the young women's emotions and actions.

Shortly after his stay in Balbec, Marcel again makes an attempt to acquire a portrait photograph, this time of Mme de Guermantes, the elegant woman he sees passing in the streets. This requires an opportunistic maneuver. When he spots her photograph in the room of his friend Robert de Saint-Loup, who is also the duchess's nephew, Marcel immediately thinks of how to obtain it:

> I was looking at the photograph of his aunt, and the thought that,
> since Saint-Loup had this photograph in his possession, he might per-
> haps give it to me, made me feel all the fonder of him and want to
> render him a thousand services, which seemed to me a very small
> exchange for it. (SLT 3, 81)

> Je regardais la photographie de sa tante et la pensée que, Saint-Loup
> possédant cette photographie, il pourrait peut-être me la donner, me
> fit le chérir davantage et souhaiter de lui rendre mille services qui me
> semblaient peu de choses en échange d'elle. (RTP 2, 379)

But Saint-Loup will later refuse to give Marcel the photograph without his aunt's permission, so the scheme ends in disappointment.
Still, at the time when Marcel finds the photograph in his friend's
room, he has plenty of time to indulge in the picture and study the
duchess's features. I will elaborate on Marcel's contemplation of this
photograph shortly, but for now only point out that he once more
tries to get his hands on a photograph from someone who is closer
to the desired woman than he is. Whereas the photograph of La
Berma could be purchased for money by anyone, the photographs of
Gilberte and Mme de Guermantes circulate in the semiprivate sphere
and can be acquired only as a favor.

If we turn to Albertine, the young woman with whom he has a
difficult relation over many years, the photographic theme becomes
more complex. As Marcel's relation to her is the most intriguing in
the novel, we might expect that Marcel longs to contemplate her
picture. But even if the novel reveals that he is in possession of such
a picture and describes how he is persuaded into showing it to Saint-
Loup, it does not depict any prolonged sequence of contemplation
related to this photograph. By contrast, some of the unpublished
fragments that Proust intended to incorporate in *The Search* depict
Marcel's way of engaging with his photographs of Albertine. In one
of these fragments, Marcel refers causally to "one of the photographs
of her that I kept in my album during these different periods of time"
(my translation) [[u]ne des photographies que j'avais d'elle dans mon
album à ces différentes époques (RTP 4, 655)] and this seems to suggest a longstanding relation to the photographs of Albertine. These
fragments have been overlooked in discussions about Proust and
photography, and I shall elaborate on one of them shortly, but for
now only point to them as a background for my brief examination
of two other scenes: the first kiss (which has often been discussed)
and the posthumous kiss (which is not often discussed). Both scenes

show Marcel's emotional involvement with Albertine, and both use photographic metaphors to describe the act of kissing and to convey a sense of both proximity and distance.

The scene of the posthumous kiss appears toward the end of the novel and depicts how Marcel attempts to kiss Albertine's "image" after her sudden death. However, this is not a proper photograph, but a mental picture that suddenly brings her near to him as he ponders upon those aspects of her life that he did not know about. The picture comes to him like an accidental snapshot photograph: "not by dint of a conscious effort of resuscitation but as though by one of those chance encounters which, as is the case with photographs that are not posed, with snapshots, always make the person appear more alive" (ISLT 5, 563) ["non grâce à un effort de résurrection mais comme par le hasard d'une de ces rencontres qui – comme dans les photographies qui ne sont pas 'posées', dans les instantanés – laissent toujours la personne plus vivante" (RTP IV, 74)]. Unlike his previous mental image of her, which has evolved over time, this "snapshot picture" shows her in a sudden and lifelike way, as an image arriving from somewhere outside of his consciousness. It gives a new aspect (or in fact a new "face" in French) to the idea of her death: "I had just approached from a new angle the idea that Albertine was dead" (ISLT 5, 563) ["je venais d'aborder par une nouvelle face cette idée qu'Albertine était morte" (RTP IV, 74)]. Moreover, the snapshot image helps him comprehend that he is only capable of realizing his feelings for her from a distance (whereas the tumult of life prevented him from understanding them in her presence). Then Marcel tries to kiss the mental snapshot picture of Albertine: "I tried to embrace the image of Albertine through my tears" (ISLT 5, 565) ["Je tâchais d'embrasser l'image d'Albertine à travers mes larmes" (RTP 4, 76)]. This pretend scene in which Marcel tries to kiss a virtual image is odd because a kiss seems to require a physical kissing object and a certain distance. Moreover, the kiss seems altogether unsatisfactory; Marcel stresses that he *tries* to kiss the picture and calls attention to his own tears, which probably blurred his vision. However, the scene is intriguing precisely because it highlights the problem of distance in relation to kissing.

In this respect, the scene of the posthumous kiss can be seen as a penchant to the famous *first* kiss described earlier in the novel; in that case, Marcel experienced a visual breakdown as he got close to Albertine with the intention of kissing her (SLT 3, 402 / RTP 2, 660). As his mouth took over for his eyes, he felt that she was dissolving in front of him, and the experience left him altogether confused. As several researchers have underlined, the narrator uses photographic metaphors to describe this sensuous experience: He explains that his imaginary picture of Albertine is two-dimensional, whereas she in real life is three-dimensional and thus appears to him like a picture viewed through a stereoscope. Confused by the fleshy three-dimensional version of Albertine, the narrator expresses his preference for the two-dimensional version of her.

Comparing these kissing scenes, we see that both highlight the problem of distance in relation to kissing, and both do so by way of photographic metaphors. Further, in both cases, the kiss is unsuccessful and Albertine dissolves in front of Marcel. Still, the posthumous kiss differs from the first kiss because of her absence and Marcel's desperate attempt to relate to her. It is as if the snapshot picture first makes him realize the distance between them and then try to overcome the distance by kissing the picture. At the same time, he knows that her death cuts her off from him permanently. Indeed, the kiss and his burst of emotions seems to be motivated by his "new" insight about her death. Even if we are here dealing with a photographic metaphor, the posthumous kiss seems to epitomize the intimate connection between photography and love, as well as the connection between photography and death: Both involve a complex relation between proximity and distance.

Yet, the photographs that most of all evoke the connection between photography and death is the portrait of Marcel's grandmother. This photograph is taken at her initiative to create a picture for Marcel to remember her by after her death. At the time of the photographic sitting in Balbec, she is seriously ill, but Marcel, who does not know this, is displeased by the whole ordeal and jealous of Saint-Loup, who takes the picture. The novel describes how Marcel contemplates this photograph after his grandmother's death, and how his responses go through various stages. First a somewhat indifferent look is replaced by sudden recognition: "It's grandmother" ["C'est grand-mère"]. Then, as Françoise tells him about his grandmother's illness and good intentions at the time of the photographic sitting, Marcel suffers a whole day in front of the picture: "It tortured me" ["Elle me torturait"]. After a few days, however, Marcel's suffering and shame wears away, and he gets used to the picture, but now his view gets more ambivalent; in it he sees both her elegant look and a look marked by death. Lastly, the narrator depicts how Marcel's mother, on her side, never got used to the photograph and saw only the grandmother's illness and tragic look (SLT 4, 194–8 / RTP 3, 172–6).[12] This episode uncovers Marcels

12. The photograph of the grandmother is commented on in illuminating ways by both Larkin and Guerlac, and Guerlac, too, stresses the photo's instability. See Larkin, *Proust Writing Photography*, 40–5; Guerlac, *Proust, Photography, and the Time of Life*, 24–30.

strong emotions with respect to the photograph and also shows how these emotions change according to the circumstances. When his reluctance to the picture disappears, it reveals his grandmother to him, and when his deep suffering wears away, Marcel sees more in the picture; now it appears ambiguous to him, capturing both the grandmother's liveliness and her death sentence.

However, Marcel is not the only one who has a passion for photographs in the novel. As we have seen, Mlle Vinteuil and her lover use a photograph in an act of revolt, and other characters, too, engage with photographs in emotional ways. This includes Saint-Loup, the Baron de Charlus, Marcel's uncle Adolphe, and, not the least, Charles Swann, the family friend who is also an art collector. The novel depicts how Swann treasures his photographs of Odette, the cocotte whom he ended up marrying.[13] Their relation is intriguing because Swann's love of her is premised upon her resemblance to Botticelli's painting of the biblical figure Zipporah, and this, of course, reveals to what degree art has influenced his preferences in love. This is evident in one particular scene where he longs for Odette, not knowing where she is, and contemplates a photograph of Zipporah:

> When he had gazed for a long time at this Botticelli, he would think of his own living Botticelli, who seemed all the lovelier in contrast, and as he drew toward him the photograph of Zipporah he would imagine that he was clasping Odette against his heart" (SLT 1, 257)

> Quand il avait regardé longtemps ce Botticelli, il pensait à son Botticelli à lui qu'il trouvait plus beau encore et, approchant de lui la photographie de Zéphora, il croyait serrer Odette contre son cœur" (RTP 1, 221–2).

This intimate way of interacting with a photograph reveals to what degree his emotions are invested in the medium, and the irony is not only that he embraces a photograph instead of a real person, but also that the photograph represents a Botticelli painting that reminds him of her rather than Odette herself.

But Swann is also in possession of photographs of the actual Odette, and his somewhat distant relation to her is revealed by the

---

13. This character was inspired by Laure Hayman, a well-known courtesan with a pink complexion, who allegedly was more cultivated than Odette. Bernard, *Le Monde de Proust*, 95.

fact that he prefers an old daguerreotype of her, taken at the time when she was an actress and a cocotte, to the more recent ones:

> Swann had in his bedroom, instead of the beautiful photographs that were now taken of his wife, in all of which the same enigmatic, victorious expression enabled one to recognize, in whatever dress and hat, her triumphant face and figure, a little old daguerreotype of her, quite plain, taken long before the appearance of this new type, and from which the youthfulness and beauty of Odette, not yet discovered by her, was absent [*semblaient absentes*]. (SLT 2, 211)

> Swann avait dans sa chambre, au lieu des belles photographies qu'on faisait maintenant de sa femme, et où la même expression énigmatique et victorieuse laissait reconnaître, quels que fussent la robe et le chapeau, sa silhouette et son visage triomphants, un petit daguerréotype ancien tout simple, antérieur à ce type, et duquel la jeunesse et la beauté d'Odette, non encore trouvée par elle, semblaient absentes. (RTP 1, 606)

The passage describes how the present Odette has learned to pose in such a way that she appears as a type; in all the new and professional pictures of her she has "the same enigmatic victorious expression." By contrast, the old photograph is marked by the absence of these features: Odette is in these pictures less self-aware and had not yet "discovered" her professional face. Swann's affection for this old picture is described in the following manner: "[Swann] enjoyed in the slender young woman with pensive eyes and tired features, caught in a pose between walking and immobility, a more Botticellian grace" (SLT 2, 211) ["goûtait-il dans la jeune femme grêle aux yeux pensifs, aux traits las, à l'attitude suspendue entre la marche et l'immobilité, une grâce plus botticellienne" (RTP 1, 607)]. His attention to Odette's "pensive eyes and tired features" suggests that he sees a self-relation in the portrait, which may be absent from more professional photographs. Adding to this is her pose "between walking and immobility," which suggests the technique of chronophotography (well known to Proust) and gives the picture a dynamic look rather than a posed one. Further, the expression "Botticellian grace" is interesting as it places Odette in the sphere of classical art rather than the atmosphere of a modern photographic studio. Perhaps Swann finds in this old daguerreotype not just a token of their happy days, but also traces of an *aura* that fails to make itself present in the more recent, professional photographs of her. The effortless

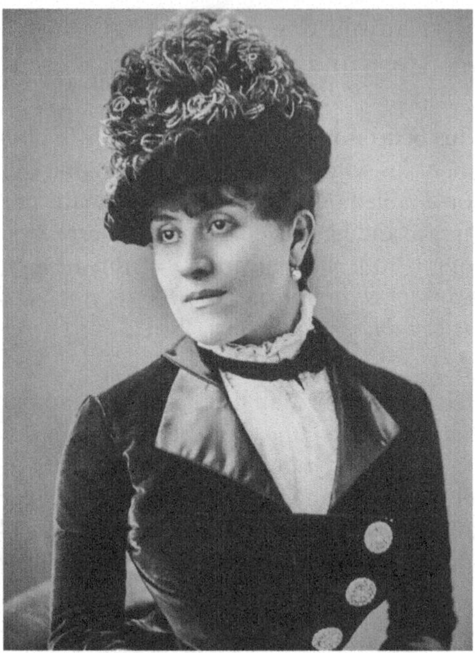

Figure 1.2   Portrait photograph of Laure Hayman by Paul Nadar, 1879.
Available in the public domain via Wikimedia Commons.

and yet graceful photograph from her early days seems to speak to
Swann, but the posed photographs do not.

Yet Monsieur Swann is not the only one who possesses pictures
of Odette. When Marcel inherits a collection of photographs from
his uncle Adolphe, mostly of actresses, he discovers a picture of a
person he knows: Odette, before she became Madame Swann, posing
as "Miss Sacripant." By the same token, he understands her various
roles and identities over the years. It should be pointed out that Uncle
Adolphe is a relative that Marcel is forbidden to see as a child because
of his dubious female companions. It is in his home that Marcel first
meets Odette, at that time just an unknown woman, but the swift
encounter is the starting point of a long story involving emerging
desire and confused identities. As a young man in Balbec, he sees a
painting of her without recognizing her, but learns from the painter
Elstir that she is an actress named Miss Sacripant. Captivated by the
picture, Marcel asks for a photograph of it: "I would very much like,
if you have such a thing, a photograph of the little portrait of Miss
Sacripant. Surely, that's not a real name?" (SLT 2, 478) ["J'aurais
beaucoup aimé, si vous en possédiez, avoir une photographie du petit

portrait de Miss Sacripant. Mais qu'est-ce que c'est que ce nom?" (RTP 2, 215)]. Marcel then suddenly realizes that Miss Sacripant and Odette Swann are the same person.

This serves as a run-up to the episode when he receives his uncle's photograph collection. The collection is brought to Marcel by a certain Morel, the son of his uncle's loyal valet, who acts with discretion:

> The object of his visit to me was as follows: his father, when going through the effects of my Uncle Adolphe, had set aside some that he felt were inappropriate to send to my parents but were, he thought, of a nature likely to interest a young man of my age. These were the photographs of the famous actresses, the notorious cocottes whom my uncle had known, the last fading pictures of that pleasure-seeking life of a man about town that he separated by a watertight compartment from his family life. (SLT 3, 288)

> Le but de sa visite était celui-ci : son père avait, parmi les souvenirs de mon oncle Adolphe, mis de côté certains qu'il avait jugé inconvenant d'envoyer à mes parents mais qui, pensait-il, étaient de nature à intéresser un jeune homme de mon âge. C'étaient les photographies des actrices célèbres, des grand cocottes que mon oncle avait connues, les dernières images de cette vie de vieux viveur qu'il séparait, par une cloison étanche, de sa vie de famille. (RTP 2, 561)

Many of these photographs are signed and thus testify to the actresses' intimate relation with Marcel's uncle. As the Pléiade editors of the novel explain, these photographs are in fact similar to the photographs that Proust inherited from his great-uncle Louis Weil, who, it appears, had a similar relation to actresses (SLT 3, 288 / RTP 2, 1653). In this collection, Marcel comes across a familiar face: "I had been greatly surprised to find among the photographs that his father had sent me one of the portrait of Miss Sacripant (otherwise Odette) by Elstir" (SLT 3, 290) ["j'avais été très étonné de trouver parmi les photographies que m'envoyait son père une du portrait de Miss Sacripant (c'est-à-dire Odette) par Elstir" (RTP 2, 563)]. Morel then relates that Marcel in fact met this woman briefly at his uncle's house as a boy, and Marcel immediately recognizes the mystery woman. He thus learns about Odette's many appearances and social maneuvering over the years.[14] In this manner, photographs play an important

14. As Suzanne Guerlac observes, Odette "relies on commercial photography to transform her social identity." Guerlac, *Proust, Photography, and the Time of Life*, 127.

role in the novel's play with uncertain identities, and they foreground the intricate game of social mobility. They help map the relations between the characters and reveal the emotions that exist on a tacit level in a society marked by conformity and facades. As such, the photographs contribute to Marcel's sentimental education.

But, above all, the gift from Uncle Adolphe demonstrates a practice that is important in the novel: the collecting of photographs. The reader understands that the uncle's collection is well placed with Marcel, and his passion for this particular kind of photographs is underlined when Morel expresses his surprise that Marcel does not keep a photograph of his uncle in his living room, as one often does in bourgeois homes. This scene is trivial, but also quite revealing: for Marcel, portrait photographs are connected with passion and desire, not with respectful family relations. The novel shows how both Uncle Adolphe and Marcel collect photographs of the women they desire and dream about, and how numerous characters in the novel entertain an intimate, affective, and tactile relation to photographs.

If we adopt a Deleuzian perspective, we could see this affective relation to photographs in Proust as an "objectivist mistake": Marcel invests his emotions in the love object, in the hope that it will yield its secrets (or, more accurately, in the hope that the "sign" will yield its "meaning"). This process is deceptive, Deleuze contends, so when Marcel learns that his kisses do not bring about any revelation in the love object, he changes his view of love, delving instead into a subjective contemplation process where he is the one who uncovers meaning.[15] Yet it is crucial that Deleuze's analysis of the objectivist mistake in Proust pertains to "real" women as love objects, whereas the issue in our context is the emotional investment in portrait photographs, whose status is highly uncertain. Portrait photographs are not persons, things, or art objects, but could be seen as the immaterial "doubles" of the depicted persons, captured on photographic paper. On the one hand, one could argue that this immateriality places them closer to truth and essence, just like art objects; on the other hand, the pictures are reproductions and do not have the unique attributes of "art." Indeed, the uncertain status of portrait photographs create uncertainty in the viewing situation and may partly explain the characters indecisive responses to them. In the novel, responses to photographs are described as ambiguous, spanning from love and affection to jealousy, confusion, and disappointment.

15. Deleuze, *Proust and Signs*, 7; 23.

These ways of engaging emotionally with portrait photographs are, it seems, crucial to Marcel's sentimental education. As they transcend both physical distances and social barriers, portrait photographs mediate between Marcel's private world and the social world. For Marcel, the absence of the material woman causes torment, but also delight insofar as this allows him to study the selected woman in privacy and feel close to her. Such pictures seem to promise love, contact, and gratification, but also provoke hesitation, despair, and reflection. In desiring, collecting, and kissing photographs, Marcel invests his emotions in the medium, but he also starts to learn about mediation processes. His love of portrait photographs thus seems to prepare for a more profound investigation of the truth of such pictures.

Reading Gestures

In *The Search*, Proust offers numerous reflections on the difficulty of reading of faces. The narrator observes that people in real life present shifting faces, so that grasping a person's face is no simple task: "The human face is indeed, like the face of the God of some Oriental theogony, a whole cluster of faces juxtaposed on different planes so that one does not see them all at once" (SLT 2, 538) ["Le visage humain est vraiment comme celui du Dieu d'une théogonie orientale, toute une grappe de visages juxtaposés dans des plans différents et qu'on ne voit pas à la fois" (RTP 2, 270)]. This multiplicity is one of the challenges that is addressed in the novel—in particular in relation to Albertine's face, which is notoriously difficult to take in and perceive clearly.[16] In this situation, the study of portrait photographs comes to the fore as a promising strategy; in a portrait photograph, time is arrested, and a person's face can be studied without interruptions. Moreover, a photograph makes visible a person's miens, gestures, and attitudes toward the world. It thus represents a privileged way of seeing, making a person's face shine forth with a new valence. Yet can a photograph, by means of this very mediation process, reveal some kind of truth? Can the reading of a portrait photograph give insight into a person's way of being? Let us examine how the connection between faces, gestures, mediality, and truth plays out in a few key passages in *The Search*.

16. André Benhaïm's study is an important reference in this respect; he examines Proust's view of faces in light of the Hebrew idea of the face as plural. See Benhaïm, Panim: *Visages de Proust*.

Of particular interest in this respect is an extended passage on faces related to Marcel's encounter with the young girls in Balbec, depicted in the second volume of the novel, *In the Shadow of Young Girls in Flower* [*À l'ombre des jeunes filles en fleurs*]. This encounter, causing confusion and distress, marks the beginning of Marcel's relationship with Albertine. The problem for Marcel is that he cannot distinguish clearly among the girls, because their faces seem fluctuating and ungraspable. In retrospect, he relates how he started to understand the reasons for this confusion when he—at a later point in life—saw a group photograph of the girls, taken when they were even younger than the time of his encounter with them in Balbec. Studying the old photograph, a *carte-album*, he realizes that the girls' faces were undergoing a process of radical change during these juvenile years:

> Later on, a photograph showed my why. Who could now have recognized in them, scarcely and yet quite definitively beyond an age in which one changes so completely, that amorphous, delicious mass, still utterly infantine, of little girls who, only a few years back, might have been seen sitting in a ring on the sand around a tent; a sort of white and vague constellation in which one would have distinguished a pair of eyes that sparkled more than the rest, a mischievous face, blond hair, only to lose them again and to confound them almost at once in the indistinct and milky nebula? (SLT 2, 438)

> Plus tard une photographie m'expliqua pourquoi. Qui eût pu reconnaître maintenant en elles, à peine mais déjà sorties d'un âge où on change si complètement, telle masse amorphe et délicieuse, encore tout enfantine, de petites filles que, quelques années seulement auparavant, on pouvait voir assises en cercle sur le sable, autour d'une tente : sorte de blanche et vague constellation où l'on n'eût distingué deux yeux plus brillants que les autres, un malicieux visage, des cheveux blonds, que pour les reperdre et les confondre bien vite au sein de la nébuleuse indistincte et lactée? (RTP 2, 180)

Looking at the young faces in the photograph, Marcel realizes that they are without distinct character; describing them as an "amorphous, delicious mass," he suggests that they are plastic and featureless.[17] The narrator concludes that, at this age, the girls have *not yet* developed a

17. Commenting on this scene, Suzanne Guerlac argues that the photograph in itself is out of focus and refers to it as a "blurry photograph." Although this question is certainly open to interpretation, I am not fully convinced by Guerlac's argument in this respect. The picture itself is not described as blurry by the narrator; rather he highlights the lack of distinguishable features in the girls' faces. In my

personality to mark their faces: "Back then those children, mere babies, had been still at that elementary stage in their formation when personality has not set its seal on each face" (SLT 2, 438) ["Alors, ces enfants trop jeunes étaient encore à ce degré élémentaire de formation où la personnalité n'a pas mis son sceau sur chaque visage" (RTP 2, 180)].

The narrator's meditation on the plasticity of young faces is picked up at a later point in the novel, and there it is connected to a reflection on how time works on the human face. The narrator points out that the young girls' flesh is still at work, "like a precious leaven" ["comme une pâte précieuse"], and that "this plasticity gives a wealth of variety and charm" (SLT 2, 526) ["cette plasticité donne beaucoup de variété et de charme" (RTP 2, 259)]. At the point when he encounters them, they are still marked by this openness, he relates, but their expressions have *started* to take on a hint of specificity suggesting an attitude toward life: "No doubt the lines of the voice, like those of the face, were not yet definitely fixed" (SLT 2, 529), but they "already gave a clear indication of the attitude that each of them had adopted toward life" (SLT 2, 530) ["Sans doute les lignes de la voix, comme celles du visage, n'étaient pas encore définitivement fixées"; "accusait déjà nettement le parti pris que chacune de ces petites personnes avaient sur la vie" (RTP 2, 262)]. Having established how a mindset slowly becomes visible in a young person's face, the narrator offers a general reflection on faces, gestures, and time:

> The features of our face are hardly more than gestures that force of habit has made permanent. Nature, like the destruction of Pompeii, like the metamorphosis of a nymph, has immobilized us in an accustomed movement. Similarly, our intonations embody our philosophy of life, what a person, at each moment, says to himself about things. (SLT 2, 530)

> Les traits de notre visage ne sont guère que des gestes devenus, par l'habitude, définitifs. La nature, comme la catastrophe de Pompéi, comme une métamorphose de nymphe, nous a immobilisés dans le mouvement accoutumé. De même nos intonations contiennent notre philosophie de la vie, ce que la personne se dit à tout moment sur les choses. (RTP 2, 262)

view, this is key to understanding the picture and the way in which it affects the narrator; it reveals something to him about the nature of young girls' faces. Thus, where Guerlac stresses the dynamic of the photograph, my analysis sees its stasis as a site for discovery and revelation. See Guerlac, *Proust, Photography, and the Time of Life*, 58–66.

Seeing the features of a face as gestures imposed upon us by long-standing habits, the narrator connects them to the passing of time. Moreover, the permanent fixing of such gestures is described as a violent act in which movement is turned into stasis, just like the mummification of the city of Pompeii after the volcano eruption.[18] Comparing such gestures to our ways of speaking, the narrator suggests that these intimate practices reveal our philosophy of life. He thus implies that there is a relation between body and mind and that a way of seeing the world is translated into one's corporeal habits. This perspective is in my view helpful to understand an important aspect of the novel: its attention to silent gestures and tacit habits as semi-conscious forms of expression and traces of life.

This insight about faces becomes even more intriguing when it is related to the medium of photography. In fact, Marcel first begins to understand the nature of faces by way of a photograph, which allows him to study the young girls' faces at close hand. What he discovers is that, in these faces, clear and distinct features are *not yet* in place. The reader thus understands Marcel's fascination for the young faces that are on the verge of everything, having just started to "flower" but without fully unfolding their petals yet. Unlike the faces of old people, these faces embody possibility as such.[19] The reader also understands his inclination for face studies generally and his attraction to portrait photographs particularly. In a portrait photograph, the gestures of a person are revealed to the beholder, suggesting his or her philosophy of life.

These reflections on faces and gestures may illuminate our understanding of the scene where Marcel studies the photograph of Mme de Guermantes. Whereas Albertine is a young girl in flower, the duchess is an adult woman, experienced in life and quite superior in her attitude. Marcel's trouble with her is that he never gets to see her clearly, but only catches a glimpse of her as she passes by, and when he discovers a photograph of her in a room where he is all by himself, it is like having a private audience with her. What he is now allowed to study is the features of her face:

18. In Proust's day, important excavation work in the city Pompeii was undertaken, and the illustrated press showed photographs of mummified bodies in contorted positions. The reference to Pompeii was thus near at hand.

19. In the last part of the novel, the narrator depicts the grotesque and masklike faces of the aging aristocracy at a reception. This part, referred to as "Le Bal des Têtes" (meaning "the masquerade ball"), reveals how the characters have aged and how they have suffered the passing of time.

For this photograph was like one more encounter, added to all those that I had already had, with Mme de Guermantes; better still, a prolonged encounter, as if, by some sudden stride forward in our relations, she had stopped beside me, in a garden hat, and had allowed me for the first time to gaze at my leisure at that plump cheek, that arched neck, that tapering eyebrow (veiled from me hitherto by the swiftness of her passage, the bewilderment of my impressions, the imperfection of memory); and the contemplation of them, as well as of the bare throat and arms of a woman whom I had never seen save in a high-necked and long-sleeved dress, was to me a voluptuous discovery, a priceless favor. Those lines, which had seemed to me almost a forbidden spectacle, I could study there, as in a textbook of the only geometry that had any value for me. (SLT 3, 81)

Car cette photographie c'était comme une rencontre de plus ajoutée à celles que j'avais déjà faites de Mme de Guermantes ; bien mieux, une rencontre prolongée, comme si, par un brusque progrès dans nos relations, elle s'était arrêtée auprès de moi, en chapeau de jardin, et m'avais laissé pour la première fois regarder à loisir ce gras de joue, ce tournant de nuque, ce coin de sourcils (jusqu'ici voilés pour moi par la rapidité de son passage, l'étourdissement de mes impressions, l'inconsistance du souvenir) ; et leur contemplation, autant que celle de la gorge et des bras d'une femme que je n'aurais jamais vue qu'en robe montante, m'était une voluptueuse découverte, une faveur. Ces lignes qu'il me semblait presque défendu de regarder, je pourrais les étudier là comme dans un traité de la seule géométrie qui eût de la valeur pour moi. (RTP 2, 379)

What kind of "reading" takes place in this scene? The words "contemplation" and "study" suggests that Marcel's emotional engagement with the picture is deep and meaningful (rather than abrupt). He refers to his engagement with the picture as an "extended encounter," which indicates that the photograph creates a feeling of presence and intimacy. It is also remarkable that that the whole scene is described in terms of secrecy and prohibition, discovery and favor; Marcel is given access to something that has been hidden from him, and the picture is described as a revelation. However, this is not a classical ekphrastic description because it does not really make the reader see; we see how Marcel sees and feel his attraction to the photograph, but *what* he sees is merely hinted at.

In return, Marcel's motivation for studying the portrait is made clear. It gives privileged access to the face of a person he dreams about, a face that his perception cannot capture clearly, and his memory cannot reproduce. The scene depicts Marcel's gaze as he looks successively at her cheek, neck, eyebrow, throat, arms, and dress, before summing up his impression by focusing on the *lines* of her face. Highlighting these lines, he refers to the art of geometry, and this underlines the fact that Marcel does not engage with a woman in flesh and blood, but with a photographic picture.[20] Whereas the passage opens on a sensual note, focusing on her neck and cheek, this final remark reveals his penchant for abstraction and formalism, as well as his tendency to study a face like a work of art.

It seems to me that the main concern here is not sensual satisfaction (projection of fantasies) or a factual interest in Mme de Guermantes's face (documentation); rather, Marcel appears to look for some kind of truth in the picture.[21] The whole scene suggest that the medium of photography performs a singular attraction on Marcel and rewards his contemplation by offering a revelation to him. In fact, his attraction to the picture seems to be premised on the promise of such a revelation. If we acknowledge that Marcel expects some kind of revelation in the picture, this allows us to reconsider the question of the unreturned gaze. As Marcel depicts the photograph, the unreturned gaze does not seem to represent a problem; rather than expecting his gaze to be met by hers, Marcel engages with the aesthetic presence created by the photograph. Whereas the expectation to have one's gaze returned is a Romantic trope based on unmediated relations, and the unreturned gaze, in comparison, comes to represent the modernist feeling of alienation, Proust suggests how this trope is reconfigured in the age of photography.[22] He

20. This is underlined by Marcel's disappointment when he gets to see Mme de Guermantes for the first time in a church during a wedding. The problem for Marcel is that she does not correspond to his mental image of her. In real life, Mme de Guermantes's face is red, and her material presence is disturbing to Marcel. In my view, this episode supports the view that the photograph he studies allows for a different way of seeing her. Proust SLT 1: 199 / RTP 1: 172.

21. In fact, Marcel explicitly denounces the identity photograph as reductionistic in an offhand remark (this is clearer in the original than in the translation): "nothing more than the mere photograph, for identification" (SLT 3: 5) ["n'est plus que la simple carte photographique d'identité" (RTP 2: 311)].

22. In her insightful Proust study, Katja Haustein argues that the expectation to have one's gaze returned is a Romantic trope and that Marcel's experience of the unreturned gaze represents the collapse of Romanticism. This collapse, she maintains, leaves "emotional cavities" in the subject, that is, a state of unfulfilled desire, and she concludes that Proust initiates a rethinking of affectivity under post-Romantic conditions. I find this argument convincing and helpful, but Haustein does not discuss the act of looking at portrait photographs; she discusses the relation between Marcel and the world generally and more specifically the sight of his ill grandmother and the sight of Albertine sleeping. See Haustein, *Regarding Lost Time*, 54–67.

implies that the unreturned gaze in a photograph is part of the enigmatic absence-presence created by the picture; it creates an aesthetic experience rather than a "real" meeting.

Further, when the lines of the Mme de Guermantes's face are described as a treatise in geometry, and as the only one that matters to Marcel, this seems to indicate that the treatise concerns her specifically; indeed, this suggests that each face may have its own geometry. This way of reading faces differs from Lavater's physiognomic approach in which a general set of rules applied to all faces. Rather, Marcel sees the duchess's face as giving its own rule, like a work of art, and he acknowledges that her singularity is made visible by way of a photograph. In fact, Proust's reference to the art of geometry finds an interesting parallel in *Against Sainte-Beuve*, where he denounces biographical approaches to literature and advocates the autonomy of literature. There he states that, in Sainte-Beuve's hands, only "a treatise on pure geometry" ["un traité de géométrie pure"] escapes the biographical method.[23] Opposing this method, Proust advocates a formalist poetics in which a literary work is an abstraction and not simply an expression of the author's personal life. A similar logic seems to be at work in the depiction of Mme de Guermantes's photograph: in the picture, she is cut off from her biographical being and her personality is conveyed through her gestures, which are enhanced by the medium.[24] This rather sophisticated way of connecting life and art, which gives primacy to aesthetic form, is key to Proust's poetics.

Also important in this context is a letter Proust wrote to the Comtesse Greffulhe, who served as a model for the Mme de Guermantes, to ask for her photographic portrait. As he tries to convince her, he argues that what photographs do is in fact something wonderful; they immobilize a woman's beauty and thus eternalize "a radiant moment" [un moment radieux].[25] This key statement shows that Proust recognized the value of portrait photographs and saw them as giving access to eternal beauty. A similar view on photographs seems to be in play in the novel, and particularly in the passage on the photograph of Mme de Guermantes. Marcel studies how her features and lines are immobilized in the photograph, revealing her beauty. The photograph

23. Proust here reiterates Sainte-Beuve's own wording. Proust, *Against Sainte-Beuve*, 12 / Proust, *Contre Sainte-Beuve*, 221.
24. In this context, we may add that Paul Nadar often retouched his photographs, removing riddles and uneven skin tones, thus making his photographs resemble art.
25. Proust, quoted in Tadié, *Marcel Proust: Biographie* 1: 549 / Tadié, *Marcel Proust: A Life* 1: 316. I will come back to this passage in the last part of the chapter.

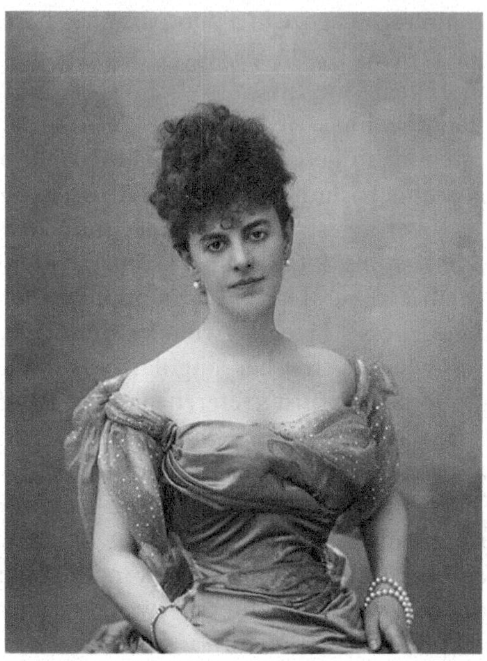

Figure 1.3   Portrait photograph of the Comtesse Élisabeth Greffulhe by Paul Nadar, 1895.

thus allows him to study her face like a work of art, and just like a work of art, the photograph seems to yield some kind of truth.

However, what kind of truth could be in play here? As we saw in the previous passage on faces and gestures, the narrator asserts that the features of a face may reveal a person's attitude toward the world and thus translate between body and mind. If we adopt this way of thinking about gestures in our understanding of Marcel's engagement with the Mme de Guermantes's photograph, we may see the photograph as making visible her philosophy of life. Yet her "philosophy" or "truth" is never explicitly conveyed to the reader and thus remains an enigma in the novel. We study the narrator's attraction and emotional response to the portrait photograph but are never allowed to see it. The picture is evoked as a place for revelation, but it is at the same time hidden from the reader. This way of thinking about portrait photographs may help us to understand why the contemplation of photographs matters so much to Marcel: he is searching for the sitter's attitude toward life, as it is revealed by silent miens and gestures.

This way of associating faces, photographs, and gestures resonates with more recent reflections on photography and gestures, and in particular the writings of Giorgio Agamben. This should not surprise us, for Agamben is an astute reader of Proust, who several places takes his cue from the French writer. In an essay on gestures and photography, where Proust plays a key role, he asserts that photographs are capable of capturing a person's gestures and making them visible to us. He sees this as a prefiguration of Judgment Day, when the final truth about a person is revealed, and he asserts that Judgment Day will find us in an "insignificant" moment of our everyday lives:

> In the supreme instant, man, each man, is given over forever to his smallest, most everyday gesture. And yet, thanks to the photographic lens, that gesture is now charged with the weight of an entire life; that insignificant or even silly moment collects and condenses in itself the meaning of an entire existence.[26]

Agamben is here concerned with the most intimate gestures of a person, which are so insignificant that we barely notice them before we see them captured in a photograph. These gestures are the carriers of what is most intimate to us and thus condenses the meaning of our lives. By exposing such gestures, a photograph thus unfolds the less noticeable aspects of our lives and charge them with meaning.

What is intriguing is the way in which Agamben refers to Proust in this essay. First, his conception of photography as Judgment Day recalls Proust's conception of gestures as issuing from a reifying catastrophe such as the destruction of Pompeii: both of them postulate a transformative moment in which time is frozen, contracted, and made visible as gesture. Second, and more specifically, Agamben picked up the Judgment Day metaphor from Proust, but from a different text: his essay on Ruskin published in 1900.[27] There, Proust comments on a seemingly insignificant stone figure in a church and considers it in terms of Judgment Day and gesturality. For Proust, the minor figure carved in stone—with its peculiar expression—demonstrates how art can address us across a temporal distance. Using this Proustian trope, which connects Judgment Day and the truth of art, Agamben thus develops his views on the *redemptive* moment of photography.

This redemptive moment is crucial because it connects the time of the sitter with the time of the beholder. For Agamben, a photograph is thus marked by a double temporality: it refers both to the

26. Agamben, "Judgment Day," 24.
27. Proust, "John Ruskin," 116–30.

chronological time of the photograph (the time of the sitter) and to eschatological time, the moment where a person's life is recognized and redeemed (the time of the beholder). He relates this to an exigency or a "mute apostrophe" in the photograph in which the sitter demands to be named and not forgotten. Here, Agamben takes his cue from Benjamin's essay on photography, but he also refers explicitly to Proust, and more specifically to the portrait photograph Proust received from a young Edgar Auber (with whom he was in love), at one of his requests.[28] On the back of the picture, the following inscription could be read in English: "Look at my face: my name is Might Have Been; I am also called No More, Too Late, Farewell." This jesting inscription may have been deceiving for Proust, but perhaps he also appreciated its bittersweet insight into the temporal paradoxes of love—and photography.[29] A photograph allows one to contemplate possibility and loss in one figure. In keeping with this, Agamben considers Auber's inscription in terms of the ethical (or messianic) demands of the photograph: It is suspended between two temporalities: the memory of a historical moment and a hope for redemption—even resurrection. The photograph thus presents itself as a dynamized moment, perpetually moving toward redemption, toward the beholder.

With his Proustian tropes, Agamben thus allows us to conceptualize the apparent agency of photographs and the relation between the sitter and the beholder. They do not belong to the same situation, but they connect in the picture's gestic moment. As the beholder looks at the picture, he succumbs to its gestural expressiveness; the photograph makes visible the sitter's attitude toward life and calls upon the beholder to remember and take part in a particular existence. In this manner, the picture encompasses the possibility of recognition and truth.

Let us now return to *The Search* and pose the following questions: How does Proust describe the act of looking at photographic pictures? What is the role of the beholder in the contemplation of such pictures? We know for sure that Proust was concerned with our subjective ways of perceiving the world, but does this imply that the beholder simply uses portrait photographs as a screen for his own

28. Agamben refers to Benjamin's claim that the photograph of a Newhaven fishwife by David Octavius Hill silently expresses a desire to be named and not forgotten. See Benjamin, "Little History," 276–7.

29. Auber's inscription alludes to Dante Gabriel Rossetti's poem "Stillborn Love" (1870), so the intertextual relations are complex. As Brassaï has shown, the words of the inscription were important to Proust, and he used them several places. Brassaï, *Marcel Proust*, 38–41.

imagination? I would like to suggest a different possibility: that the contemplation of portrait photographs in Proust is motivated by a search for truth and the expectation of a possible revelation.[30] As the picture acts on the beholder, it seems to promise contact, revelation, truth. Even if the photograph may prove to be disappointing, frustrating, or only partly rewarding, the picture is active, and the beholder responds to something he or she sees in the picture.

Yet what the beholder looks for appears to exist as a latency in the photographic picture and seems to require a reading process. This reading process, in turn, is associated with solitude and the private room; we have seen how Marcel contemplates photographs when he is all by himself, both with respect to La Berma and Mme de Guermantes. Now, also with respect to *mental* images, Proust describes a reading process that takes place in the private room, and as the two processes seem to have something in common, comparing them might be helpful. As many researchers have pointed out, Proust uses photographic metaphors to describe the subjective processing of mental images. In the following two passages, we see how this photographic metaphor is used to describe how ephemeral impressions, to become discernable, require a process of "development" that takes place once someone has retreated to their private room:

> Pleasure in this respect is like photography. What we take, in the presence of the beloved object, is merely a negative that we develop later, when we are back at home, and have again found at our disposal that inner darkroom, the entrance to which is barred to us so long as we are with other people. (SLT 2, 490)

> We barely notice this remark if we are with friends: we are merry all the evening, a certain image never enters our mind; during those hours it remains dipped in the necessary solution: when we return home we find the plate developed and perfectly clear. (SLT 4, 217)

> Il en est des plaisirs comme des photographies. Ce qu'on prend en présence de l'être aimé, n'est qu'un cliché négatif, on le développe plus tard, une fois chez soi, quand on a retrouvé à sa disposition cette chambre noire intérieure dont l'entrée est « condamnée » tant qu'on voit du monde. (RTP 2, 227)

30. Here I build on Kaja Silverman's understanding of photography in terms of reception and revelation rather than projection, which stresses the nonhuman agency of the picture. In one of her chapters, Silverman offers an insightful reading of Proust in terms of photography, focusing on the figure of the chiasm and the relationship between Marcel and Albertine. See Silverman, *The Miracle of Analogy.*

> On ne fait guère attention à cette phrase si on est avec des amis ; on est
> gai toute la soirée, on ne s'occupe pas d'une certaine image ; pendant
> ce temps-là elle baigne dans le mélange nécessaire ; en rentrant on
> trouve le cliché, qui est développé et parfaitement net. (RTP 3, 193)

Marcel here establishes a contrast between ephemeral impressions
from social life and the deep experiences that can be developed in
hindsight when we withdraw to our private chamber, where the private chamber seems to work like a private darkroom. This *meta-
phorical* development process pertaining to perception images is
in many respects similar to the "reading" of actual portrait photographs.[31] Both activities take place in the private room, and in
both cases, a deeper truth is exposed on the basis of a latent or
underexposed image. The difference is that in the reading of photographs, the picture—with its trace of reality—acts on the beholder
and reveals something to him or her. In the case of mental images,
by contrast, the imagination appears to have the upper hand. The
photographic portrait reveals to Marcel something that lies outside
of him; it suggests a person's way of being and philosophy of life.

It should be pointed out that development is not the same as projection and that this way of understanding Proust recognizes the
subjective element in the reading process while also granting the
photograph an active role. Where projection requires a blank screen
on which the subject can project his fantasies, development starts
out from a visible trace and works toward exposing a latent picture.
As the processes in question are quite subtle, the choice of metaphor
matters. Of course, the projection model may be pertinent for an
understanding of Proust generally, but the problem is that it risks
simplifying the relation between picture and beholder. With respect
to the development model, one could argue that the beholder may be

31. Many researchers have commented on the importance of the principle of
    latency in Proust's work, including Larkin, who argues that "temporal latency
    characterizes Marcel's process of perception and reception," and Silverman,
    who asserts that the psyche is described by Proust as a "receptive surface, like
    a photographic plate, on which sensory 'impressions' are traced" and explains
    that these images are invisible until we illuminate them once we are back home.
    Further, Guerlac sees the time of the latent image as important for the novel's
    depiction of lived experience and dynamic time. Moreover, Silverman uses the
    term "development" to describe the workings of the involuntary memory, but,
    in my view, it could also be used in a wider sense, to describe a way of studying
    photographs. Larkin, *Proust Writing Photography*, 55; Silverman, *The Miracle
    of Analogy*, 117; Guerlac, *Proust, Photography, and the Time of Life*, 91–3.

more or less loyal to the trace in the photograph, but this is the case in all interpretation processes. My point is that Proust seems to endow portrait photographs with the capacity of exposing something truthful to the beholders. Portrait photographs incite us to engage with someone else's worlds—not as biographical persons, but as ways of being and as possible philosophies of life. Proust's description of the process of "reading" portrait photographs suggests that the truth of a face in a photograph is revealed through silent contemplation, and it suggests that this form of "development" involving the *beholder* is necessary to fully appreciate a portrait photograph. This mediation process brings about the "redemptive" moment of a portrait photograph, the moment when a person is recognized.

Confronting the Other

We have seen that portrait photographs inspire a love of the medium and in this regard are related to *desire*. We have also seen that photographs invite the reading of faces and gestures as if they were works of art and in this respect induce a search for *truth*. Now we will look at a third aspect that is explored in Proust's novel: how a photograph may create a *collision* in which one's subjective image of a person clashes with a photograph's unsentimental and seemingly objective rendering of the same person. Such collisions provoke feelings of stupefaction and alienation, but they also lead to insight about the difference between a subjective and an external gaze. By indicating the existence of a different field of vision, they contribute to a visual education and thus represent important steps in Marcel's learning process.

Proust's treatment of this topic needs to be seen against the background of his thoughts about the subjective life world of each human being. In the first volume, the narrator depicts subjective vision as a privilege allowing us to imbue the world with value. An external eye, by contrast, is described as having no value: "by the eyes of an observer who sees things only from without, that is to say, who sees nothing" (SLT 1, 444) ["aux yeux d'un observateur qui ne voit les choses que du dehors, c'est-à-dire qui ne voit rien" (RTP 1, 383)]. The narrator also describes one's inability to reach out of the subjective consciousness as part of the human condition: "Man is the creature who cannot escape from himself, who knows other people only in himself" (ISLT 5, 515) ["L'homme est l'être qui ne peut sortir de soi, qui ne connaît les autres qu'en soi" (RTP 4, 34]. Yet, he also expresses a longing to reach outside of the subjective consciousness and break through to the exterior world, as in the following paragraph from the first volume:

> For even if we have the sensation of being surrounded by our own soul, still it does not seem an immobile prison; rather do we seem to be borne away with it in a perpetual struggle to pass beyond it, to break out into the world [*pour atteindre à l'extérieur*], with a kind of discouragement, hearing endlessly, all around us, that unvarying sound which is no echo from without, but the resonance of a vibration from within. (SLT 1, 98)

> Car si on a la sensation d'être toujours entouré de son âme, ce n'est pas comme d'une prison immobile ; plutôt on est comme emporté avec elle dans un perpétuel élan pour la dépasser, pour atteindre à l'extérieur, avec une sorte de découragement, entendant toujours autour de soi cette sonorité identique qui n'est pas écho du dehors, mais retentissement d'une vibration interne. (RTP 1, 85–6)

In the novel, the idea that it is possible to escape the prison of our own consciousness and break out into the world is nurtured by the medium of photography, which offers an "external gaze" of the world to the beholder and indicates the deficiencies of his own field of vision. Indeed, Proust was one of the first to understand that photographs allow us to see the world without the mediation of subjective consciousness and thus to adopt an external gaze. As many researchers have pointed out, Proust's thoughts on vision and photography herald the theories of photography that started to take form early in the twentieth century. However, in exploring this aspect of photography, he pursues his own train of thought. In the following, I will therefore assess Proust's stance in relation to emergent theories of photography and consider how these issues are treated in *The Search*.

Two scenes in the novel and a few fragments from Proust's manuscripts are particularly revealing with respect to this exterior point of view. The first is the renowned scene in which Marcel, entering a room, unexpectedly sees his grandmother alone by herself but does not recognize her.[32] For a brief moment, Marcel's usual way of looking at his grandmother is not yet in place, and he views this unfamiliar

---

32. The role of "photographic vision" in this scene has been discussed by numerous critics, from Siegfried Kracauer's early observations (published in 1960) to Larkin's more recent examination. See Kracauer *Theory of Film*, 15–16; Larkin, *Proust Writing Photography*, 39.

woman as from outside, without any emotional commitment—as a witness, an observer, a stranger or *a photographer* would have seen her, he explains:

> there was present only the witness, the observer, with a hat and traveling coat, the stranger who does not belong to the house, the photographer who has called to take a photograph of places that one will never see again. The process that automatically occurred in my eyes when I caught sight of my grandmother was indeed a photograph. We never see the people who are dear to us except in the animated system, the perpetual motion of our incessant love for them, which, before allowing the images that their faces present to reach us, catches them in its vortex, flings them back upon the idea that we have always had of them, makes them adhere to it, coincide with it. (SLT 3, 149)

> il n'y avait là que le témoin, l'observateur, en chapeau et manteau de voyage, l'étranger qui n'est pas de la maison, le photographe qui vient prendre un cliché des lieux qu'on ne reverra plus. Ce qui, mécaniquement, se fit à ce moment dans mes yeux quand j'aperçus ma grand-mère, ce fut bien une photographie. Nous ne voyons jamais les êtres chéris que dans le système animé, le mouvement perpétuel de notre incessante tendresse, laquelle, avant de laisser les images que nous présente leur visage arriver jusqu'à nous, les prend dans son tourbillon, les rejette sur l'idée que nous nous faisons d'eux depuis toujours, les fait adhérer à elle, coïncider avec elle. (RTP 2, 438)

In this passage, Marcel depicts the contrast between a subjective gaze, colored by personal emotions, and a gaze that suddenly takes in something without having the time to establish the usual way of seeing. Describing the latter visual capacity further, he stresses how it occurs like an accident, allowing us to see something that it never should have witnessed. This happens because one's consciousness is not yet in place and the eyes work only at a mechanical level—like a camera:

> So it is when some cruel ruse of chance prevents our intelligence and pious affection from coming forward in time to hide from our eyes what they ought never to behold, when it is forestalled by our eyes, and they, arising first in the field and having it to themselves, set to work mechanically, like films [*pellicules*] (SLT 3, 149–50)

> Il en est de même quand quelque cruelle ruse du hasard empêche notre intelligente et pieuse tendresse d'accourir à temps pour cacher à nos

regards ce qu'ils ne doivent jamais contempler, quand elle est devancée par eux qui, arrivés les premiers sur place et laissés à eux-mêmes fonctionnent mécaniquement à la façon de pellicules. (RTP 2, 439)

This collision creates a radical feeling of estrangement, where Marcel experiences his grandmother as a stranger: "I saw, sitting on the sofa, beneath the lamp, red-faced, heavy, and common, sick, daydreaming, following the lines of a book with eyes that seemed hardly sane, a stricken old woman whom I did not know" (SLT 3, 150) ["j'aperçus sur le canapé, sous la lampe, rouge, lourde et vulgaire, malade, rêvassant, promenant au-dessus d'un livre des yeux un peu fous, une vielle femme accablée que je ne connaissais pas" (RTP 2, 440)]. We should note that this is a two-way process in which the grandmother appears as a stranger to Marcel and he himself feels estranged, being unable to connect with her. He recognizes neither his grandmother nor himself, simply because he has been granted access to a different field of vision. This is described as an extraordinary visual faculty, "the faculty of being suddenly the spectator of one's own absence (SLT 3, 149) ["la faculté d'assister brusquement à notre propre absence" (RTP 2, 438)]. By comparing this perspective with the photographer's perspective, Proust thus succeeds in conceptualizing a feeling of radical estrangement, of being outside oneself. At the same time, he succeeds in describing in a striking manner how photographic technology offers new visual experiences. Photographs bring about experiences of *otherness*, and this implies a feeling of being *alienated* and not recognizing the other person. This insight has been key to theories of photography after Proust.

The second scene in which a photograph provokes a collision occurs later in the novel, when Marcel shows his friend Robert de Saint-Loup a photograph of Albertine. Saint-Loup is already convinced that she must be beautiful because Marcel is so much in love with her. Yet when Saint-Loup finally gets to see her photograph, Marcel understands from his friend's face that it does not correspond to his expectations and that he sees something other than Marcel does:

> At last I had found the photograph. "She's bound to be wonderful," Robert was still saying, not yet having seen that I was holding out the photograph to him. All at once he caught sight of it, and held it for a moment between his hands. His face expressed a stupefaction which amounted to stupidity. "Is this the girl you love?" he said at length in a tone in which astonishment was curbed by his fear of offending me. (ISLT 5, 499)

Enfin je venais de trouver la photographie. « Elle est sûrement merveil-
leuse », continuait à dire Robert, qui n'avait pas vu que je lui tendais la
photographie. Soudain il l'aperçut, il la tint un instant dans ses mains.
Sa figure exprimait une stupéfaction qui allait jusqu'à la stupidité.
« C'est ça, la jeune fille que tu aimes ? » finit-il par me dire d'un ton où
l'étonnement était maté par la crainte de me fâcher. (RTP 4, 21)

Seeing Saint-Loup's confusion, Marcel understands that his own
enamored gaze is different from the gaze of the camera, and that the
photograph Saint-Loup looks at shows a different woman than the
one Marcel sees. As the two ways of seeing Albertine collide, Marcel
reflects critically upon the difference between them:

In short, Albertine was merely, like a stone round which snow has
gathered, the generating centre of an immense structure which rose
above the plane of my heart. Robert, to whom all this stratification
of sensations was invisible, grasped only a residue which it prevented
me, on the contrary, from perceiving. (ISLT 5, 500)

Bref Albertine n'était, comme une pierre autour de laquelle il a neigé,
que le centre générateur d'une immense construction qui passait par
le plan de mon cœur. Robert, pour qui était invisible toute cette stratification de sensations, ne saisissait qu'un résidu qu'elle m'empêchait
au contraire d'apercevoir. (RTP 4, 22)

In the novel's final volume, Marcel returns to this scene in a digressive
remark where he refers to "the expression on the face of Saint-Loup
when he had looked at the photograph of Albertine" (ISLT 6, 275) ["le
regard de Saint-Loup sur la photographie d'Albertine" (RTP 4, 491)].
This time he describes its effect as one of liberation; it helped him to
free himself for a moment from his "belief in the pure objectivity of
this feeling" (ISLT 6, 275) ["ma croyance en la pure objectivité de
celle-ci" (RTP 4, 491)]. Because of Saint-Loups's surprised response to
the photograph of Albertine, Marcel was for a moment liberated from
his illusion; he understood that his gaze was not objective but a subjective, enamored gaze. This insight is in fact key to Marcel's understanding of himself and his relation to others. It makes him realize that he
sees others through a subjective filter and that a different field of vision
exists, unfiltered, so to speak. This is the world as it is seen by the camera eye. Yet the "liberation" conveyed by the gaze of the camera also
entails alienation with respect to Albertine, for, without his subjective
filter, Marcel simply does not recognize her.

In addition to these important scenes, some of the material that Proust intended to include in *The Search* is interesting in this context, for there, too, the alienating effect of looking at photographs is highlighted in relation to Albertine.[33] In Proust's manuscripts, we find a few fragments depicting scenes where Marcel looks at photographs of Albertine and perceives her as a stranger. The following fragment is especially noteworthy:

> I looked at a photograph of her taken the very year, it seemed, when I knew her in Balbec, but it might have been the different hairstyle, it appeared to me that the face was inhabited by a stranger.
>
> She was already someone else during these last months when she was by my side than she had been when I knew her in Paris and Balbec. One of the photographs of her that I kept in my album during these different periods of time had the air of being inhabited by a new person more and more familiar and for whom the woman who inhabited the older pictures might have been just as strange as for me, although they were quite beautiful; those of a pleasant and serious girl but inspired by a God that I had never known and that had also disappeared from the Albertine that I had known. To such a degree that between the first years in Balbec and the last moments, the bond of personality seemed not to have been able to unite these twenty sorts of time with a continuous solution for the identity of the inhabitant of the various faces. (my translation)

> Je regardais une photographie d'elle faite la même année où je l'avais connue paraît-il à Balbec, mais était-ce la coiffure différente, le visage me semblait habité par une étrangère.
>
> Elle était déjà une autre pendant ces derniers mois où elle était auprès de moi que quand je l'avais connue à Paris, et à Balbec. Une des photographies que j'avais d'elle dans mon album à ces différentes époques avait l'air d'être habitée par une nouvelle personne de plus en plus familière et pour qui était aussi étrangère que pour moi-même la femme qui habitait les photographies plus anciennes, bien belles pourtant, celles d'une fillette accorte et grave mais inspirée d'un dieu que je n'avais pas connu et qui avait disparu aussi de l'Albertine que j'avais connue. Si bien qu'entre les premières années de Balbec et les derniers moments, le lien de la personnalité semblait n'avoir pas pu joindre ces vingt espèces de temps et une solution de continuité entre l'identité de l'habitante des divers visages. (RTP 4, 655)

33. These fragments are published as sketches (*esquisses*) to the work in an appendix section of the French Pléiade edition entitled "Les photographies d'Albertine" and preceded by Proust's note "À mettre quelque part" ("To be placed somewhere"). See RTP 4:655–6. These sketches are not included in the English translations.

In this rich passage, the narrator describes the picture of Albertine as "inhabited" by a stranger and thus points to a discrepancy between his own perception of Albertine and her picture. Further, he points to a discrepancy between the different pictures of her and suggests that the person in the most recent photograph might feel estranged with respect to the person in the former photographs. For the narrator, Albertine in these pictures fails to add up to one recognizable person; only the last manifestation of her is somewhat recognizable to him. The scene thus expounds on one of the novel's key motifs, that is, Albertine's many faces, and it shows how the narrator, in studying her photographs, discovers her profound strangeness.

In this manner, the sketch describing Albertine's picture offers further proof of Proust's interest in the alienating effect of photography: Just as in the grandmother scene and the scene where Marcel glances at Saint-Loup looking at Albertine's photograph, this scene shows how photographs create a collision. Yet by giving access to an external vision, they also make Marcel aware of his own limited viewpoint, and this proves to be important for the novel as a whole. Well aware that we do not see things objectively, the narrator asserts toward the end of the novel that "[w]e see, we hear, we conceive the world in a lopsided fashion" and that this creates a "perpetual error, which is precisely 'life'" (ISLT 5, 656) ["Nous voyons, nous entendons, nous concevons le monde tout de travers"; "Cette perpétuelle erreur qui est précisément la « vie »" (RTP 4, 153–4)]. This insight seems to be related to Marcel's encounters with photographs and different ways of seeing, and photographs could thus be seen as playing an important role in his visual education.

But this also prompts the question of whether photographs can do more than *liberate* a person from a subjective illusion: To what degree can they also give access to a different field of vision in such a way that the premises of human perception and interaction are radically altered? In the early days of photography theory, the idea of a new vision was groundbreaking and fueled multiple creative and theoretical endeavors.[34] The surrealists experimented with the visual potential of photographs during the 1920s, Moholy-Nagy claimed that photographs offered a "new vision" (1925), and Benjamin suggested that photographs gave access to the "optical unconscious" (1931).[35] Moreover, Epstein (1924),

34. Many researchers bypass this important context, but an exception is Suzanne Guerlac's recent study, which situates Proust's novel in the context of emerging theories of photography; see Guerlac, *Proust, Photography, and the Time of Life*, 42–3.
35. Moholy-Nagy, *Malerei, Fotografie, Film*; Benjamin. "Little History." Recently, Kaja Silverman has offered similar perspectives on photography; see *The Miracle of Analogy*.

Balázs (1925), and Woolf (1926) made similar claims with respect to film.[36] The insight that photography and film allowed viewers to see the world without the mediation of subjective consciousness was revolutionary, and the new media were consequently invested with utopian ideals. The belief was that photography and film gave access to an external, common, or shared world and that the spread of these media opened up a new era in the history of humanity.

Proust's novel predates these theories by several years and informed them as they developed from the 1920s onward. It offers early insight into the workings of photography, demonstrating that the medium represents a possible exit from solipsism and allowing us to see without the mediation of our subjective consciousness. In the scenes described above, a veil is lifted from Marcel's eyes, allowing him to see first his grandmother, and later Albertine, without his usual projections, the result being a feeling of alienation. Yet there are important differences between Proust's stance and early theories of photography: Proust never invested the medium with ideals of intersubjectivity. In Proust's novel, the external gaze is depicted as exceptional and momentary and never gains permanence. It is described as an accident, a shock, causing feelings of alienation, but also leading to insight.

To capture the accident-like quality of this gaze, we may borrow a term from Roland Barthes: what takes place here is a *confrontation* between a subjective gaze and "reality," as it is conveyed by photographs (in Lacanian terms, a confrontation between "the imaginary" and "the real"). Barthes uses the word "confrontation" [affrontement] in the syllabus for a planned seminar on Proust and photography dedicated to Paul Nadar's photographs of people from Proust's circles. The seminar was experimental in that it ventured to explore the effects of such confrontations on his students and make them appreciate the modus operandi of photography: the way they affect us and disturb us, challenge our subjective worlds, and offer access to something radically *other*.[37] In a similar manner, we may venture to say that, for Proust, part of the fascination with portrait photographs stems from

36. Epstein, "On Certain Characteristics of *Photogénie*"; Balázs, *Early Film Theory*; Woolf, "The Cinema."
37. Barthes planned the seminar as an experiment where the students examined (but did not analyze or comment on) Paul Nadar's portraits of the persons from Proust's circle (who served as models for the novel's characters). The aim was to "produce an intoxication, a fascination, an action particular to the Image," he stated. Barthes explained that the experiment was directed toward "marcellians" (not those interested in Proust as an author), who knew the novel intimately and had developed their own ideas of the characters. For these persons, a meeting

the way they may disturb our mental images of a person and give access to *otherness*. Even if it is momentary, even it occurs in a sudden and violent manner, this external gaze contributes to Marcel's visual education, teaching him the existence of a world to which he usually does not have access.

Describing this visual experience, Proust does not invest it with utopian ideas (like the early theories of photography), nor does he see it as changing the premises of human thought (like Deleuze would do later with respect to film), but he acknowledges how it momentarily shakes Marcel's visual and epistemological ground and reveals to him the uncertain foundation of the subject. In this manner, Proust's novel heralds important insights about photography and its epistemological implications.

However, even if Proust seems to acknowledge that photography may momentarily provide experiences of otherness, it ultimately plays a secondary role in *The Search*, whereas art is the privileged medium, and the novel in particular. Concluding his reflections in the last volume, the narrator contends that it is art that allows us to see what others see:

> Through art alone are we able to emerge from ourselves, to know what another person sees of a universe which is not the same as our own and of which, without art, the landscapes would remain as unknown to us as those that may exist on the moon. (ISLT 6, 254)

> Par l'art seulement nous pouvons sortir de nous, savoir ce que voit un autre de cet univers qui n'est pas le même que le nôtre et dont les paysages nous seraient restés aussi inconnus que ceux qu'il peut y avoir dans la lune. (RTP 4, 474)

Proust here acknowledges that each sees the world differently, and that there exists a visual landscape that is unknown to us, as unknown as the landscapes on the moon. In this manner, he continues his conceptualization of that which Benjamin would later refer

with the photographs of Proust's real-life models would bring about a confrontation [un affrontement] between their imaginary world and the "real" world, *le réel*. This experiment was no doubt inspired by Proust's novel and its insight about the shock caused by "conflicting perspectives." What interests Barthes is how the reader/beholder indulges in his or her subjective imagination, but also must bear intrusion from *le réel*. Even if the confrontation with such photographs creates disappointment, uneasiness, or surprise, they have a hold over us, he asserts. See Barthes, "Proust and Photography." For an illuminating discussion of the seminar notes, see Yacavone, "Reading through Photography." See also Yacavone, "Barthes et Proust."

to as our "optical unconscious," but this time in relation to art. This insight emerges at the point when the narrator is ready to withdraw from social life to write his novel, having been disillusioned with all human relations—friendship, love, and social acquaintances.

Yet one could ask whether Proust's—and Marcel's—experience with photography has contributed to this insight about the novel as a medium. Not only are the previous passages on photography described as revelatory and leading to insight, but Proust also resorts to photographic metaphors to depict the merits of the novel as an art form. He describes it as an optical instrument that the reader can use in order to perceive more than he is usually capable of: "The writer's work is merely a kind of optical instrument which he offers to the reader to enable him to discern what, without this book, he would perhaps never have perceived in himself" (ISLT 6, 273) ["L'ouvrage de l'écrivain n'est qu'une espèce d'instrument optique qu'il offre au lecteur afin de lui permettre de discerner ce que sans ce livre il n'eût peut-être pas vu en soi-même." (RTP 4, 489–90)]. The novel is thus described as a visual technology that allows readers to see differently, through someone else's "lenses." Of course, the novel as an aesthetic form works in a different way than a photograph insofar as it uses words rather than images and the reading process is stretched out in time. So how does a novel make us see? According to Proust, this is a question of literary style: Just like color used by a painter, the style of the writer is "a question not of technique but of vision" (ISLT 6, 254) ["car le style pour l'écrivain aussi bien que la couleur pour le peintre est une question non de technique mais de vision" (RTP 4, 474)]. Indeed, Proust's prose style has a strong visual quality; through an extensive use of photographic metaphors and motifs, he makes the reader see, and he also offer a reflection on our ways of seeing. At the end of the novel, it thus seems that Marcel's experiences with photographs—what we could call his visual training—has become an integrated part of his insight as a writer. He has learned that people see in different manners, he has become aware of the limitation of his own viewpoint, and he has acknowledged that a visual landscape exists that is as unknown to us as the landscape on the moon. *The Search* is premised on this insight.

The Explosion of the Private into the Public

Toward the end of *The Search*, Proust's timely engagement with photography is thus abandoned and translated into a series of photographic metaphors related to art and literature. This leaves some unanswered questions to the photographically inclined reader. Certainly, it is not surprising that a novelist ends up praising the novel as an art form, and especially a novel that is about the process of becoming a writer. But the narrator's fascination with photography proper, in tandem with his use of photographic metaphors to describe the merit of the novel, creates uncertainty in the value system of Proust's own novel. Adding to this is the variety of approaches to photography. As we have seen, Marcel's contemplation of different photographs creates different responses: Looking at La Berma's picture, Marcel understands that she shows always the *same* face, whereas the contemplation of Mme de Guermantes's picture is like revelation to him, giving access to her *singular* way of being. But the encounters with Albertine's pictures show that she always differs from herself and has *numerous* ways of appearing. Moreover, the novel in some cases convey negative views on the medium as a mechanical technology. For instance, Marcel's grandmother sees the mechanical nature of photographic reproductions as vulgar (SLT 1, 45 / RTP 1, 39).[38] However, a general remark suggests that photographs can transcend their technological basis and enter the aesthetic sphere; as soon as they cease to refer to reality, they acquire dignity as aesthetic objects bearing a trace of the past:

> I keep a photograph of the house, when it was still unspoiled, just as I keep one of the princess before her large eyes had learned to gaze on anyone but my cousin. A photograph acquires something of the dignity that it ordinarily lacks when it ceases to be a reproduction of reality and shows us things that no longer exists. (SLT 2: 374)

> [Je] conserve la photographie de la première encore intacte, comme celle de la princesse quand ses grands yeux n'avaient de regards que pour mon cousin. La photographie acquiert un peu de la dignité qui lui manque quand elle cesse d'être une reproduction du réel et nous montre des choses qui n'existent plus. (RTP 2: 123)

How, then, should we understand the novel's stance on photography? In my view, *The Search* could be seen as exploring the uncertain status of photographic pictures early in the twentieth century. As "immaterial" representations of persons, portrait photographs create

---

38. The grandmother thus presents a common accusation against photography from the perspective of artists and writers (from Baudelaire onward): photographs are merely mechanical devices. Further, the narrator suggests that the spread of landscape photographs has diminished the value of Elstir's landscape paintings, making banal the laws that art first discovered: "an industry has vulgarized them [the laws]," he claims (SLT 2, 454) ["une industrie les a vulgarisées" (RTP 2, 194)].

a strange absence-presence; they resemble art but are produced by means of technological reproduction. What status should one grant such objects? Indeed, the relation between photographs, art, and truth is key with respect to Proust's view of photography. *The Search* depicts a situation where portrait photographs are, on the one hand, associated with an enigmatic presence and, on the other, associated with a person's vulgar appearance. What's more, they seem to give access to a different field of vision. As Proust describes how Marcel and other characters engage with portrait photographs, he offers insight into the attraction and beauty of portrait photographs around 1900, while at the same time describing a rapidly changing media culture. Accordingly, his ambivalent engagement with photographs can be better understood in light of the developments of the visual culture of his day, pulling him toward a negative verdict on the medium. With the rise of the illustrated press, a more vulgar use of photographed faces started to dominate and diminished the possibilities for finding truth in photographs.

When photographed faces started to proliferate in the illustrated press, a new phase began in the cultural history of the human face.[39] Where individuals appearing in the press were previously referred to by their proper names and sometimes an engraved portrait, they would now more and more often be referred to through a portrait photograph as well.[40] Their "real" faces, which were previously reserved for face-to-face encounters, were now exposed to a mass audience. This change was already prepared by the circulation of celebrity cards (which individuals could buy and take home) and the exchange of family portraits (used mostly in the private sphere). However, the illustrated press increased the circulation of photographed faces and changed the structural conditions pertaining to portrait photographs: they were increasingly in the hands of media houses rather than in the hands of private citizens.[41]. This media change had large-scale consequences, but it worked in subtle rather than spectacular ways.

39. According to press historian Gisèle Freund, press pictures were introduced in the newspapers during the two first decades of the twentieth century, whereas the weekly and monthly magazines printed photographs from 1885 onward. Freund, *Photography and Society*, 104.
40. Freund asserts that the press photographs made the faces of famous people familiar: "The introduction of newspaper photography was a phenomenon of immense importance [. . .] The faces of public personalities became familiar and things that happened all over the globe were to his share. As the reader's outlook expanded, the world began to shrink." Freund, *Photography and Society*, 103.
41. Marien, *Photography*, 241.

With this "professional" use of faces and photographs, the distinction between the private and the public spheres started to dissolve. Indeed, it could be argued that the increased use of mediated faces in the press contributed to a reconfiguration of the relation between the private and the public spheres.

An important element in this development was the growth of a celebrity culture that made extensive use of photographs. Yet also the faces of private citizens were preyed upon and could find their way to the public without the consent of the sitter. The contrast between the celebrity culture profiting from the new media situation and more restricted circles appreciating discretion and privacy becomes abundantly clear if we look at two women whom Proust admired and their relation to photographs: the actress Sarah Bernhardt and the Comtesse Greffulhe. Bernhardt served as a model for La Berma in *The Search*, whereas Greffulhe served as a model for Mme de Guermantes. In Proust's novel, we understand that acquiring a photograph of La Berma is easy; Marcel simply buys a celebrity photograph of her in an open-air stall in Paris, and he kisses it when he is all by himself. He also studies theater posters for her performances, which typically included photographs. By contrast, obtaining a picture of Mme de Guermantes proves difficult. She will refuse to give him the photograph he asks for, and Marcel only gets to study a picture of her in a "stolen moment" in her nephew's room.

These episodes depict two different circuits for photographs, and even if they are fictive, they correspond to historical conditions that are well documented. As is well known, Sarah Bernhardt was at the center of the new celebrity culture and her fame was promoted, to a large degree, through photographs (celebrity cards, posters, advertisements, and pictures in the illustrated press). In her study of this celebrity culture, Sharon Marcus describes how Bernhardt became a star by "multiplying" herself in photographs.[42] She also asserts that in purchasing such photographs the audience sought a sense of "intimacy, connection, and proximity" with and to the celebrity culture.[43] In this light, we may see Marcel kissing La Berma's picture as the typical behavior of early "fandom culture" induced by the mass media. In this culture, the multiplication of photographs does not usually represent a problem and does not diminish the value of the picture. As Marcus states, "copies do not dim the celebrity's halo:

42. Marcus, *The Drama of Celebrity*, 131–2.
43. Marcus, *The Drama of Celebrity*, 96.

they brighten it."[44] Yet in Proust's novel we see how Marcel starts to reflect upon the multiplication of La Berma's picture and to feel jealous of the other "fans" who also get to kiss her picture. He seems partly excited to engage with a mass audience, partly dissatisfied to share his love object with others, and this ambivalence ties in with his ambivalent view of La Berma in the novel.

As for the Comtesse Greffulhe, she belonged to an exclusive circle in high society that was not open to outsiders. When Proust asked her for a photograph, she declined, but of course with polite excuses. A letter from Proust to the countess, written in January 1920, shows how he responded to her rejection:

> May I be allowed to remind you of my request for a photograph (even if it is of the portrait by Laszlo). When you refused me before, you offered a very poor excuse, to the effect that a photograph immobilizes and reduces [arrête] a woman's beauty. Yet is it not a wonderful thing to immobilize, that is to say perpetuate, a radiant moment? It is the effigy of a youth that is eternal; I may add that a photograph I once saw at Robert de Montesquiou's seemed to me to be more beautiful than the portrait by Laszlo. As for Helleu's portrait, I have it in my copy of Montesquiou's book, but it doesn't look like you.[45]

> Je me permets de vous rappeler ma demande d'une photographie (fût-ce du portrait de Laszlo). Pour me la refuser jadis, vous aviez allégué une bien mauvaise raison, à savoir que la photographie immobilise et arrête la beauté de la femme. Mais n'est-il pas beau d'immobiliser, c'est-à-dire d'éterniser un moment radieux. C'est l'effigie d'une éternelle jeunesse ; j'ajoute qu'une photographie vue jadis chez Robert de Montesquiou me paraît plus belle que celle du portrait de Laszlo. Quant à celle du portrait d'Helleu, je l'ai dans le livre de Montesquiou mais elle ne vous ressemble pas.[46]

Proust here implores the Comtesse Greffulhe once more to give him her photograph, stressing that photographs reveal the eternal beauty of women. As we have already seen, the letter testifies to his view of the temporality of photographs, but it also demonstrates Proust's habit of requesting photographs from people he loved and admired and shows that this endeavor sometimes proved to be difficult.

44. Marcus, *The Drama of Celebrity*, 127.
45. Proust, quoted in Tadié, *Marcel Proust: A Life*, 316.
46. Proust, quoted in Tadié, *Marcel Proust: Biographie*, 1:549. Cf. Proust, *Corr.* XIX, 82.

Much later, the Comtesse Greffulhe commented on Proust's request in an interview, explaining that in those days "photographs were considered private and intimate."[47] Jean-Pierre Sirois-Trahan describes this as the *paradoxe Greffulhe*: while she was a celebrated beauty during the Belle Époque, she disapproved of having her photograph published.[48] Seeing a photograph of herself published, she expressed her discontentment: "It is not proper to do that. A woman should not let photographs of herself circulate" ["Cela ne se fait pas. Une femme ne doit pas laisser circuler des photographies d'elle"]. And the countess added that she had in fact offered the picture in question to her daughter ["Celle-ci, je l'avais donnée à ma fille Gramont"].[49] This shows that the Comtesse Greffulhe distinguished clearly between private and public photographs and preferred her own photographs to remain within the private sphere. Her refusal

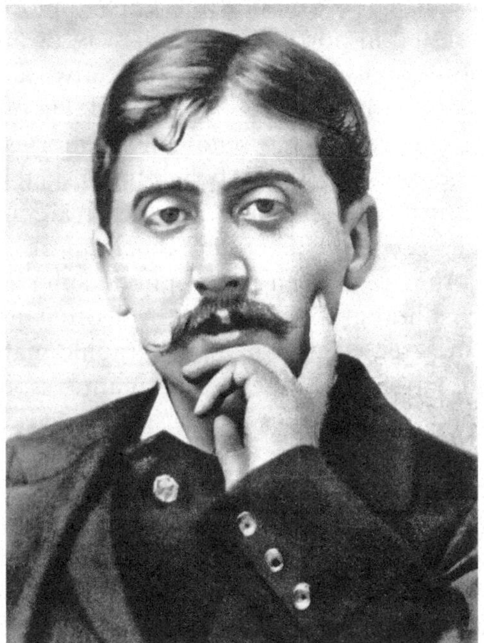

Figure 1.4   Portrait photograph of Marcel Proust by Otto Wegener, 1895. Available in the public domain via Wikimedia Commons.

47. The Comtesse Greffulhe, quoted in Bergstein, *In Looking Back One Learns to See*, 101.
48. Sirois-Trahan, "Un spectre passa . . . Marcel Proust retrouvé".
49. Bataillard, "Un personnage de Marcel Proust: La Comtesse Greffulhe." My translation.

to let her picture circulate freely indicates that some groups saw the spread of portrait photographs as a breach of privacy. They would assert their "right to their own image" and to their own face, and they would try to control the circulation of their photographs. What is at stake here is not merely the question of copyright and conditions of use, but the relation between body and image, original and copy. A private picture circulating widely in the public could easily affect the value of the original, and it would certainly change the relation between someone's public and private appearances.

By contrast, the exchange of photographs between individuals was a sign that they had entered into closer relations. Jean-Yves Tadié describes Proust's practice of asking for photographs in the following manner: "The gift of a photograph was, in Marcel's emotional life, an obligatory milestone, which he achieved as easily with men as he did with women." He adds that Proust in this manner created an important collection of photographs and points out that he was only interested in portraits: "In this way Proust assembled a collection of photographs: never landscapes, always human beings whom he had known, loved or simply admired. He often toyed with these photographs in order to resuscitate his memories or his dreams; those of women he found particularly helpful in sketching his female characters."[50] Proust's private collection of private and semiprivate portraits thus represented something much more exclusive than the photographs that were seen in the public sphere. Similarly, the engagement with photographs in the novel often has this private and exclusive character, even if the photographic material is mixed. Marcel's contemplation of Mme de Guermantes's picture is exemplary in this respect; he describes it as a "prolonged encounter" and a "priceless favor."

The scenes involving the pictures of the Comtesse Greffulhe / Mme de Guermantes and of Sarah Bernhardt / La Berma thus reflect upon different kinds of pictures and different ways of engaging with them. Yet the latter picture—the celebrity picture circulating in the public—had started to dominate in Proust's day. Indeed, the rise of the illustrated press is depicted in the novel and seems to be integrated into its value system. For instance, Marcel several times refers to the illustrated press in casual remarks. He points to a public image of Mme de Guermantes in an "illustrated magazine" (SLT 1, 199) ["revue illustrée" (RTP 1, 172)] taken at a costume ball held by the

---

50. Tadié, *Marcel Proust: A Life*, 162.

Princesse de Léon.[51] Later on, the narrator refers to illustrated magazines in a pejorative way when disparaging a statue that he finds unsatisfactory: "It gave me just about as much pleasure as a photograph of it in one of the 'illustrateds' might give a patient who was turning its pages in the surgeon's waiting room" (SLT 2, 263–4) ["Elle me causa à peu près autant de plaisir que son image au milieu d'un « illustré » peut en procurer au malade qui le feuillette dans le cabinet d'attente d'un chirurgien" (RTP 2, 25)]. With this offhand remark, the narrator implies that such photographs were perceived as dull, superficial, and surrogates for the real thing.

It is further important that the illustrated press fostered an interest in the author figure that must have displeased Proust. As Elisabeth Emery has shown, a decisive element in the new celebrity culture was a public obsession with the private lives of literary celebrities; through author interviews and photographic reportages from writers' homes, the private spaces of authors developed into "public institutions."[52] An interesting case is Robert de Montesquiou—the notorious dandy writer who served as a model for Proust's character Baron de Charlus. A popular figure in the illustrated press, he tried to control his photographic image, but experienced that the fame game was difficult to play.[53] The emergence of photojournalism and the illustrated press thus entailed large-scale consequences for the author figure, who was no longer conceived of merely as a voice or a written style, but as a face, a persona, a star.

As we may suspect, this development did not escape Proust. In *The Search*, Marcel complains about the recent interest in the writer's figure: "on the one hand, in proportion as society grew more corrupt, notions of morality became increasingly refined, while on the other hand the public learned far more than it had ever known about the private lives of writers" (SLT 2, 146) ["d'une part, au fur et à mesure que se corrompait la société, les notions de la moralité allaient s'épurant, et que d'autre part le public s'était mis au courant plus qu'il avait encore fait jusque-là de la vie privée des écrivains" (RTP 1, 549)]. This means that the author figure was being exposed in the public in a new way, and for Proust this tendency was deplorable because it detracted attention from the work of literature and

51. The notes in the Pléiade edition inform us that the Princesse de Léon indeed hosted a costume ball in 1891, which was photographed by Paul Nadar and became famous. See RTP 1, 1178.
52. Emery, *Photojournalism*, 4–5.
53. Emery, *Photojournalism*, 158.

directed it toward the biographical author. In Proust's view literature and art did not convey truth about the author's life, but offered a general truth: "the artist offers a solution in the terms not of his own personal life but of what is for him the true life, a general, a literary solution" (SLT 2, 145) ["l'artiste donne une solution non pas dans le plan de sa vie individuelle, mais de ce qui est pour lui sa vraie vie, une solution générale, littéraire" (RTP 1, 548)]. Here we are at the core of Proust's views on literature. The new interest in the author figure in the illustrated press may have buttressed Proust's criticism of biographical approaches to literature in the pamphlet *Against Sainte-Beuve* (begun in 1908, but published posthumously).[54] The biographic school in literary criticism dominating in this period was certainly in agreement with the celebrity culture in the press. In fact, one could see the illustrated press as a twentieth-century version of the salon institution that both Proust and Sainte-Beuve knew and that Proust saw as deceitful.

Countering this interest in the author figure, Proust advocates a formalist poetics, seeing the work of literature as enclosed upon itself. *The Search* performs this poetic principle: the protagonist eventually withdraws from society to his private chamber to write his novel in solitude, advocating art's truthfulness and society's deceitfulness. Similarly, Proust wrote the last parts of the novel in solitude, withdrawn to his chamber. Yet an album of carefully selected portrait photographs accompanied Proust in his seclusion, allowing him to

54. Proust there presents a severe critique of Sainte-Beuve, the beacon of biographical criticism, who saw knowledge about an author's life—his appearance in the salons as well as his diet and moral character—as the road to a work's truth. Fervently opposing this view, Proust insists on a formalist criticism that addresses the work of literature solely and dismisses biographical and contextual factors. He argued that a writer's insights in literature could not possibly be referred back to his social appearance simply because the writer appearing in society was not the same "self" as the writer alone with his literary work: "[a] book is the product of a self other than that which we display in our habits, in company, in our vices. If we want to try to understand this self, it is deep inside us, by trying to recreate it within us, that we may succeed." Proust, *Against Sainte-Beuve*, 12. [[u]n livre est le produit d'un autre moi que celui que nous manifestons dans nos habitudes, dans la société, dans nos vices. Ce moi-là, si nous voulons essayer de le comprendre, c'est au fond de nous-mêmes, en essayant de le recréer en nous, que nous pouvons y parvenir. Proust, *Contre Sainte-Beuve*, 221–2.] Today, this view may be accused of isolating the work of literature in the aesthetic sphere, but Proust had his reasons. Having spent a considerable amount of time in the Parisian salons, he firmly believed that they were ill-adapted to the pursuit of truth because of the vanity and pettiness that dominated there.

engage with a series of mediated faces. If we acknowledge that these "privileged" encounters were of great importance to Proust, we could add some nuances to the story about the writer's solitude. And if we acknowledge that the contemplation of portrait photographs was a part of Proust's life, we could perhaps better understand his various views on the medium.

The changing status of photographs in the decades before and after 1900 may in my view help us understand Proust's ways of engaging with the medium in *The Search*. Key in this respect is the difference between the photographs circulating in this private or semiprivate sphere and the photographs circulating in the wider public sphere. Proust's novel depicts a historical tipping point in the history of photography, one where photographs belonged between the hands of the beholder as much as in a printed magazine, where they belong to the private sphere as much as the public sphere. It could be argued that the rise of the illustrated press created a new media situation that reconfigured the relation between private and public faces and changed the relation between the picture and the beholder. The new media culture promoting mass-produced photographs diminished the possibilities for finding truth in photographs, and, of course, neither Proust nor Marcel endorsed this development. The writer and his narrator protagonist represented a way of engaging with photographs in decline, giving way to a new industry and a new face ideology. Today, when the dominance of this industry and this ideology is taken for granted, we should look to Proust to learn something about the lives and loves of photographs early in the twentieth century.

Chapter 2

Power in Photographs: Franz Kafka

In his fiction, Franz Kafka explores a set of inscrutable power relations and the precarious situations they create for his characters. Both metaphysical and profane forces seem to be at work, along with various technological entanglements. Portrait photography plays a role in this blend; in a variety of texts, Kafka displays a remarkable awareness of the powers of photographs. He depicts how they play a role in emotional life, creating attraction, longing, and sympathy as well as distrust and distress. He shows that they can be captivating in a limiting way, but also suggests that they can instigate processes of liberation. This engagement with portrait photographs reveals the fragile relation between human beings and technology and discloses how the premises for contact, communication, and identity formation were subject to change in Kafka's day.

Just like Proust, Kafka was passionate about portrait photographs in his personal life. The strongest evidence of this is his correspondence with Felice Bauer in the period 1912–17, which included an exchange of almost forty photographs. Kafka's letters testify to a deep emotional investment in Felice's photographs, and they reveal that he had a jealous eye and an obsessive interest in details. These letters show that photographs play a key role in creating intimacy and distant love. In Kafka's fiction as well, photographs proliferate, and especially family photographs play a key role. The characters' relation to such photographs reveal their ties of loyalty, emotional attachments, and imaginary lives. Kafka shows how photographs have a sway over the characters and serve as the compensatory gazes of the family members. Upon closer inspection, however, the photographs are ambivalent; they depict silent gestures and suppressed emotions. Beholding such photographs, his characters undergo both emotional and intellectual processes, sometimes immersing themselves in the pictures, sometimes attempting to interpret them, and sometimes considering their own relation to the photographs.

Yet Kafka not only explores the role of portrait photographs in love relationships and in family relationships—that is, their role in private life—but also problematizes more broadly the role of photographs in the visual culture of his day. In several cases, photographs serve as connecting devices between Kafka's fictive universe and the historical-political world he lived in. Especially interesting is his treatment of politically charged photographs, such as lynching photographs and photographs from the First World War. Kafka questions what kind of identification such images create and explores the role of the beholder as a witness to mediated events. In this manner, he explores the impact of the sinister and violent photographs circulating early in the twentieth century.

In previous research on Kafka and photography, a few works stand out as especially influential. Walter Benjamin's essay on photography explores the iconic childhood photograph that was taken of Kafka, stressing how his sad eyes tried to elude the conventions of bourgeois family photographs and how the photographic studio appeared like a fusion of a throne and a torture chamber.[1] Using the Kafka picture as an emblem, he highlighted the ambivalent forces related to portrait photography in the late nineteenth century. Portrait photographs also play an important role in Deleuze and Guattari's book on Kafka, and here, too, power relations are a key issue.[2] Seeing power as intimately connected with desire, they argue that portrait photographs—in particular family photographs—contribute both to binding up and unleashing flows of desire. In addition to these theoretical contributions, Carolin Duttlinger's book *Kafka and Photography* is important insofar as it maps and discusses virtually every aspect of Kafka's relationship with photographs and has opened up a large field of research.[3] As I discuss

1. Benjamin, "Little History."
2. For Deleuze and Guattari, photographs have to do with framing and serve as placeholders of bourgeois identities, intimately connected to conventional (oedipal) family structures. They serve to arrest and block desire. Yet Deleuze and Guattari acknowledge that photographs may also become the sites of *deterritorialization* and thus unleash insurgent forces. This may happen through *schizophrenic proliferation*. Deleuze and Guattari see both processes at work in Kafka's fiction and thus acknowledge Kafka's deep insight into the power of photographs as well as his capacity to turn these forces against themselves. Deleuze and Guattari, *Kafka*, 5; 61–2.
3. Duttlinger, *Kafka and Photography*. In addition, Gesa Schneider's book on Kafka's photographic poetics is a noteworthy contribution within this research field. Schneider's key argument is that photography in Kafka becomes a catalyst for a different kind of writing. Referring to Jonathan Crary's work on the technologies of vision, she asserts that Kafka engages with "real" photographs in his fiction, on the one hand, and produces a camera gaze in his texts, on the other.

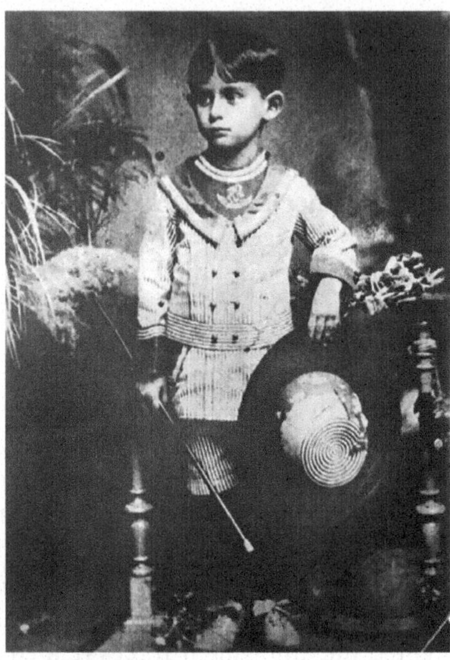

Figure 2.1   Portrait photograph of Franz Kafka as a child, taken between 1887 and 1889. Unknown photographer. Available in the public domain via Wikimedia Commons.

Kafka's engagement with the power of portrait photographs, I build on these pioneering works, while also drawing on the work of Giorgio Agamben. Yet my aim is to tease out Kafka's own way of addressing the power of photographs.

What interests me is Kafka's description of the "dual action" of portrait photographs; how they create both emotions and reflection, both attachment and detachment, in the beholder. In Kafka's writings we see how emotional investment in photographs creates and sustains affective ties to others, but also how reflection and detachment loosen up such ties and open up new possibilities. Moreover, I am interested in the relation between identity and anonymity in Kafka's engagement with photographs. Where the spread of portrait photography around 1900 has been seen as bolstering the bourgeois notion of identity, I would like to discuss whether photographs could also have a say in the creation of anonymity.

Further, Hanns Zischler's book on Kafka and film offers a "portrait of Franz Kafka as a moviegoer" and thus contributes to our understanding of Kafka's engagement with the new visual media. See Schneider, *Das Andere schreiben*, 19–20; Zischler, *Kafka Goes to the Movies*, 6.

In this chapter I study how Kafka's writings explore the ambivalent power of photographs and discuss especially their emotional and relational bearings. I first discuss the exchange of letters and photographs between Kafka and Felice Bauer, highlighting Kafka's attempt at interpreting the photographs and his concern with "unreturned gazes" and gestures. Next, I examine the role of photographs in *The Man Who Disappeared* (*Der Verschollene*, first published in German under the title *Amerika*), suggesting that the contemplation of photographs in Kafka's fiction reveals the characters' ties of loyalty and emotional attachments, while at the same time exposing ambivalences and dissonances that promote a liberation process. My argument here is that key scenes involving portrait photographs invite questions regarding identity and anonymity and tie in with some of the major topics in Kafka's oeuvre. In a third section, I discuss Kafka's treatment of politically charged photographs, such as photographs from the First World War. Focusing especially on the story "Blumfeld, an Elderly Bachelor" ("Blumfeld, ein älterer Junggeselle"), I argue that Kafka questions what kind of identification such images create. Finally, I discuss how the photographed subject in Kafka's day was inscribed in a set of power relations that pulled toward identity (in a family photograph) or anonymity (in a lynching photograph). I propose that Kafka's engagement with portrait photographs and power should be seen in light of this tension.

Photographs and Distant Love

What role could portrait photographs play in a love relationship in Kafka's day? Where Proust gave us insight into the attraction of photographs, Kafka's love letters expand our understanding of how photographs are invested with emotions and longings. His correspondence with Felice Bauer begins a month after their first meeting in Prague in August 1912. It soon becomes a passionate affair in which the exchange of studio portraits, childhood pictures, group photographs, and other kinds of photography plays a central role. In total, they exchanged around forty such photographs from 1912 to 1917, of which around half were sent during the initial phase from September 1912 to March 1913.[4] Kafka's letters comment extensively on these photographs; he describes them, tries to interpret them, and lets Felice know how he touches and kisses them. From

---

4. Duttlinger, *Kafka and Photography*, 127

the letters we thus understand that photographs play an important role in establishing and sustaining a long-distance relationship; in creating distant love.

Kafka's letters, the only part of their correspondence that is preserved, repeatedly draw Felice's attention to their first meeting on August 13, 1912, where photographs played a central role. It had taken place in Max Brod's home, where Kafka was unpleasantly surprised at first to find a stranger, because he had intended to discuss his current manuscript with Brod. In a letter from October 27 the same year, Kafka recalls how the three of them had instead looked at a series of photographs from a journey he and Brod had taken to Weimar and the Goethe House the same summer.[5] As Kafka repeatedly returns to this meeting in his letters, it is established as the *Urszene* of their relationship. He stresses Felice's thoughtful engagement with the photographs: "You took the pictures very seriously" (LF, 14) ["Sie nahmen das Anschauen der Bilder sehr ernst" (BFB, 23)].[6] Further, he refers to the way she had let her gaze wander around the table: "The changing view of your face, as you slowly turned your head, left an indelible impression on me" (LF, 65) ["Diese langsame Kopfwendung und den hiebei natürlich verschiedenartigen Anblick Deines Gesichtes habe ich unvergänglich behalten" (BFB, 105)]. Commenting on one of the photographs she sends him, he also asks her about a gesture he believes is typical of her: "[I]sn't it a habit of yours to keep pushing your hair off your forehead, especially when you are holding a picture and want to look down at it? Does my memory betray me? For I sometimes see you that way" (LF, 125) ["[H]ast Du nicht die Gewohnheit, öfters das Haar aus der Stirn zu streichen, besonders wenn Du z.B. ein Bild in der Hand hältst und niederschauen willst. Ein Irrtum der Erinnerung? Ich sehe Dich nämlich manchmal so" (BFB, 200)]. Thus, it appears that Kafka had been closely looking at her while she looked at his photographs during their first meeting. And photographs, gazes, and gestures will play key roles in his letters to Felice.

Kafka's letters are very emotional, especially the letters written during the first six months of their acquaintance. He quite soon opens up to her, without hiding his anxieties and nervous manners,

5. Stach, *Kafka*, 98; Duttlinger, *Kafka and Photography*, 126.
6. References are to the following edition and translation, abbreviated as shown: BFB: Franz Kafka, *Briefe an Felice Bauer*, edited by Hans-Gerd Koch. Frankfurt am Main: Fischer, 2015. LF: Franz Kafka. *Letters to Felice*, edited by Erich Heller and Jürgen Born, translated by James Stern and Elisabeth Duckworth. New York: Schocken Books, 2016.

and tells her about his writing, his work at the insurance company, his health, and his peculiar *Lebensweise*. The letters bear witness to an intimate relationship, and it may be seen as a paradox that this intimacy is created by letter writing, which presupposes a distance. One may ask if this form of intimacy was easier for Kafka to endure; for a nervous man like Kafka, distant love may have been preferable to a "real" relationship.

What is curious about these letters is the fact that two of their main topics are precisely letter writing and the exchange of photographs. This could be described in Roman Jakobson's terms as a focus on the channel of communication itself, that is, the *phatic* function of utterances. (This is the function that is activated if, for instance, someone is speaking on the phone and asks the interlocutor, "Can you hear me?") Kafka continually asks Felice if she has received his letters and reproaches her for not writing at regular intervals. In a letter from November 20, he asks her with bewilderment if she has not received any of the fourteen or fifteen letters he has sent her since last Friday, while in a letter from December 24, he complains that it has been sixty-six hours since he last received a letter from her (BFB, 83, 196). He thus tries frantically to keep the channel between them open and to confirm their common presence in the communication circuit. Curiously, Kafka saw the inefficiency of the postal system as a disturbing factor in this regard, causing numerous delays and altering the order of their letters. He refers to this postal problem as "a regular misfortune in our relationship" (LF, 49) ["ein regelmäßiges Unglück unseres Verkehrs" (BFB, 77)], and claims that they are "persecuted by the post office" (LF, 53) ["die Post verfolgt uns wirklich" (BFB, 85)].

A feeling of connectedness is established through these letters, but it is vulnerable and depends on the frequency and rhythm of their correspondence. Kafka is notoriously indecisive about his preferences in this regard: sometimes he pleads with Felice to write more often; other times he forbids her to write to him because his longing for her letters disturbs his work. He describes the effect of this long-distance relationship as a painful hybrid of presence and absence: "We are lashing each other with all these letters. They can't create a presence, only a mixture of presence and distance that becomes unbearable" (LF, 73) ["Wir peitschen einander mit diesen häufigen Briefen. Gegenwart wird ja dadurch nicht erzeugt, aber ein Zwitter zwischen Gegenwart und Entfernung, der unerträglich ist" (BFB, 117)]. Even if the exchange of letters continues, this remark highlights a key problem in their relationship: the uncertain relation between absence and presence. What helps creating a feeling of presence, however, is Kafka's imagination, which allows Felice's face to emerge from the letters. He asserts that, to be able to write to someone, "one has to have an idea of the face one is addressing" (LF, 40) ["muß man sich doch vorstellen, daß man sein Gesicht vor sich hat, an das man sich wendet" (BFB, 64)]. A week later he expresses the same idea, writing that "your letters were as present to me as is the expression on the face of someone I am talking to" (LF, 55) ["denn deine Briefe waren mir wie immer so auch diesmal so gegenwärtig wie der Gesichtsausdruck des Menschen, mit dem ich spreche" (BFB, 87)]. Yet a new stage in their relationship begins when they start exchanging photographs and the imaginary face is replaced by a series of photographs where Felice's face can be studied carefully.

Having several times hinted that he would have appreciated a picture of her, Kafka finally receives one late in November 1912. Soon he starts to expect new photographs, and he also sends his own photographs to her. In this manner, a new channel of communication is opened up, and Kafka highlights this twofold form of communication by describing himself as a double figure, as both a letter writer and a person represented in a photograph. Felice has to deal with and care for both: "Forgive us both, the writer of letter and the subject of the photograph, and in our duality let us also benefit with kisses" (LF, 89) ["Verzeih uns beiden, dem Briefschreiber und dem Photographierten und laß uns durch unsere Zweigestalt auch an Küssen profitieren" (BFB, 143)]. From now on, the photographs act as "doubles" in their relationship, and Kafka engages in a highly emotional and physical engagement with them.

It is moving to read about Kafka's emotional investment in these photographs; he touches them, kisses them, and brings them with him wherever he goes. He thus discloses a veritable "love of the medium," caring for the photographs as physical objects. It starts when Kafka receives the first photograph of her; he is about to go on a work trip (an undertaking that does not please him the least) and is thrilled because the picture may serve as a travel companion:

> As I told you yesterday, I am going away this evening, alone, at night, into the mountains, and though you couldn't have known, you send me this charming little companion. What a delightful little girl! The narrow shoulders! So fragile and easy to hold! She is so modest, but calm. No one had worried her in those days, and made her cry, and her heart beats the way it should. Looked at for any length of time, you know, the picture could easily bring tears to one's eyes. (LF, 65)

> Wie ich Dir gestern schrieb, fahre ich heute abend weg, allein, in der Nacht, ins Gebirge und da schickst Du mir ohne daß Du es ausdrücklich wüßtest, die liebe kleine Begleiterin. Was für ein liebes kleines Mädchen ist das! Die schmalen Schultern! So schwach und leicht zu fassen ist sie! Bescheiden ist sie, aber ruhig. Damals hat sie noch niemand geplagt und zum Weinen gebracht und das Herz schlägt wie es soll. Weißt Du, daß man leicht Tränen in die Augen bekommt, wenn man das Bild länger ansieht. (BFB, 104)

This passage shows how Kafka indulges in the photograph, contemplating Felice's tenderness, and it shows the emotional impact the picture has on him; it even has the capacity to provoke a physical reaction in the form of tears. At his return, he discloses that he kept the image by his bed during the trip and thus treated it as a companion: "During the whole trip your photograph was looked at now and then for comfort, and for comfort your photograph spent the night on a chair beside my bed" (LF, 67) ["Dein Bild würde während der ganzen Reise hie und da zum Troste angesehn, Dein Bild lag auch in der Nacht zum Troste auf dem Sessel neben meinem Bett" (BFB, 108)]. Further, Kafka soon takes on the habit of bringing the photographs with him in a little purse that Felice has sent him for that very purpose:

> The little case you sent me is a magic case. It is making a different, calmer, better man of me. The possibility of looking at the picture wherever I happen to be, or at least of pulling out the little case (the notion of carrying it constantly in my hand has not proved successful), is again a new delight, which I owe to you. Whenever I look at your picture – it is standing in front of me now – I marvel at the strength which binds us together. (LF, 126)

> Dieses kleine Täschchen, das Du mir geschickt hast, ist ein Wundertäschchen. Ich werde ein anderer ruhiger besserer Mensch dadurch. Diese Möglichkeit, wo immer ich bin, das Bildchen anzusehn oder wenigstens das Täschchen hervorzuziehn (die Methode es ständig in der Hand zu halten, hat sich nicht bewährt) ist wieder eines neues Glück, das ich Dir verdanke. Wenn ich Dein Bildchen – es steht vor mir – anschaue, geht beim Anschauen immer wieder ein Staunen darüber mit, mit welcher Stärke wir zwei zusammengehören. (BFB, 201)

The purse allows him to contemplate her photograph wherever he is, and he can immediately connect with her and make her present:

> There are times when my longing for you overwhelms me. The case is ripped open, and in a friendly and charming manner you at once

present yourself to my insatiable scrutiny. In the light of street lamps, outside illuminated shop windows, at my desk in the office, at a sudden standstill in the corridors. (LF, 127)

Manchmal geht mir das Verlangen nach Dir an die Kehle. Das Täschchen wird ausgerissen und freundlich und lieb zeigst Du Dich gleich dem unersättlichen Blick. Unter dem Licht der Straßenlaternen, an den beleuchteten Auslagen, am Schreibtisch im Bureau, beim plötzlichen Innehalten auf den Korridoren. (BFB, 203)

A similar phrase is used earlier, when he describes his delight at opening a letter from her and discovering a photograph in it: "one finds a picture inside and you yourself slip out of it" (LF, 82) ["da ist ein Bild darin gewesen und Du schlüpfst selbst heraus" (BFB, 132)]. These comments show how Kafka treats the photographs as her doubles and how he starts including them in his everyday life. This, however, creates a peculiar relation between presence and absence, which causes frustration and longing.[7]

To compensate for Felice's absence, Kafka emphasizes the photographs' materiality and enters into a tactile and affective relation with them. The photographs gain value as material objects that Kafka can bring with him, just like talisman figures. As Duttlinger has argued, this exchange of photographs can be described as fetishistic.[8] We should note, however, that Kafka envisions this "fetishism" as reciprocal; he not only describes to Felice how he touches and kisses the photographs, but also discloses that he envisions himself as an image in her hands: "to me it means so much that you should hold me in your hands, at least in a photograph" (LF, 83) ["soviel liegt mir daran, wenigstens als Bild in Deiner Hand zu sein" (BFB, 133)]. The photographs thus serve as objects in which their longing, affection, and erotic desire can be invested. In this regard, Kafka's relation with images resembles the one described by Proust. Yet more than Proust, Kafka is painfully aware of the ambivalent powers of photographs:

Dearest, how powerful one is, face to face with a picture, and how powerless in reality! I can easily imagine your whole family stepping aside and removing themselves, leaving you on your own, while I lean across the big table searching for your eyes, finding them, and

7.   In her reading of the role of photography in these letters, Schneider, too, highlights the relation between presence and absence and how the photographs make Felice come to life for Kafka, even if she is absent. Schneider, *Das Andere schreiben*, 41–58.
8.   Duttlinger, *Kafka and Photography*, 125ff.

dying of joy. Dearest, pictures are wonderful, pictures are indispensable, but they are torture as well. (LF, 92)

Liebste wie mächtig ist man gegenüber Bildern und wie ohnmächtig in Wirklichkeit! Ich kann mir leicht vorstellen, daß die ganze Familie beiseite tritt und sich entfernt, daß nur Du allein zurückbleibst und ich mich über den großen Tisch zu Dir hinüberlehne, um Deinen Blick zu suchen, zu erhalten und vor Glück zu vergehn. Liebste, Bilder sind schön, Bilder sind nicht zu entbehren, aber eine Qual sind sie auch. (BFB, 148)

Kafka is tortured by pictures, and he is dying of joy from them. These violent emotions show how intensely Kafka experiences the power of portrait photographs. Where Proust mostly depicts responses of a less violent kind (only the picture of his grandmother tortures Marcel, and the torture lasts only a day), Kafka seems to be in the power of photographic pictures.

Kafka also differs from Proust in his detailed inspection and description of photographs, which could be described as belonging to the genre of ekphrasis. Carefully describing to Felice what he finds noteworthy in the images of her, he speculates about the situation they are taken in, and inquires about details. Using ekphrasis as an investigating mode, he displays both curiosity and suspicion. Yet there seems to be a conflict between Kafka's aim to fully understand the pictures and their muteness; the images he scrutinizes cannot be fully deciphered but appear to keep their secret. This link between photographs and secrets is clearly expressed in the following passage:

That photograph, dearest, brings me far, far closer to you again. [. . .] The lightning, the position, and the mood of those in the picture make it all look most mysterious, and the key to the mystery is on the table in front, lying beside its box, but this does not make the whole thing any clearer. You have a wistful smile, or it may be my fancy that invents this smile for you. I mustn't look at you too much, or I won't be able to take my eyes off you at all. (LF, 91–2)

Diese Photographie Liebste bringt Dich mir wieder ein großes, großes Stück näher. [. . .] Der Ganze sieht übrigens in der Beleuchtung, Gruppierung und Laune der Abgebildeten ganz geheimnisvoll aus und der Schlüssel des Geheimnisses, der vorne auf dem Tisch neben der zu ihm gehörigen Schachtel liegt, macht die Sache um nicht klärer. Du lächelst wehmüthig oder es ist meine Laune, die dir dieses Lächeln andichtet. Ich darf Dich nicht ordentlich ansehn, sonst bekomme ich den Blick nicht von Dir los. (BFB, 147)

Here Kafka simply cannot figure out exactly what is going on in the image and what kind of emotions are in play. Duttlinger is certainly right in pointing out that Kafka perceives Felice's photographs as mysteries to be deciphered and as hermeneutic puzzles, but it should be added that this is an emotional as well as an intellectual undertaking.[9] The frustration these images create in Kafka appears to stem from their muteness; the way in which they resist reduction and definite interpretation. A photograph offers a multitude of details to the eye and numerous ways of seeing, and without verbal coding (a key), it may be perceived as enigmatic or confusing. Another letter shows how frustrated Kafka is by the inexhaustible nature of the image:

> And because this little photograph is so inexhaustible, it actually produces as much pleasure as pain. It does not fade away, it does not disintegrate like a living thing; instead it will survive forever, a permanent comfort; it cannot altogether satisfy me, but it won't leave me, either. (LF, 127)

> Und daß dieses Bildchen so unerschöpflich ist, das ist freilich ebenso viel Freude wie Leid. Es vergeht nicht, es löst sich nicht auf wie Lebendiges, dafür aber bleibt es wieder für immer erhalten und ein dauernder Trost, es will mich nicht durchdringen, aber es verläßt mich auch nicht. (BFB, 203)

Thus, Kafka perceives that he can neither find a satisfactory reading of the image nor remain indifferent to it, and interestingly, he describes the image as having agency in this regard; it appears to haunt him.

The inscrutable character of the images is particularly painful to Kafka because of his jealousy, and he repeatedly asks Felice to explain details to him. For instance, he is disturbed by a photograph in which a part has been cut out: "By the way, what was this photograph of which you send only part? Why don't I get all of it?" (LF, 70) ["Was war das übrigens für eine Photographie, deren Abschnitt Du mir schickst? Warum bekomme ich sie nicht ganz?" (BFB, 112–13)]. He adds that it is a sin to tear images apart. A photograph is always already a decontextualized fragment, and this one has also been cut, so it stimulates

9.   Duttlinger, *Kafka and Photography*, 136. Schneider and Caygill, too, observe that the photographs in Kafka's fiction invite the characters to engage in interpretation processes. Schneider, *Das Andere schreiben*, 72; Caygill, "Kafka and the Missing Photograph," 92.

Kafka's curiosity and jealousy and makes him ponder about the omitted context. When he receives the full picture, a group photograph, suspicion makes him inquire about details. He is anxious because he cannot see where she has placed her second hand and pleads with her to explain everything to him: "But where is your other hand [. . .] Never could you explain this picture to me in too much detail" (LF, 99) ["Wo ist aber Deine zweite Hand? [. . .] Zu dem Bild könntest Du mir gar nicht genug Erklärungen geben" (BFB, 160)].

Kafka is also jealous because Felice stands too close to the men, as he cannot kiss the picture without also kissing the men:

> Now at last the whole girl has arrived! [. . .] But unfortunately held so tightly on either side that it would take immense strength to pry her loose. And unfortunately so close to her partner that should one want to kiss her, one would have to kiss Herr Rosenbaum [. . .] as well. (LF, 99)

> Nun ist also endlich das ganze liebe Mädchen da! [. . .] Nur leider so festgehalten auf beiden Seiten, daß man Riesenkräfte haben müßte, um sie hervorzureißen. Und leider so nahe neben ihrem Herrn, daß man, wenn man sie küssen will, notwendig diesen Herrn Rosenbaum [. . .] mitküssen müßte. (BFB, 159)

These passages show that Felice's colleagues and working environments, as these are depicted in the photograph, disturb the vision Kafka has of her and evokes his jealousy. This is partly acknowledged by Kafka in a letter where he comments on the background of the photograph she has sent him: "I have surrounded you with so many wishes and hopes that in no way fit a real business organization, but would be perfect in an unreal one" (LF, 83) ["daß ich Dich so fest mit Wünschen und Hoffnungen umgeben habe, die in einen wirklichen Geschäftsbetrief gar nicht, in einen unwirklichen dagegen ausgezeichnet passen" (BFB, 134)]. Whereas Kafka's imagination is romantic and selective, the camera gaze is not, and as it captures the reality surrounding Felice, this interferes with the intimate relation he sees developing between them. If he is dissatisfied when he receives the photographic fragment, he is equally displeased when he sees the full context of a picture. Once his attention is drawn to the boundaries of the photographs, this seems to disturb the illusion that the picture addresses him directly.

This leads us toward one of the most intriguing features of Kafka's responses to these photographs: his attention to Felice's gaze. He describes how his attempts to meet Felice's eyes in the photographs repeatedly fails. Kafka complains that she sometimes appears to deliberately look away, but at the same time seems to be aware of his gaze, so the impression she gives is ambiguous and confusing. Commenting on a specific photograph, he praises her lively attitude but reproaches her for not turning toward him: "You hold yourself magnificently; I call you by your name, but you don't turn toward me, though I expected you to" (LF, 105) ["Deine Haltung ist prachtvoll, ich rufe Dich bei Deinem Namen an und Du wendest Dich mir nicht zu, trotzdem ich es erwartet habe" (BFB, 169)]. The same kind of expectation is described in a later letter, when he longs for her and finds that her gaze in the image capriciously avoids him:

> But now I am tired and dull, and more than your kisses I should need that lively look of yours, which can be detected in today's photograph. Today I shall tell you only what I object to in that picture: Your eyes refuse to meet mine, they always ignore me; I turn the picture this way and that, you invariably manage to look the other way, calmly and as though deliberately to look the other way. On the other hand I have the opportunity of pulling the whole face toward me by kissing it, which I do, and shall do again just before going to sleep, and shall do again when I wake up. (LF, 125)

> Nun aber bin ich müde und dumpf und würde noch mehr als Küsse Deinen lebendigen Blick brauchen, wie er in der heutigen Photographie zu ahnen ist. Heute sage ich nur, was ich an dem Bild auszusetzen habe; Dein Blick will mich nicht treffen, immer geht er über mich hinweg, ich drehe das Bild nach allen Seiten, immer aber findest Du eine Möglichkeit, wegzusehn und ruhig und wie mit durchdachter Absicht wegzusehn. Allerdings habe ich die Möglichkeit, das ganze Gesicht mich zu reißen, indem ich es küsse und das tue ich und will es noch einmal tun, knapp ehe ich einschlafe und will es nochmals tun, wenn ich aufwache. (BFB, 199–200)

Experiencing that Felice fails to meet his gaze, Kafka tries to find the right angle, as if not realizing that flat photographs do not offer any privileged vantage points (this requires depth). When the endeavor proves unsuccessful, he still finds a way to compensate for the unreturned gaze; by kissing the photograph repeatedly, he demonstrates his ability to command the photographic object, if not her gaze. He thus engages with the photograph as a physical object and invests his emotions in it, even integrating it in his daily routines.

Indeed, Kafka's trouble with Felice's gaze may be considered in a wider historical context and related to Benjamin's comments on the unreturned gaze as a truly modern experience.[10] Insofar as portrait photographs do not return one's gaze, they create a new and more distant relation to others, and with the spread of this medium, people would thus have to learn to live with unreturned gazes. Kafka's comments are thought-provoking because they vividly demonstrate the disappointment of the beholder in such cases: the unreturned gaze creates frustration and yearning. Kafka seems to think that Felice avoids him on purpose, without acknowledging that this is an effect created by photographic technology. Still, we should note his slightly mocking tone, which suggests that he knew full well that his hope to have his gaze returned in a photograph could not be fulfilled in a wholly satisfactory manner.

However, Kafka not only expresses his own longing and frustration, but also shows that he is sensitive to *her* situation and her way of expressing herself. In one letter he observes that "You look at me so warily and suspiciously" (LF, 82) ["Wie vorsichtig und mißtrauisch Du mich ansiehst" (BFB, 132)], and in another letter he exclaims "What a searching look you give me from that picture" (LF, 111) ["Mit welchem prüfenden Blick Du aus dem Bild hervorschaust!"

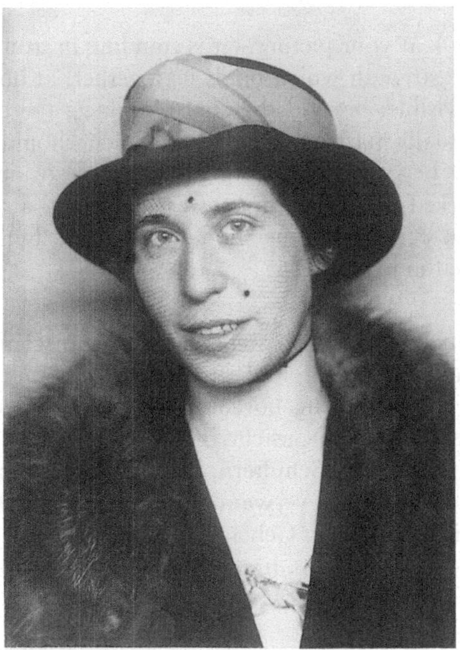

Figure 2.2   Portrait photograph of Felice Bauer. Unknown photographer and date. Photo: (c) Archiv S. Fischer Verlag GmbH.

10. Benjamin, "On Some Motifs in Baudelaire," 204.

(BFB, 178)]. Surely, Kafka was well aware of the vulnerable situation of its sitter in front of the camera, but the comments suggest that he sees more in the picture than an uneasy photographic situation. He pays attention to her look in the photograph, considering how it is sent off into the world with wariness and sensibility. It is a "searching" look, sent by someone who is not sure of what to expect and remains both open and cautious. This searching look says something about Felice's self-relation, and we may assume that this is what intrigues Kafka. Even if her look is cautious, he gets to study her way of appearing in the photograph, her way of both showing and hiding. Engaging in face studies, he thus learns something about her that is not about her "inner" character, but about her way of appearing to others.

Indeed, Kafka seems to be well aware that he does not have access to Felice's inner world and must contemplate her as a mystery. This inaccessibility—which is reinforced by the distance between them—seems to contribute to his fascination with her; it is the "secret" that he searches for in all the pictures. In one of his letters, he comments explicitly on that which is invisible in her picture and lies beyond her face:

> Whenever I look at your picture – it is standing in front of me now – I marvel at the strength which binds us together; at how, beyond all this which is visible, beyond the charming face, the calm eyes, the smile, the (actually narrow) shoulders, which should promptly be hugged – how beyond all this, forces so close, so indispensable to me, are at work; I marvel at the mystery of it all – a mystery which an insignificant person like me shouldn't look at, he should simply immerse himself in it. (LF, 126)

> Wenn ich Dein Bildchen – es steht vor mir – anschaue, geht beim Anschauen immer wieder ein Staunen darüber mit, mit welcher Stärke wir zwei zusammengehören. Wie hinter alledem, was da zu sehen ist, hinter dem lieben Gesicht, den ruhigen Augen, dem Lächeln, den (eigentlich schmalen) Schultern, die man eiligst umfangen sollte, wir hinter alledem, mir so verwandte, mir so unentbehrliche Kräfte wirken und wie das alles ein Geheimnis ist, das man als geringfügiger Mensch gar nicht anschauen, in das man nur ergeben untertauschen dürfte. (BFB, 201–2)

Studying Felice's picture, Kafka is captivated by that which appears to lie behind her smile and eyes, which is merely suggested. Referring to the invisible powers at work in the picture, he appears to depict the power of attraction, as it is mediated by photographic technology. Kafka even suggests that these powers should not be looked at directly, and thus appears to consider them in an almost metaphysical light.

Yet the workings of time represent a problem in this uncertain love affair, and Kafka is concerned with the temporality of portrait photographs. He worries about the delay that is created between the time when a photograph is taken and the time when he beholds it, which makes each photograph quickly outdated. Realizing that Felice changes from picture to picture, he presents the idea that they send each other monthly pictures to keep up, but dismisses the idea immediately (LF, 127 / BFB, 203). However, temporal gaps do not necessarily create distance, for Kafka is immensely fond of a childhood photograph of Felice, the very first picture of Felice he receives (the one he brings with him on a work trip as a travel companion). What is the cause of Kafka's attachment to it? He explains how it depicts a serious and pale little girl, and it seems that, for Kafka, this girl is very approachable. When he later receives a new and updated photograph of her, he states that he prefers the first one because he feels close to the girl, whereas he has too much respect for the adult Felice:

> The new photograph makes me feel strange. I feel closer to the little girl, could say anything to her, but for the young lady I feel too much respect. [. . .] If I had to choose between them in real life, I wouldn't rush up to the little girl without hesitating – no, I wouldn't do that, but I would nevertheless advance, even though very slowly, toward the little girl, while all the time turning to glance at the young lady, never letting her out of my sight. Nicest of course would be if the little girl then took me up to the young lady, and commended me to her. (LF, 70)

> Mit der neuen Photographie geht es mir sonderbar. Dem kleinen Mädchen fühle ich mir näher, dem könnte ich alles sage, vor der Dame habe ich zuviel Respekt [. . .] Wenn ich zwischen beiden im Leben zu wählen hätte, so würde ich keineswegs ohne Überlegung auf das kleine Mädchen zulaufen, das will ich nicht sagen, aber ich würde doch, wenn auch sehr langsam, nur zum kleinen Mädchen hingehn, allerdings immerfort nach dem großen Fräulein mich umsehn und es nicht aus den Augen lassen. Das Beste wäre freilich, wenn das kleine Mädchen dann mich zu dem großen Fräulein hinführen und mich ihm anempfehlen würde. (BFB, 112)

Kafka's curious comment that he wished that the girl could have introduced him to the woman points to the temporal gap between the two

Felices and suggests that it is difficult for him to link the photographs and see how they overlap. In a later letter Kafka points out that the girl in the photograph does not exist anymore: "The first photograph of yours is very dear to me, for the little girl no longer exists, and so the photograph is all there is" (LF, 75) ["Deine erste Photographie ist mir unendlich lieb, denn dieses kleine Mädchen existiert nicht mehr und die Photographie ist diesmal alles" (BFB, 121)]. Duttlinger compares this comment on Felice's childhood photograph with Barthes's comment on his mother's childhood photograph: none of them longer has a referent, and the photographs thus depict someone who no longer exists, so that "[t]he true message is the absence of its sitter."[11] To be sure, this is what gives a sense of melancholy to childhood pictures. Yet, at issue here is not merely time and melancholy, but also, I suggest, the relation between dissimilation and sincerity in the two photographs. When Kafka connects with the childhood photograph, we may suppose that this is partly due to the innocence of the sitter, who presumably acted less self-consciously than the adult woman. As an adult, Felice has surely developed a more complex self-relation; she poses with a cautious look, which instills him with respect. We may therefore suppose that Felice's adult picture testifies to alternations in her attitude toward the world and hence also to herself.

When Kafka later receives adult photographs of Felice that remind him of the little girl, he is delighted and reflects on her way of presenting herself. Here his care for her is clearly perceivable, as is his self-consciousness: "In these pictures you again look very much like the little girl in the first picture you sent me. You sit there so quietly, your left hand completely idle, yet it cannot be seized, something requiring thought is being dictated" (LF, 154) [Auf diesen Bildern gleichst Du wieder sehr dem kleinen Mädchen auf dem ersten Bild, das du mir schicktest. So still sitzt Du da, die linke Hand, ganz unbeschäftigt, darf doch nicht erfaßt werden, etwas sehr Nachdenkliches wird diktiert" (BFB, 248)]. The picture, taken in Felice's office, presumably depicts her as she pays attention to something that is being dictated to her, and which makes her thoughtful. As Kafka studies the picture, this thoughtfulness is transposed to him. Paying attention to her quietness and her idle hand, Kafka seems to see in her bodily habits something that is typical of her and something that makes her dear to him. Her quiet way suggests innocence and artlessness, just like the photograph of her as a child, and it makes her appear vulnerable. Kafka thinks of seizing her hand, perhaps wishing to protect her, but knows that this cannot be done. And this is what

11. Duttlinger, *Kafka and Photography*, 131.

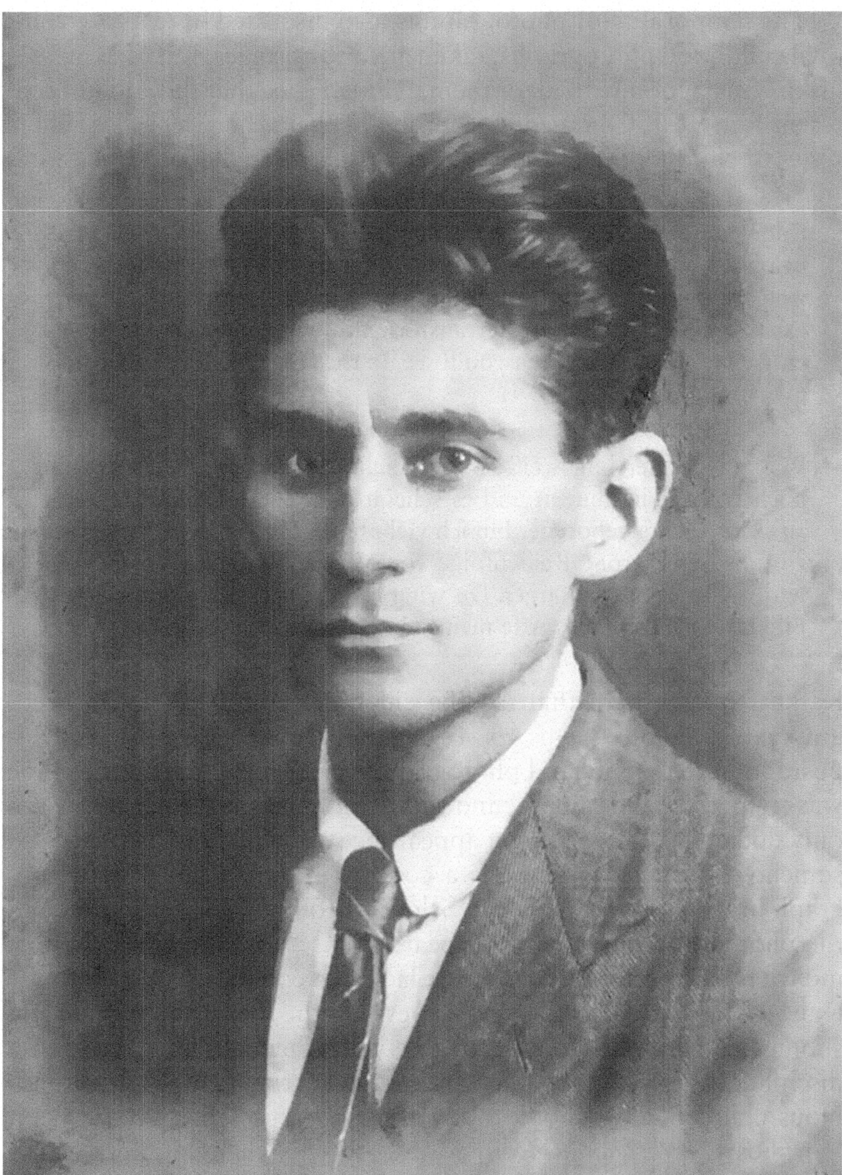

Figure 2.3   Portrait photograph of Franz Kafka in 1917. Unknown photographer. Available in the public domain via Wikimedia Commons.

provokes his pensive mode; the emotional impact the picture has on him combined with his awareness of his inability to respond in a way that she can perceive. It is thus the impossibility of responding, not of receiving, that puzzles Kafka. Or rather, it is the ambivalent emotions instigated by the picture—both affection and helplessness—that cause his thoughtfulness.

The temporality of photograph is also discussed in relation to his own childhood photographs, taken at various stages. Kafka expresses his dissatisfaction with all of them, telling Felice that they do not represent him well. Commenting on one of them, he refers to a whole series of childhood pictures that depicts his altered appearances:

> I don't know how old I was in this one. At that time I think I still belonged completely to myself, and it seems to have suited me very well. As the eldest, I was constantly being photographed and there exists a long succession of transformations. From now on it gets worse in every picture, but you'll see. In the very next one I appear as my parents' ape. (LF, 73–4)

> Wie alt ich hier bin, weiß ich gar nicht. Damals gehörte ich wohl noch vollständig mir an und es scheint mir sehr behaglich gewesen zu sein. Als Erstgeborener bin ich viel photographiert worden und es gibt also eine große Reihenfolge von Verwandlungen. Von jetzt an wird es in jedem Bild ärger, Du wirst es ja sehn. Gleich im nächsten Bild trete ich schon als Affe meiner Eltern auf. (BFB, 118)

Kafka explains here that, as the eldest son, he was often photographed, and thus seems to see a fatalist connection between his position in the family and photographic technology. It is just as if he was trained for the camera, and this could mean that the camera not only documents his changing appearance as he grows older, but also somehow furthers it. There is a contrast between the early photograph in which Kafka says he "belonged completely" to himself and the photograph in which he appears as his "parents' ape"; the first indicates autonomy and perhaps a lack of a conscious attitude to the external world, whereas the second evokes the image of a trained and subjugated child. What happened between them? It may seem that a disciplinary process took place that erased every trace of the autonomous child. But we should note that Kafka uses the word "metamorphosis" [*Verwandlungen*] to describe his changing appearance in the photographs, and this may suggest more complex processes. The word, of course, recalls Kafka's story about a young man's transformation from man to insect and his cumbersome family situation granting him almost no leeway. It also recalls Deleuze and Guattari's reading of the story, where the process of "becoming-animal" is seen as a "line of escape" from limiting family constellations.[12]

12. Deleuze and Guattari, *Kafka*, 12–15.

In a similar manner, the word *Verwandlung* is here used to describe the process of transformations through which he becomes an "ape," and this may suggest that the ape and the insect have something in common; they have escaped the limitations that were set for the boy / the son. Thus, when Kafka describes himself as his parents' ape, he may not be referring merely to his submissive attitude. He may also be suggesting that he has succeeded in becoming someone radically *other* in the photograph; he is not simply his parents' obedient son, but instead their *jesting ape*.

Summing up, how should we describe Kafka's relation to Felice's pictures? His many ways of engaging with the photographs, in combination with his careful descriptions of his efforts in this respect, suggest that he was well aware of the power of technical images. Knowing that they caused both gratification and torment, he seems also to acknowledge that they create an interlacing of presence and absence and that there is an overlapping between the pictures and his imagination. Yet this knowledge does not prevent him from engaging emotionally with her pictures. Rather, it causes an *ambivalence* in his descriptions and provokes reflections on the power of photographs. Indeed, Kafka's responses to photographs—fictive and real—are marked with both emotion and critical reflection, and this is what creates his ambivalent view of the medium.[13]

We may further ask what role the photographs play in Kafka and Felice's love relation. Clearly, the photographs create a peculiar feeling of both absence and presence, and this keeps their relation going, both arousing desire and preventing its fulfillment. The exchange of photographs contributes to creating intimacy between them and

13. Duttlinger's skillful analysis of Kafka's letters to Felice also stresses Kafka's ambivalence toward photographs, but she seems to underscore especially his skepticism toward photographs, and she argues that a letter from the end of December 1912 marks a turning point in Kafka's view of photographs: "In subsequent letters, Kafka never rekindles the earlier, ecstatic sense of recognition, stressing instead the inadequate and even deceptive character of the photographic medium." Duttlinger, *Kafka and Photography*, 147. In the book's conclusion, she states: "Alongside an intense, at times obsessive fascination with photographic images, it is the critique of photography as a representational paradigm and social phenomenon which acts as one of the principal driving forces behind his literary explorations. Duttlinger *Kafka and Photography*, 255. Although I do not disagree with these views, I stress other aspects than Duttlinger, seeing Kafka's stance as marked by both emotion and reflection, absorption and detachment.

gives them the possibility to enter into each other's private rooms, with attention to the silent communication conveyed by gazes, gestures, and postures. Even if Kafka does not succeed in teasing out every secret in Felice's photographs, and even if she never returns his gaze, he learns to appreciate a self-relation in these pictures, to care for her vulnerability and to reflect on his own possibilities for responding. This suggests that a level of intimacy is sharable through photographs, even if they may fail to satisfy completely.

A slightly different question is what role the photographs play in Kafka's love letters. As we have seen, Kafka comments extensively on the photographs, seeing no detail as too small to be addressed in the letters. He writes about his uncertain reading of the photographs, as well as his emotional responses to them and his physical way of interacting with them. One could venture to say that their peculiar communication situation brings Kafka to write down some of the silent protocols of private life; the observation of the faces, gazes, and gestures that takes place in intimate relations. Because photographs here serve as stand-ins for real faces, Kafka's response is not directly visible to Felice and must be put down in writing. This allows him to assure her that he sees her, cares for her, and thinks about her constantly. Indeed, this is the kind of discourse one would expect in a love letter, but it revolves around specific photographs serving as her double. Writing in this manner, Kafka creates intimacy and draws her closer, while trusting that his emotional letters will be well received. Yet Kafka knows full well that the reading of photographs is a never-ending process. Insofar as such pictures are in perpetual need of interpretation, comments, or "captions," they are generative and cause even more writing from Kafka's hand.

In the Power of Photographs

What will interest us next is the relation between portrait photographs, identity, and power, first in a family context and subsequently also in a wider context. As is well known, family photographs were an established genre in bourgeois culture around 1900. Group photographs and individual portraits were produced for circulation within the family and served to bolster bourgeois identities. We saw that the narrator in Proust's novel was only moderately interested in family photographs; instead, his interest in photographs was related to his passions and love relations. But, in Kafka's fiction, family photographs play a significant role; they appear in the characters' surroundings and work on them in inscrutable ways. To be sure, this way of deploying family photographs testifies to Kafka's sensitivity to their powers in a bourgeois society.

When Benjamin commented on a childhood studio photograph of Kafka in "Little History of Photography," the question of power was key. Paying attention to the boy's "humiliatingly tight child's suit" and the alienating requisites in the picture, Benjamin underscored the limiting role ascribed to the subject in such photographs:

> This was the period of those studios – with their draperies and palm trees, their tapestries and easels – which occupied so ambiguous a place between execution and representation, between torture chamber and throne room, and to which an early portrait of Kafka bears pathetic witness. There the boy stands, perhaps six years old, dressed up in a humiliatingly tight child's suit overloaded with trimming, in a sort of greenhouse landscape. The background is thick with palm fronds. And as if to make these upholstered tropics even stuffier and more oppressive, the subject holds in his left hand an inordinately large broad-brimmed hat, such as Spaniards wear. He would surely be lost in the setting were it not for his immensely sad eyes, which master this landscape predestined for them.[14]

At the time when he wrote this ekphrastic passage, Benjamin was familiar with Kafka's own writings on photographs, which a few decades before had explored similar issues. Commenting on the photographic portrait, he captured an important aspect of nineteenth-century portraits: the photographic studio appeared at the same time as a torture chamber and a throne room, signaling both extreme suffering and sovereign power. As we will see, this ambivalent power relation is also in play when Kafka engages with portrait photography in his writings.

To explore this issue further, I now turn to Kafka's least-known novel, *The Man Who Disappeared*.[15] First, I consider how the depiction

---

14. Benjamin, "Little History," 282. A similar passage is found in Benjamin's essay on Kafka: "Franz Kafka," 800.
15. We also find intriguing scenes involving family photographs and other private photographs in *The Trial* [*Der Process*] and *The Castle* [*Das Schloss*]. For instance, in the first chapter of *The Trial*, Fräulein Bürstner's photographs exert a magnetic attraction on the men in K's room, and we later learn that they have left the photographs in disorder. The tendency is for pictures to be associated with desire and attraction, but also with obscurity, damage, and disorder. As Duttlinger aptly puts it, photographs in Kafka "attract, enhance, and mediate desire." Duttlinger, *Kafka*, 182.

of family photographs in the novel is marked by both absorption and detachment, and thus how the work shows a somewhat uncertain relation to photographs. Second, I show that there are similarities between Kafka's views on family photographs and his broader consideration of photographs and power. Politically charged photographs play a central role in my discussion of this novel; this is where the ambivalence between torture chamber and sovereign power most clearly come into play.

The Man Who Disappeared is a true anti-Bildungsroman, telling the story of a young, German immigrant's misfortunes in America. The protagonist, Karl Rossmann, is a naïve character, who passively accepts what happens to him, including his parents' arrangement to send him to America (to cover up for his involvement in the maid's pregnancy). He is expected to start a career and live the "American dream," but when his rich uncle cuts off relations with him, a process of social decline begins. Without a job and a home, he spends the night at an inn, and in this precarious situation, he takes a photograph of his parents out of his suitcase and considers it affectionately. The scene reveals his emotional ties to his family and home country but involves complex and ambivalent emotions. Whereas Deleuze and Guattari list this as an example of the subjugating forces of photographs, I find that the scene invites a more nuanced reading.[16]

The scene is particularly interesting because the contemplation of the family photograph is here contrasted with the reading of the Bible, and the photograph is described as more attractive than the Holy Scripture. This seems to suggest that the contemplation of photographs represents a new kind of metaphysics, but "softer" and more ambiguous. Karl's absorption in the photograph is not total, and he goes through several phases as he looks at it. First, he looks at his father:

> [Karl] leafed through the bible a little without reading anything. Then he picked up his parents' photograph, in which his little father was standing upright, while his mother sat leaning back a bit in the armchair in front of him. His father was holding the back of the armchair with one hand, while the other, clenched to form a fist, was placed on an illustrated book which was lying open on a fragile ornamental table beside him. There was also a photograph on which Karl was portrayed with his parents, his father and mother were looking at him intently, while he, following the instructions of the photographer, had had to look at the camera. That photograph, however, had not been given to him for his journey.

16. Deleuze and Guattari, *Kafka*, 3.

He looked all the more carefully at the one in front of him and tried to meet his father's gaze from various angles. But his father, however much he changed his view by holding the candle in different positions, wouldn't come to life, and his thick horizontal moustache didn't at all resemble the reality, it was not a good picture. (MWD, 69)[17]

[Karl] blätterte ein wenig in der Bibel, ohne etwas zu lesen. Dann nahm er die Photographie der Eltern zur Hand, auf der der kleine Vater hoch aufgerichtet stand, während die Mutter in dem Fauteuil vor ihm ein wenig eingesunken dasaß. Die eine Hand hielt der Vater auf der Rückenlehne des Fauteuils, die andere zur Faust geballt, auf einem illustrierten Buch, das aufgeschlagen auf einem schwachen Schmucktischchen ihm zur Seite lag. Es gab auch eine Photographie, auf welcher Karl mit seinen Eltern abgebildet war, Vater und Mutter sahen ihn dort scharf an, während er nach dem Auftrag des Photographen den Apparat hatte anschauen müssen. Diese Photographie hatte er aber auf die Reise nicht mitbekommen.

Desto genauer sah er die vor ihm liegende an und suchte von verschiedenen Seiten den Blick des Vaters aufzufangen. Aber der Vater wollte, wie er auch den Anblick durch verschiedene Kerzenstellungen änderte, nicht lebendiger werden, sein wagrechter starker Schnurrbart sah der Wirklichkeit auch gar nicht ähnlich, es war keine gute Aufnahme. (V, 105–6)

The frustrated attempt to meet his father's gaze in a photograph in many respects resembles Kafka's attempts to meet Felice's gaze in her photographs. Just like Felice, Karl's father persistently refuses to return the beholder's gaze. When Karl interacts physically with the photograph, trying out various angles and lighting, this may be seen as an effort to compensate for this deficiency. But the photograph will not come alive; just like the Bible, his father's photograph fails to speak to him. Moreover, the claim that the picture does not resemble the reality and accordingly is not a good picture may seem to reproduce well-established ideas about photographs rather than Karl's own judgment. He seems to be drawn to the photograph precisely because it does not resemble reality, but then tries to reduce the hold it has on him by denouncing it as a bad photograph.

17. References are to the following edition and translation, abbreviated as shown: MWD: Franz Kafka, *The Man Who Disappeared*. Trans. Ritchie Robertson. Oxford: Oxford University Press. 2012. V: Franz Kafka, *Der Verschollene*. Frankfurt am Main: Fischer Taschenbuch, 2008.

Karl then examines his mother's appearance in the photograph and is disturbed by a strange gesture she makes:

> His mother, though, was portrayed much better, her lips were twisted as though she had been hurt and were trying to smile. Karl felt that anyone looking at the picture must find this so obvious that the next moment he felt this impression was too powerful and almost absurd. How could a picture impart so strongly the unshakable conviction that the person portrayed was concealing their emotion? And he looked away from the picture for a while. (MWD, 69)

> Die Mutter dagegen war schon besser abgebildet, ihr Mund war so verzogen, als sei ihr ein Leid angetan worden und als zwinge sie sich zu lächeln. Karl schien es, als müsse dies jedem der das Bild ansah, so sehr auffallen, daß es ihm im nächsten Augenblick wieder schien, die Deutlichkeit dieses Eindrucks sei zu stark und fast widersinnig. Wie könne man von einem Bild so sehr die unumstößliche Überzeugung eines verborgenen Gefühls des Abgebildeten erhalten. Und er sah vom Bild ein Weilchen lang weg. (V, 106)

As Karl studies his mother's way of appearing in the photograph, he notices her twisted lips and sees this as an indication of a suppressed feeling. The twisted lips could perhaps be attributed to her discomfort before the camera, but they could just as well be seen as covering up a deeper emotion. The picture creates strong emotions in Karl; he feels that the impression it makes is "powerful and almost absurd." At the same time, however, he experiences a growing consciousness with respect to the impact a picture may have on the beholder. Then, as his mind ponders the question about the power of photographs, Karl "looked away from the picture for a while." This part of the passage is crucial because it testifies to a degree of detachment on Karl's side.

However, the scene ends not with philosophical pondering, but rather with physical intimacy. As Karl gets tired, the photograph falls out of his hand, and he ends up sleeping on it, as if it were a pillow, feeling its coolness against his chin. Where Karl first interacts with the photograph by way of his hands and his gaze, he ends up pressing his chin against it, sensing its materiality, with his eyes closed:

> While thus gazing, he soon noticed that he was very tired and would hardly be able to stay awake all night. The picture dropped from his hands, then he laid his face on the picture, the coolness of which did his cheek good, and with a pleasant feeling he went to sleep. (MWD, 70)

In diesem Anschauen merkte er bald, daß er doch sehr müde war und kaum die Nacht werde durchwachen können. Das Bild entfiel seinen Händen, dann legte er das Gesicht auf das Bild, dessen Kühle seiner Wange wohltat und mit einem angenehmen Gefühle schlief er ein. (V, 107)

The description of Karl's interaction with the photograph is highly ambiguous: It encompasses both absorption and detachment, both deep emotions and self-conscious reflection. Just like reading the Bible, the experience of the photograph proves to be emotionally unsatisfactory, and if Karl finally finds comfort in it, it is because he feels the coolness of the physical object against his chin. It is perhaps this ambivalent and largely unsatisfactory experience of his parents' photograph that eventually makes it possible for Karl to free himself from the subjugating forces of his family. Looking at the image of his parents, Karl endeavors to connect with them but feels that they are sealed off from him, and he starts to reflect upon the effect the image has on him. In this manner, the scene explores question of the agency of photographs. It could thus be argued that Karl's emotional bindings to his parents are now loosened.[18] Moreover, it could be argued that he has started his visual education, gradually becoming more aware of the impact of such pictures.[19]

When Karl a little later loses the photograph of his parents, these ties are so to speak cut off, and this marks a turning point in the narrative. This happens when he is "on the road," having joined the two vagabonds Delamarche and Robinson, who turn out to be crooks sponging on Karl. Having left them for a short while to get food for the three of them, Karl discovers upon his return that they have searched through his suitcase and that the photograph has disappeared. While anxiously looking for it, Karl explains that it is irreplaceable: "It mattered to me more than anything else in the suitcase [. . .] 'You see, it's irreplaceable, I can't get another [. . .] It was the only picture of my parents that I have'" (MWD, 85) ["'Sie war mir wichtiger, als alles

---

18. The scene could, in fact, be read in light of Deleuze and Guattari's views on the proliferating power of photographs. They claim that photographs "have the power to metamorphose those who look at them [. . .] In short, the portrait or the photo that marked a sort of artificial territoriality of desire now becomes a center for the perturbation of situations and characters, a connector that precipitates the movement of deterritorialization." Deleuze and Guattari, *Kafka*, 61–2.
19. Here I side with Schneider, who observes that Karl in contemplating this picture goes through a liberation process. Schneider, *Das Andere schreiben*, 78.

was ich sonst im Koffer habe,' sagte Karl [. . .]. 'Sie ist nämlich uner-
setzlich, ich bekomme keine zweite. [. . .] Es war das einzige Bild, das
ich von meinen Eltern besaß'" (V, 130–1)]. The loss of the photograph
underlines the fact that Europe and Karl's parents are now left behind
and the original models no longer available. The family photograph
thus plays a central role in the story about Karl's loss of connections
with his homeland and his family.[20] First he is separated physically
from his family and left merely with a photograph of his parents, then
he starts developing an ambivalent relation with the photograph, and,
finally, he loses the photograph and no longer has a connection with
his former life. As we will see, however, this does not simply liberate
him but rather opens him up to new loyalties and ties.

But Karl gets a last chance to look at photographs from the Old
World when he gets a job at the Hotel Occidental. There he meets
other European immigrants, and among them is the head cook from
Prague. When Karl enters her apartment in the hotel, where he is to
spend his first night, he notices a display of family photographs from
Europe and is drawn to them:

> On a low chest of drawers, with a loosely woven woollen blanket
> spread over it, there were various photographs, framed and behind
> glass, while inspecting the room Karl paused there and looked at
> them. They were mostly old photographs, the majority showing girls
> in outdated uncomfortable clothes, with small but high hats placed
> loosely on their heads, their right hands resting on parasols, facing
> the viewer and yet avoiding his gaze. Among the likenesses of men,
> Karl noticed especially the picture of a young soldier who had put
> his cap on a small table and was standing to attention with his wild
> black hair and was filled with proud but suppressed laughter. The
> buttons on his uniform had been gilded after the photograph was
> taken. All these photographs must come from Europe, as one could
> probably have read on their backs, but Karl did not want to pick any
> of them up. The way the photographs were standing here was the
> way he would have liked to put the photographs of his parents in the
> room he was going to have. (MWD, 90)

> Auf einem niedrigen Schrank mit Schiebefächern, über den eine
> großmaschige wollene Decke gezogen war, standen verschiedene
> Photographien in Rahmen und unter Glas, bei der Besichtigung

20. Howard Caygill argues that the novel "sets out in pursuit of loss: the loss of
    memory, the loss of concentration, the loss of objects such as umbrellas, suitcases,
    hats, and in the midst of this, the loss and eventual recovery of a photograph."
    Caygill, "The Missing Photograph," 89.

des Zimmers blieb Karl dort stehn und sah sie an. Es waren meist alte Photographien und stellten in der Mehrzahl Mädchen dar, die in unmodernen unbehaglichen Kleidern, mit locker aufgesetzten kleinen aber hochgehenden Hüten, die rechte Hand auf einen Schirm gestützt, dem Beschauer zugewendet waren und doch mit den Blicken auswichen. Unter den Herrenbildnissen fiel Karl besonders das Bild eines jungen Soldaten auf, der das Käppi auf ein Tischchen gelegt hatte, stramm mit seinem wilden schwarzen Haar dastand und voll von einem stolzen aber unterdrückten Lachen war. Die Knöpfe seiner Uniform waren auf der Photographie nachträglich vergoldet worden. Alle diese Photographien stammten wohl noch aus Europa, man hätte dies auf der Rückseite wahrscheinlich auch genau ablesen können, aber Karl wollte sie nicht in der Hand nehmen. So wie diese Photographien hier standen, so hatte er auch die Photographie seiner Eltern in seinem künftigen Zimmer aufstellen mögen. (V, 138–9)

The description of poses, gestures, and miens in these photographs is remarkable. The passage highlights the way the girls in the photographs pose and make gestures, while their uncomfortable clothes constrain their movements. It underscores that they are facing the beholder but still dodge his gaze; they are thus enticing yet avoidant. Among the photographs of men, Karl's attention is drawn toward a soldier posing in an unusual manner: he has taken his hat off and appears to be at ease, his hair is wild and black, and he is smiling. Although this is obviously an informal photograph that breaks with the conventions of the official portraits of soldiers, it appears to depict a person who is still constraining himself to some degree. His body is full of laughter, but he controls it. What these portraits have in common is that they are full of ambivalence; they simultaneously show and hide, reveal and withhold. They attract Karl, but he also keeps his distance, and he has a keen eye for their ambiguity.

We should note that these old photographs from Europe make him long for his own family photograph, not his own family. Even if the subjects are strangers to him, these photographs appeal to him and serve a compensatory role. What especially pleases Karl is this way of displaying photographs in frames on a dresser (whereas he used to keep the photograph of his parents in his suitcase) and he wishes that he could display his own photograph in a similar manner. Such a display calls for a less intimate way of relating to photographs; it invites visual inspection, but not physical interaction, as proven by the fact that Karl does not wish to hold these pictures in his hands. The scene thus indicates that Karl has found the correct distance in relation to such pictures.

This compensatory scene is the last mention of Karl's family photograph in the novel, and his connection with his family is now lost altogether. We follow him through a series of unfortunate events: he gets fired from the hotel, runs to escape the police, receives unexpected help from his crook "friends," and ends up as a servant in Delamarche's apartment. This is where Kafka ended the first draft of the novel, which was never completed. Yet one of the fragments that he added to the manuscript, written shortly after the outbreak of the First World War, gives a new ending to the story. There, he gets a new job and a new opportunity at the great Oklahama Theater, which recruits anyone who wants to join them.[21] As Karl is now open to new loyalties and new commitments, he puts his trust in the theater. What is interesting is that Kafka in this fragment addresses questions regarding photography, identity, and power in a context that exceeds the family and intimate relations: At stake here are the topics of class and racial identity as well as political loyalty.

With the Oklahama fragment, Kafka gives the novel an ambiguous ending, for it is highly uncertain what the theater actually represents.[22]

21. Two contradictory statements contribute to making the status of the theater uncertain: A comment made by Kafka and transmitted by Max Brod indicates that he considered the Oklahama Theater to be a social utopia and intended the novel to end on a "happy" note: "I know from our conversations that the incomplete chapter we have about the 'Nature Theater of Oklahoma' (Kafka especially loved the beginning of this chapter, and read it aloud in a heartrendingly beautiful manner) was to be the final chapter of the novel and would close on a conciliatory note. Kafka hinted with a smile and baffling words that his young hero would again find a profession, freedom, support, and even his homeland and parents in this 'nearly limitless' theater, as if by heavenly magic" ["Aus Gesprächen weiß ich, daß das vorliegende unvollendete Kapitel über das 'Naturtheater in Oklahoma', ein Kapitel, dessen Einleitung Kafka besonders liebte und herzergreifend schön vorlas, das Schlußkapitel sein und versöhnlich ausklingen sollte. Mit rätselhaften Worten deutete Kafka lächelnd an, daß sein junger Held in diesem 'fast grenzenlosen' Theater Beruf, Freiheit, Rückhalt, ja sogar die Heimat und die Eltern wie durch paradiesischen Zauber wiederfinden werde"]. However, a passage from Kafka's notebook (written in September 1915) indicates a less fortunate outcome for Karl. There Kafka compares Karl's fate with the fate of K., the protagonist of *The Trial*: "Rossmann and K., the innocent and the guilty, both ultimately put to death indiscriminately, the innocent with a lighter hand, more pushed aside than struck down" ["Roßmann und K., der Schuldlose und der Schuldige, schließlich beide unterschiedslos strafweise umgebracht, der Schuldlose mit leichterer Hand, mehr zu Seite geschoben als niedergeschlagen"]. Stach, *Kafka: The Decisive Years*, 248–9; Engel and Auerochs, *Kafka Handbuch*, 181.
22. Should the theater be seen as Karl's rescue or as his demise? Presumably, Max Brod's view of *The Man Who Disappeared* as a comic novel as well as his editing of the first published version precluded more serious readings of the

As we follow Karl's attempt to figure out what kind of institution the theater is, the text alludes to traumatic events in American history: the discrimination against African Americans, the American Civil War, and the murder of President Abraham Lincoln. In the fragment, two photographs serve as connecting devices between the fictive story and this historical context. These photographs depict socially or politically motivated killings: a lynching photograph depicting two hanged African Americans and a photograph from Ford's Theater representing the assassination of Lincoln. It is well known that both lynching photographs and various images commemorating Lincoln's death were circulating in the visual culture around 1900.[23] We may therefore see Kafka's use of such photographs as an exploration of the impact of violent photographs circulating in the public sphere. Yet what power relations are in play in such pictures, and are they in some respects similar to the power relations in portrait photographs? Let us take a close look at the Oklahama fragment, and how it connects photographs to questions regarding life and death.[24]

novel at an early stage. Brod certainly influenced Benjamin's messianic interpretation of the novel in which the theatre represented a happy ending for Karl. Further, Hanna Arendt's political reading of Kafka's novels is influenced by Benjamin and seems strangely ignorant of the ideological stakes of this particular novel. See Benjamin "Franz Kafka," 800; Arendt, "The Jew as Pariah," 87; Arendt, "Franz Kafka, Appreciated Anew," 108. Knowing the allusion Kafka makes to the lynching photograph however, it is difficult to overlook the sinister aspects of the theater, and more recently, several readers have highlighted the somber and uncanny character of Kafka's fictive theater. See Duttlinger, *Kafka and Photography*, 62–99; Caygill "The Fate of the Pariah"; Hillis-Miller, *The Conflagration of Community*, 45–66; Grøtta, "At the Door of the Theater." In my own article on Kafka's Oklahama Theater, I argue that it can be seen as an early twentieth-century blend of ultra-German and ultra-American ideologies, operating through an "inclusive exclusion."

23. Apel and Smith, *Lynching Photographs*; Borchard and Bulla, *Lincoln Mediated*, 41; Lowry, *The Photographer and the President*, 13–14; 189–90.
24. Carolin Duttlinger and Howard Caygill have previously analyzed the role of these two photographs in perceptive and illuminating ways. My analysis to some degree overlaps with theirs but my framework and emphasis differs. Duttlinger focuses mainly on the picture from Ford's Theater and the representation of power, whereas I explore the role of the lynching photograph to a larger degree. Countering Benjamin and Arendt, Caygill reads the novel in a somber light, focusing on the loss of the family photograph Karl brought with him from Germany. Discussing the novel's ending, he highlights the two "sinister" photographs, seeing them as significant to the understanding of the novel, but his discussion is rather brief. Building on these important works, I explore in more depth the significance of the two photographs in question. Duttlinger, *Kafka and Photography* and Caygill, "The Fate of the Pariah."

The lynching photograph is not explicitly described in the text but is rather alluded to in the name Kafka gave to the theater. "The Theater of Oklahama" refers to a caption in a bestselling book about America that Kafka consulted when he wrote the novel, Arthur Holitscher's *Amerika heute und morgen: Reiseerlebnisse* (1911–12).[25] In a chapter entitled "Der Neger" [The Negro], Holitscher discusses the discrimination against Black Americans, comparing it to the discrimination against Jews in Germany. He addresses the lynching processes during the Civil War, stressing that no one seemed to protest against them but rather tacitly accepted them.[26] The chapter includes a photograph, apparently taken in Oklahoma, which illustrates this illegal and murderous practice and makes visible the anonymous deaths in America. It depicts an otherwise idyllic grove used as a "lynching court," and in the middle, we see two hanged Black Americans, still suspended with their necks in an unnatural position. They are surrounded by white men in elegant suits and hats, posing with the victims as if they were trophies. Most of the men look directly into the camera, whereas one of them looks straight at the victim in front, thus embodying the role of the witness. The caption from the 1912 edition reads, "Idyll aus Oklahama."[27] It is from this caption that Kafka picked up the misspelling of the state Oklahoma, and as we will see, it appears that he also picked up Holitscher's morbid irony concerning the deceptively beautiful scenery that was used as a "lynching court."[28] When Kafka

25. Holitscher's travel reports were first published in *Die neue Rundschau* in 1911–12 and then as a book in 1912, and it became immensely popular. Kafka owned a copy of the book, and its influence on his Amerika novel has been noted by several critics. See, especially, Wirkner, *Kafka und die Außenwelt*; Heimböckel, "Amerika im Kopf"; and Engel and Auerochs, *Kafka Handbuch*.
26. Holitscher discusses the way Black Americans are treated as second-class citizens and are excluded from the free job market. This clearly reflects Karl's own situation as an unskilled immigrant in America. Holitscher is also concerned with the lack of rights of African Americans and asserts that they are presumed to be guilty rather than innocent. Depicting the lynching processes, he points out that the country's democratic institutions (he refers to the Congress and the Senate) as well as the media prefer to keep silent about them. It is also interesting that Holitscher compares the plight of African Americans with that of Jews in Europe, with both groups being excluded, persecuted, and considered an "internal enemy." Holitscher, who was himself a Jew, was highly aware of the social similarities between America and Europe with respect to the questions of discrimination, exclusion, power, and justice. He appears to have contributed to Kafka's description of the life of an outcast in America, excluded, persecuted, and without rights. Holitscher, *Amerika*, 333–47.
27. Holitscher, *Amerika*, 339. The misspelling has been amended in later editions.
28. This connection is acknowledged in Engel and Auerochs, *Kafka Handbuch*.

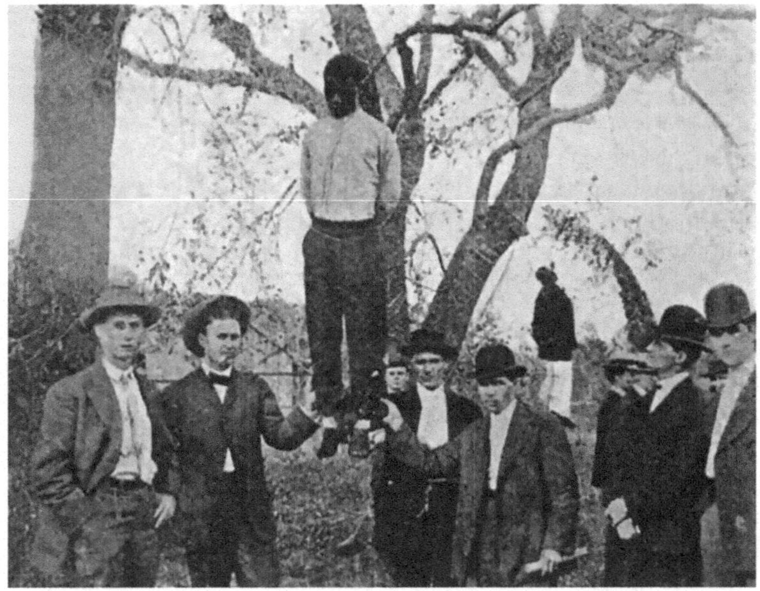

Figure 2.4   Lynching photograph from Arthur Holitscher's book *Amerika heute und morgen: Reiseerlebnisse* (Berlin: S. Fischer Verlag, 1912).

chooses to name the theater representing Karl's last hope in a way that alludes to this photograph, he offers a gruesome context for its understanding. In this light, the Oklahama Theater could be interpreted as an idyllic site for execution, and we may assume that death is awaiting Karl.

The allusion to Holitscher's chapter and the lynching photograph is also activated when Karl goes through the bureaucratic process for recruitment at the theater. When he is asked for his name, Karl hesitates to give his real name, and decides to use the nickname he was given in his former job, "Negro" (written in English by Kafka).[29] As

29. Reading the novel in a postcolonial context, Rolf J. Goebel sees his registered name "Negro, ein europäischer Mittelschüler" ("Negro, a European middle school pupil") as "a deeply emblematic signifier for his hybrid position between cultures." Stressing the importance of "crosscultural translation," he asserts that Karl, the immigrant, is not until this point in the novel "willing and able to undergo that total erasure of personal identity, cultural origins and national affiliation." He further suggests that this transformation may either liberate him or lead to his disappearance. See Goebel, "Kafka and Postcolonial Critique," 196. Although I find Goebel's postcolonial perspective valuable, his reading in my view underplays the dark aspects of Karl's fate in America. He does not refer to the lynching photograph or to Holitscher's book.

he chooses to become a "nobody" in America, Karl Rossmann, born from German parents, starts to disappear:

> He did not answer immediately, he was shy of giving his real name and having it written down. Once he had been given a job, however tiny, and done it satisfactorily, then people could learn his name, but not now, he had concealed it for so long that he wasn't going to reveal it now. So, as no other name occurred to him at that moment, he gave the name by which he had been called in his last few posts: "Negro." "Negro?" asked the manager, turning his head and pulling a face as though Karl's untrustworthiness had reached its limit. The clerk too looked searchingly at Karl for a while, but then he repeated "Negro" and wrote the name down. (MWD, 203)

> Er antwortete nicht gleich, er hatte eine Scheu, seinen wirklichen Namen zu nennen und aufschreiben zu lassen. Bis er hier auch nur die kleinste Stelle erhalten und zur Zufriedenheit ausfüllen würde, dann mochte man seinen Namen erfahren, jetzt aber nicht, allzulang hatte er ihn verschweigen, als daß er ihn jetzt hätte verraten sollen. Er nannte daher, da ihm im Augenblick kein anderer Name einfiel, nur den Rufnamen aus seinen letzten Stellung: "Negro". "Negro?" fragte der Leiter, drehte den Kopf und machte eine Grimasse, als hätte Karl jetzt den Höhepunkt der Unglaubwürdigkeit erreicht. Auch der Schreiber sah Karl eine Weile prüfend an, dann aber wiederholte er "Negro" und schrieb den Namen ein. (V, 306–7)

The theater manager offers his mild protests to Karl's claim that his name is "Negro," but then consents to the arrangement. The whole passage demonstrates that the question of identity is in play in the fragment, which of course fits well with the context of the theater. Indeed, identity papers are often in question in Kafka's work and should be related to his interest in portrait photographs. In this scene, Karl appears to be aware of the danger of being inscribed in this institution under his real name and thus abandons his bourgeois identity, conscious of the fact that he has no identity papers to confirm it.

The new name "Negro" reflects Karl's low status in America and represents an act of solidarity with African Americans, who found themselves at the very bottom of the social ladder. Paradoxically, Kafka's protagonist thus becomes an American by becoming an outcast, excluded, persecuted, and without rights. Holitscher's book is a crucial intertext in this respect; insofar as the name "Negro" connects Kafka's story to the lynching photograph from Holitscher's book, one could say that the book haunts the novel and is part of its political unconsciousness. In this manner, the novel's fixation on family and identity is undercut, and its title, *The Man Who Disappeared*, is given a new meaning. As a nobody (an immigrant or an African American), outside the constraints of the bourgeois family, one risks becoming someone that society does not care to protect. What Karl may be facing is thus anonymity and death.

The second photograph in question ties in with the context of racism and inequality in America. Toward the end of the fragment, before the train leaves for Oklahama, a number of photographs from the theater circulate among the newly recruited. Only one of them reaches the end of the table where Karl sits, but this particular photograph fascinates him greatly. It represents the presidential box at the theater—empty, but richly adorned:

This picture showed the box of the President of the United States. At first glance you might have thought it was not a box but the stage, the curved balustrade projected so far into the free space. This balustrade was made entirely of gold in all its parts. Between the slender columns which seemed to have been cut out with the finest scissors, medallions of earlier presidents were fixed in a row, one had a remarkably straight nose, thick lips, and eyes staring downwards under their arched lids. All round the box, from the sides and from above, there came rays of light; the foreground of the box was revealed in white yet soft light, while its recesses, behind folds of red velvet in many shades that hung down all round the sides and could be moved by cords, seemed to be a dark, reddish, shimmering emptiness. One could hardly imagine people in the box, it all seemed so autocratic. (MWD, 208)

Dieses Bild stellte die Loge des Präsidenten der Vereinigten Staaten dar. Beim ersten Anblick konnte man denken, es sei nicht eine Loge, sondern die Bühne, so weit geschwungen ragte die Brüstung in den freien Raum. Diese Brüstung war ganz aus Gold in allen ihren Teilen. Zwischen den wie mit der feinsten Scheere ausgeschnittenen Säulchen waren nebeneinander Medaillons frühere Präsidenten angebracht, einer hatte eine auffallend gerade Nase, aufgeworfene Lippen und unter gewölbten Lidern starr gesenkte Augen. Rings um die Loge, von den Seiten und von der Höhe kamen Strahlen von Licht; weißes und doch mildes Licht enthüllte förmlich den Vordergrund der Loge, während ihre Tiefe hinter rotem, unter vielen Tönungen sich faltendem Sammt der an der ganzen Umrandung niederfiel und durch Schnüre gelenkt wurde, als eine dunkle rötlich schimmernde Leere erschien. Man konnte sich in dieser Loge kaum Menschen vorstellen, so selbstherrlich sah alles aus. (V, 314)

This passage shows Karl's attention to the depth and perspective of the photograph, which gives a strong sense of space. He also notices that the aesthetic adornments of the theater box dominate the photograph, and he perceives the light surrounding the box; it comes from all sides and does not seem to have a primary source. The passage shows how power is constituted and consecrated, namely, through aesthetic effects. Indeed, it seems almost self-evident that the box is empty because the picture is all about *representation* of power. Moreover, the passage demonstrates how effectively profane powers can be given a religious veil in a "selbstherrlich" look (the English translation "autocratic" does not have the same religious connotations).

Although this is clearly not a portrait photograph, its features are in a way akin to nineteenth-century portraiture: It is just as if the subject has been removed and the staging and props have been moved into the foreground. Moreover, the passage depicts a series of medallions portraying former presidents, highlighting one of them in particular; its features tally well with representations of Abraham Lincoln (conspicuously straight nose, raised lips, arched eyebrows, and fixed gaze). We could thus see the photograph as an "inverted" or transmuted Lincoln portrait. As soon as one recognizes the Lincoln reference, it becomes clear that the fictive photograph alludes to an *actual* photograph that was widely distributed at the turn of the century and became something of an icon: the photograph of the empty theater box where Lincoln was assassinated on April 14, 1865, by the actor and Confederate sympathizer John Wilkes Booth.[30] The event took place toward the end of the American Civil War after a speech in which Lincoln envisioned how the franchise could be extended to some African Americans. Strongly opposed to granting African Americans civil rights, Booth assassinated Lincoln a few days later, in his theater box at the Washington theater in the middle of a play.[31]

30. Duttlinger, *Kafka and Photography*, 96; Lowry, *The President*, 185. Although the picture has sometimes been attributed to Matthew Brady, it was probably taken by Alexander Gardner, Brady's associate. Gardner was also assigned the mission of taking pictures of those involved in the Lincoln murder on death row, as well as their execution by hanging. This series of photographs included the infamous picture of Lewis Payne on death row, which Roland Barthes considers in his book on photography. For Barthes, the Payne picture demonstrates how time (or death) can be the "punctum," or the piercing force, of a picture. In the book, the picture's caption is "He is dead and he is going to die . . ." See Barthes, *Camera Lucida*, 95.
31. Lowry, *The President*, 183–5.

There is thus an uncanny resemblance between these historical events and Kafka's novel; in both cases, political questions regarding rights and inclusion are related to the theater, and in both cases, politics, power, and aesthetics seem to go hand in hand. Crucial elements from Lincoln's assassination thus appear to be incorporated into the Oklahoma fragment, and although no crime takes place in it, the fragment suggests that Karl—who has taken the nickname "Negro"—is at risk. Having cut all ties to his former life and identity, he has placed his life in the hands of an uncanny theater institution, representing an almost supreme power.

Together with the allusion to the lynching photograph, the image alluding to Lincoln's assassination makes us see Karl's fate in light of somber historical events. The photographs thus work as ways of crossing the boundaries between fiction and nonfiction, priming the reader toward a more somber reading of the story. Indeed, it is remarkable that Kafka in the Oklahoma fragment refers to two photographs from the visual culture of his day that both represent socially or politically motivated killings.[32] These photographs play a key role in the novel; they speak silently about injustice and violence—topics that are treated in a "light" manner at the narrative level.

We have now moved from the submissive poses in family photographs to the representation of death in politically charged photographs, and the question that emerges is what relation there is

32. Lynching photographs were widely circulated in the period when lynching was most common (1880–1930), and the lynchings were staged to such a degree that one could say that they were intended for the camera's eye. See Leigh Raiford. "Consumption of Lynching Photographs." At first they were sold as postcards and souvenirs, and when the newspapers started to print photographs they were also published in the local press. Such photographs were first distributed to create a feeling of supremacy among the white beholders and to produce fear among the Black ones, making the lynching known beyond those who were present. However, when lynching photographs started to circulate also in the northern states and beyond the communities in which the lynching took place, they created horror and became part of anti-lynching campaigns. See Allen et al., *Without Sanctuary*; Apel, *Imagery of Lynching*; Apel and Smith, *Lynching Photographs*. Holitscher's use of the lynching photograph in a German book testifies to this critical approach, and Kafka's view of it is critical as well. As for the Lincoln photograph, it circulated as part of a series of stereographic cards from the civil war published originally around 1865. It was thus intended for private or semipublic use by the numerous owners of stereoscopes (a popular device in the second half of the twentieth century). As such it was used to commemorate the brutal death of a remarkable president and to document the dramatic events. See Lowry, *The President*.

between these different kinds of pictures. As we have seen, all the pictures represent power relations where individuals are subjugated and exposed, yet in ambivalent ways. The family photograph where Karl's parents pose in a well-known studio fashion represents authority and restricted possibilities for Karl. The two political photographs, too, represent power and dominance, and they, too, depict power relations in combination with theatricality. If we now return to Benjamin's notion of the studio portrait as resembling both a torture chamber and throne room, we may recognize how Kafka's two political photographs are marked by similar features: The lynching photograph represents the torture of an individual, *post mortem*, whereas the Lincoln photograph represents the power throne, *post mortem*. We may thus see a similarity between the staging of power in the family photograph and the staging of power in the politically charged photographs. Whereas the family photograph appears both as a torture chamber and a throne room, the pictures Kafka refer to show an even more brutal dynamic; both the "torture" picture (representing suffering) and the "throne" picture (representing sovereign power) are marked by theatricality as well as death.

In light of these photographs, we may outline the novel's plotline in the following manner: Karl was once his parent's prince, placed on an ambivalent throne (the family photograph), then becomes a "Negro," unprotected (the lynching photograph). Next, he is subjected to the uncanny powers of the Oklahama Theater, covered up by aesthetic and theatrical effects (the photograph of the presidential box), and, eventually, he disappears ("the man who disappears"). Referring to photographs, Kafka thus offers a reflection on the power relations Karl is caught up in. Even if Karl seems to be on guard when a new authority (the Oklahama Theater) replaces his parents, this does not save him from an uncanny fate at the theater—unless disappearance is seen as the ultimate freedom; a leap into true anonymity. The only problem is that this kind of anonymity could amount to death. But then this may be precisely the brutal "logic" of the novel, with its relentless, machine-like dynamics, narrating Karl's fall from "identity" to "anonymity."

Yet Kafka's way of using the motif of looking at photographs indicates that there may be something to learn from such an activity; a self-awareness may slowly emerge. We saw that Karl was capable of both absorption and detachment in his engagement with family photographs, and that he seemed to learn how to consider them with more distance. This may be interpreted as a step toward visual literacy. But in his meeting with the Lincoln photograph, his visual education appears to have made a halt; Karl seems more immersed in this picture and its "grandiose" look than in the family photograph. Although he notices its aesthetic features, the picture does not really cause any critical reflection in him about the institution he is joining; rather, the picture's staging of power is described with a certain awe. It is at this point that Karl is truly at risk. Indeed, the novel depicts the theater institution as a greater power and a more acute danger than the family institution, which he has already left behind.

Thus, Kafka seems to target political photographs in particular. In fact, there is reason to believe that the audience in Kafka's day had less training in the "reading" of news photographs and public photographs than in the reading of family photographs, which were well known from mid-nineteenth century onward. This point should not be exaggerated, though, for the real Lincoln photograph dated from 1865, the year of Lincoln's death. Still, one could argue that critical reflection on the power of public images was still nascent in Kafka's day, and that Karl's naïve response reflects this state of affairs. In this perspective, one could argue that the motif of beholding such photographs in Kafka's writings offered possibilities for meta-reflection and prompted questions about the power of images at the beginning of the twentieth century. Pursuing this question, we will now look at the role of the "media witness." What will interest us is the witness's distance from the events shown and the relation between immersion and detachment.

War, Death, and Witnessing

With the circulation of politically charged photographs and the emergence of photojournalism early in the twentieth century, the public was gradually trained to process news events visually. A new role thus started to take shape: the *media witness* beholding political events as they were mediated through photographs. Such photographs were important not only for their information value, but also for the emotional responses they prompted and for the moral reflection they spurred (more or less consciously). Through such photographs, political sympathy was created and distributed.

Among the news photographs from this period, photographs from the First World War must have had a strong effect, because they gave a new sense of realism as to what war was about. Reading about war is a very different thing than witnessing photographic scenes from the war. Compared to the abstractedness of journalistic texts, war photographs are more visceral, offering specificity and myriad details. It is therefore interesting to see that in two places Kafka refers to photographs of soldiers and political leaders in the context of war, once related to the outbreak of the First Balkan War in 1912 and once related to the outbreak of the First World War in 1914. In both cases, Kafka, highlighted the realism of the photographs and displayed sensitivity to the experience of witnessing at a distance.

Kafka's active days as a writer coincided with a period of great distress in Europe, marked by international crisis and preparations for war, first the Balkan Wars (1912–13) and then the First World War (1914–18). Both affected the politics and national status of the Austrian-Hungarian Empire of which Kafka was a citizen; the Balkan Wars took place on the borders of the empire, and the First World War led to its end. The newspapers from the period were filled with disturbing news from the wars, and photographs made the events feel even more real. Yet Kafka appears to be strangely unaffected by these events. As we have already seen, however, it would be simplistic to dismiss Kafka as an apolitical writer; even if his writings may appear abstract and ahistorical, they comment on contemporary issues in subtle ways. With respect to the Balkan Wars and the First World War, Carolin Duttlinger and Thomas Anz have done important work in situating Kafka within that historical context.[33] Admittedly, Kafka's writings include a quite limited number of references to the war, but those that can be found are worthy of consideration.

It is probably safe to say that the Balkan Wars and the First World War were the first wars that were covered to a certain extent through photojournalism (the photographic covering of the Crimean War was more limited, even if it was pioneering, as was the covering of the American Civil War and the Boer Wars). The photographers were, however, not allowed to cover the battles, and their undertakings were subject to political censorship. Official photographs would document the pre-battle situation of military parades and posing soldiers as well as the post-battle situation of battlefields and ruins. Photographs of soldiers in action, including soldiers shot to death, were first published during the Spanish Civil War (as commented upon by Virginia Woolf). Furthermore, there was a considerable delay in the publication of photographs from the war. Since the images had to travel over land and could not be telegraphed, as news reports could, the images that were shown documented last week's events.

33. Duttlinger, "Snapshots of History"; Duttlinger, *Kafka and Photography*, 206–19; Anz, "Das größte Theater der Welt."

Kafka's biographer Reiner Stach has dedicated a chapter in his biography to the First Balkan War, with the heading "Balkan War: The Massacre Next Door."[34] According to Stach, the press was soon to call the war a "Balkan slaughterhouse," and photographs played an important role in making the brutality of the war known to civilians. He recounts that "[p]hotographs were being circulated of corpses stacked up on horse carts and people in tatters slowly moving eastwards."[35] Pointing to the conflicts that emerged regarding these shocking pictures, he suggests that Kafka saw pictures that were "unprintable":

> The initial thirst for adventure on the part of the frontline photographers and war correspondents, which was bitterly denounced by Karl Kraus, dissipated rapidly. Even Erwin Egon Kisch, who was anything but thin-skinned, and had traveled through the Balkans for the Prague newspaper *Bohemia* in May 1913, found that he was no longer able to apply his customary light touch to help his readers cope with the shattering images he encountered. It is possible, although there are no documents to prove it, that Brod and Kafka learned things from him firsthand that would have been unprintable.[36]

Stach thus suggests that Kafka and Brod saw war photographs that were more brutal than the ones printed in newspapers. Kafka himself commented on the unsettling news from Balkan in several letters to Felice Bauer written in November 1912. On November 1, he relates that he does not sleep well and depicts a dream that keep haunting him. It is about Montenegrins in elaborate costumes: "for a whole week I saw nothing but Montenegrins in my sleep, in extremely disagreeable clarity, which gave me headaches, I saw every detail of their complicated dress" (LF, 22) ["eine Woche lang habe ich in diesem Schlaf nur Montegriner gesehn mit einer außerst widerlichen, Kopfschmerzen verursachenden Deutlichkeit jedes Details ihrer komplicierten Kleidung" (BFB, 35)]. This dream may have been a reminiscence of photographs from the First Balkan War,

34. Stach, *Franz Kafka*, 226–41. The war was fought between the Balkan League (consisting of Bulgaria, Greece, Montenegro, and Serbia) and the Ottoman Empire between October 1912 and May 1913, after Montenegro declared war on the Ottomans on October 8. Even if Austria-Hungary was not involved in the war, they considered the Balkan League a threat and feared its expansion, so the war caused tension there as well.
35. Stach, *Kafka*, 226–7.
36. Stach, *Kafka*, 229.

depicting Montenegrin soldiers in their uniforms.[37] As the letter was written on November 1, three weeks after the war had started (with Montenegro's declaration of war), it is probable that the first photographs from the war had recently been published. This brief comment is significant because it says something important about Kafka's response to photographs from the war and ties in well with his other comment on photographs. He stresses how much the dream disturbs him and will not let him go, and this suggests that he perceives the pictures as having some kind of agency. When he relates that he saw nothing but Montenegrins the whole week, this means that the dream was recurrent; the war image thus multiplied in his dreams, in the same way as photographs from the war multiplied in the newspapers.

Kafka's letter about his dream reveals that the war disturbed him profoundly, and Duttlinger has perceptibly noted that an echo of this comment appears in his fiction. One of the fragments in *The Trial*, which Kafka began in August 1914 shortly after the outbreak of the First World War, describes a scene that is in many respects similar to the one described in Kafka's dream. Here, too, dream images appear to mix with photographic images. The scene depicts K. as he dozes in the sofa in his office, visiting in his thoughts a court building where people move around in a confused, dreamlike manner. He suddenly sees Fräulein Bürstner surrounded by two men, and we are told that this vision is only the "indelible memory of a photo" ["die unauslöschliche Erinnerung an eine Photographie"] he has seen of her previously. He then sees a man in a foreign costume. This time, there is no explicit comment on a photograph, but the scene still seems to depict the act of looking at a photograph:

> [D]etails kept impressing themselves on his brain with painful clarity, a foreigner, for example, was taking a walk in one of the anterooms, his dress was similar to a bullfighter's, the waist cut in sharply, as if with knives, his very short jacket, wrapped stiffly round him, consisted entirely of yellowish lace made of coarse threads, and this man exposed himself the whole time to K.'s astonished gaze without for a moment interrupting his walk. K. crept round him, bent low, and gaped at him, straining to keep his eyes wide open. He knew all the patterning of the lace, all the missing fringes, all the undulations of the little jacket, and still could not take his eyes off it. Or rather, he could have taken his eyes off it long ago, or, to be more precise, he

37. Stach, *Kafka*, 229; Duttlinger, *Kafka and Photography*, 200.

had never wanted to look at it, but it kept a hold of him. 'What fancy outfits they have abroad!' he thought, opening his eyes even wider. And he continued in this man's wake until he turned over on the sofa and pressed his face into the leather.[38]

Einzelheiten drückten sich ihm mit schmerzlichster Deutlichkeit immer wieder ins Hirn, ein Ausländer z. B. spazierte in einem Vorsaal, er war gekleidet ähnlich einem Stierfechter, die Taille war eingeschnitten wie mit Messern, sein ganz kurzes ihn steif umgebendes Röckchen bestand aus gelblichen grobfädigen Spitzen und dieser Mann ließ sich, ohne sein Spazierengehn einen Augenblick einzustellen, unaufhörlich von K. bestaunen. Gebückt umschlich ihn K. und staunte ihn mit angestrengt aufgerissenen Augen an. Er kannte alle Zeichnungen der Spitzen, alle fehlerhaften Fransen, alle Schwingungen des Röckchens und hatte sich doch nicht sattgesehn. Oder vielmehr er hatte sich schon längst satt-gesehn oder noch richtiger er hatte es niemals ansehen wollen aber es ließ ihn nicht. 'Was für Maskeraden bietet das Ausland!' dachte er und riß die Augen noch stärker auf. Und im Gefolge dieses Mannes blieb er bis er sich auf dem Kanapee herumwarf und das Gesicht ins Leder drückte.[39]

As Duttlinger has pointed out, this passage has many similarities with the dream image of the Montenegrin soldier from the outbreak of the Balkan War in fall 1912.[40] Here, the soldier is transformed into a foreign guard, wearing the costume of a bullfighter and serving in an obscure legal system. We may ask if it is the bullfighter's attitude that troubles K.: Just like a soldier, a bullfighter is merciless, yet elegant— he is both a butcher and an aesthete. Further, in both passages, Kafka stresses the clarity of the visions as well as the strong effects they have on the one dreaming. In his letter to Felice, Kafka tells her that he sees Montenegrins in his dreams in "extremely disagreeable clarity" and that he "saw every detail of their complicated dress." He also tells Felice that the detailed outline of this recurrent dream gave him head-aches. The same level of precision characterizes the passage from *The Trial*, as well as the painful physical effect: "details kept impressing themselves on his brain with the painful clarity."

Moreover, when the passage describes how the marching man willingly allowed K.'s gaze without being disturbed by it, this may seem to refer to the sealed off world of the photograph. Indeed, a man

38. Kafka, *The Trial*, 184.
39. Kafka, *Der Process*, 271.
40. Duttlinger, *Kafka and Photography*, 198–201.

depicted in a photograph is completely indifferent with respect to the beholder, and the relation between the observer and the observed is thus in play here. The observer has no influence over a photograph, whereas the photograph can have a strong effect on the observer. Insofar as it can infect pain and haunt us, the photograph seems to have some kind of agency. In fact, this way of responding to images bears some similarities to Kafka's response to Felice's picture: K. is troubled by the fact that the man in the picture does not return his gaze, just as Kafka was troubled by the fact that Felice did not return his gaze.

We may also note that K. is utterly captivated by what he sees in his dream. He cannot take his eyes off the man, or rather, the image will not let him go, so he remains "in this man's wake." This lasts until the moment when K. fervently throws himself around in the sofa and hides his face. Thus, in the scene, there is a dynamic between visual immersion and visual resistance, or between opening one's eyes widely and hiding one's eyes. A similar visual dynamic was in play in *The Man Who Disappeared*, although it was played out much more quietly: In that case, Karl looked at the photograph of his parents, reflecting on the strong impact it had on him, and then "looked away from the picture for a while." In both cases, Kafka describes deep absorption in images as well as a capacity to resist their power, and in this manner, he subtly grants the protagonists a nascent capacity for critical ways of responding.

The question of the powerlessness of the viewer is especially disturbing when it comes to images of war. When the events of war were reported for the first time through newspaper photographs, offering detailed images of the soldiers in their uniforms and with their weapons, ordinary newspaper readers were turned into witnesses of threatening world events, without possibilities for interfering. A newspaper reader is typically left to either witness the events after the fact or imagine the events that followed the photographic moment. In the case of war photographs, the temporality that haunts every photograph is thus exacerbated. They create moments of suspense, leaving the predications of the *before* and *after* to the viewer. In this manner, war photographs are steeped in the pathos of the moment.

A second case in point is a detailed description of a war photograph in "Blumfeld, an Elderly Bachelor," one of Kafka's posthumously published stories, originally written in 1915. The story, about a lonely bachelor who wants someone to witness his life, includes a scene in which the protagonist browses through a magazine and has his attention caught by a photograph. As the photograph is described in great detail, it is easy to recognize the historical event it alludes to: a state visit to the Russian czar Nicholas II in St Petersburg by the French president Raymond Poincaré, taking place during the prelude to the First World War, the so-called July Crisis. Kafka's description of the photograph reveals his perceptiveness regarding the historical moment and raises questions about what it means to witness images of war.

The order of the events is worthy of a reminder: The July Crisis followed the assassination of Austrian archduke Franz Ferdinand in Sarajevo on June 28, 1914. In the wake of this event, Austria-Hungary formulated an ultimatum to Serbia (accused of being complicit in the murder) that was signed by Emperor Franz Joseph on July 21, but not delivered until July 23, as soon as the afore-mentioned Franco-Russian summit had concluded. As Duttlinger has pointed out, Austria-Hungary and its ally Germany did not want to deliver the ultimatum while the heads of France and Russia, their two main rivals, were meeting and thus well placed to devise a joint strategy. In Duttlinger's words, "Photographs of the state visit provide a snapshot of Europe on the brink of war, in the process of frantic diplomatic and military preparations."[41]

Kafka's story and the magazine reading scene thus depict how a reader perceives an image from the buildup to the war. Blumfeld comes across the photograph when he, following his routine, sits down with a French magazine that has just arrived. Feeling more impatient than usual, he does not have the calmness to read it carefully and only browses it. A large photograph on one of the pages catches his attention, and it is described in great detail (a lengthy quotation is required here):

> Above the table, within reach, a shelf is nailed to the wall on which stands the bottle of kirsch surrounded by little glasses. Beside it, in a pile, lie several copies of the French magazine. (This very day the latest issue has arrived and Blumfeld takes it down. He quite forgets the kirsch; he even has the feeling that today he is proceeding with his usual activities only to console himself, for he feels no genuine desire to read. Contrary to his usual habit of carefully turning one page after the other, he opens the magazine at random and there finds a large photograph. He forces himself to examine it in detail. It shows a meeting between the Czar of Russia and the President of France.

---

41. Duttlinger, *Kafka and Photography*, 211. See also Duttlinger, "Snapshots of History." Again, my analysis overlaps with Duttlinger's, but my framework and my emphasis differ from hers.

This takes place on a ship. All about as far can be seen are many other ships, the smoke from their funnels vanishing in the bright sky. Both Czar and President have rushed toward each other with long strides and are clasping one another by the hand. Behind the Czar as well as behind the President stand two men. By comparison with the gay faces of the Czar and the President, the faces of their attendants are very solemn, the eyes of each group focused on their master [vereinigen sich auf ihren Herrscher]. Lower down – the scene evidently takes place on the top deck – stand long lines of saluting sailors cut off by the margin. Gradually Blumfeld contemplates the picture with more interest, then holds it a little further away and looks at it with blinking eyes. He has always had a taste for such imposing scenes. The way the chief personages clasp each other's hand so naturally, so cordially and light-heartedly, this he finds most lifelike. And it's just as appropriate that the attendants – high-ranking gentlemen, of course, with their names printed beneath – express in their bearing the solemnity of the historical moment.)[42]

Über dem Tisch ist in Griffnähe an der Wand ein Brett angebracht, auf dem die Flasche mit dem Kirschenschnaps von kleinen Gläschen umgeben steht. Neben ihr liegt ein Stoß von Heften der französischen Zeitschrift. (Gerade heute ist ein neues Heft gekommen und Blumfeld holt es herunter. Den Schnaps vergißt er ganz, er hat selbst das Gefühl, als ob er heute nur aus Trost an seinen gewöhnlichen Beschäftigungen sich nicht hindern ließe, auch ein wirkliches Bedürfnis zu lesen hat er nicht. Er schlägt das Heft, entgegen seiner sonstigen Gewohnheit, Blatt für Blatt sorgfältig zu wenden, an einer beliebigen Stelle auf und findet dort ein großes Bild. Er zwingt sich es genauer anzusehn. Es stellt die Begegnung zwischen dem Kaiser von Rußland und dem Präsidenten von Frankreich dar. Sie findet auf einem Schiff statt. Ringsherum bis in die Ferne sind noch viele andere Schiffe, der Rauch ihrer Schornsteine verflüchtigt sich im hellen Himmel. Beide, der Kaiser und der Präsident, sind eben in langen Schritten einander entgegengeeilt und fassen einander gerade bei der Hand. Hinter dem Kaiser wie hinter dem Präsidenten stehen je zwei Herren. Gegenüber den freudigen Gesichtern des Kaisers und des Präsidenten sind die Gesichter der Begleiter sehr ernst, die Blicke jeder Begleitgruppe vereinigen sich auf ihren Herrscher. Tiefer unten, der Vorgang spielt sich offenbar auf dem höchsten Deck des Schiffes ab, stehen vom Bildrand abgeschnitten lange Reihen salutierender Matrosen. Blumfeld betrachtet allmählich das Bild mit mehr Teilnahme, hält es dann ein wenig entfernt und sieht es so mit blinzelnden Augen an.

42. Kafka, "Blumfeld," 187.

Er hat immer viel Sinn für solche großartige Szenen gehabt. Daß die Hauptpersonen so unbefangen, herzlich und leichtsinnig einander die Hände drücken, findet er sehr wahrheitsgetreu. Und ebenso richtig ist es, daß die Begleiter – übrigens natürlich sehr hohe Herren, deren Namen unten verzeichnet sind – in ihrer Haltung den Ernst des historischen Augenblicks wahren.)[43]

As with other ekphrastic passages from Kafka's hand, this description (which was omitted from the final version of the story) is full of interesting details and subtle nuances. First, we should observe that Kafka here depicts a new reading habit: browsing through the pages rather than reading carefully, and getting absorbed in images rather than in texts. The same tendency was described in *The Man Who Disappeared*, where Karl puts down the Bible to contemplate a family photograph. The question of distraction versus absorption is thus in play here, as is the relation between image and text. An amusing detail is that the magazine does not here compete with the Bible, but with a bottle of kirsch. This shows how subtly Kafka depicts changes in everyday bourgeois rituals and how the profane and the religious negotiate.

Second, it is interesting to note that Blumfeld is depicted as an embodied reader who engages physically with the image and gradually takes it in. In this respect, his approach to photographs resembles Karl Rossmann's. He begins by forcing himself to examine the photograph in detail and in this first phase identifies the persons depicted in it and the place of the scene. He then contemplates it with more involvement ("mehr Teilnahme") and so to speak tests the relation between his body and the photograph, holding it away and looking at it with blinking eyes. It is as if he turns his bodily and sensory organs into a testing instrument for the photograph, allowing it to have an impact on him.

Third, Blumfeld pays close attention to the composition and aesthetics of the picture, making this part of his final verdict: "He has always had a taste for such imposing scenes." He follows the lines of the horizon with his eyes and notices how the lines of sailors are cut off by the margin [Bildrand]. Likewise, he is interested in the theatrical qualities of the scene, commenting not only on its formal setup (the hierarchy between the leaders, attendants, and sailors) but also on the realism of the scene ("natural," "lifelike," "appropriate"), as

43. Kafka, "Blumfeld," 147–8.

if it were a scene from a movie. Yet the realism of the picture could be contested. As has been demonstrated by Duttlinger, the two state leaders that form the center of the photograph are described in a manner that suggests both stillness and movement, and what Kafka describes could thus be considered a hybrid image (or a photomontage) that could not have existed.[44]

Fourth, Blumfeld considers the expression of faces and the direction of gazes in the photograph, noticing the hierarchic order in it. The political leaders are at the center of the picture, the attendants stand behind them, looking at their masters (in fact, they *unite* with their masters through their gazes ["die Blicke jeder Begleitgruppe vereinigen sich auf ihren Herrscher"]), and the sailors stand in the margins of the picture, saluting the masters. Blumfeld's conclusion to the scene concerns the solemnness of the attendants' faces, which is judged worthy of the historical moment. Further, he pays attention to the names of these attendants, printed in the caption below the picture and appears pleased to see their rank and role acknowledged by the newspaper. The passage whole passage reveals that Blumfeld in this picture not only sees a meeting between two political leaders, but considers how the attendants' gazes and the sailors' salutary gestures contribute to creating the historical moment. He thus appears to acknowledge the role of the witnesses, without which the historical moment could not have come about.

Further, there is a detail in this passage which speaks loudly of Blumfeld's response to the picture. When Blumfeld sits quietly by himself in his living room, looking at this large photograph in a magazine, he does so with blinking gaze ("mit blinzelnden Augen"). He does not look away (as Karl did when he looked at his parents' photograph); he blinks. This indicates a disturbance in the established order—a bodily hiccup—that is caused by the photograph. In fact, the description gives associations to how the flash in a photographic session causes blinking eyes, and this give a sense of intensity to an otherwise restrained ekphrastic description. How should we interpret this hiccup? It seems to be an effect created by the picture and may perhaps be caused by its *closeness*. When Blumfeld engages physically with the photograph, holding the magazine in his hands and observing how the lines of soldiers are "cut off by the margins" of the image, an overlapping is created between his own witnessing situation from home and the witnessing of the attendants on the ship. He is drawn into the photograph as a cum-witness, uniting with

44. Duttlinger, "Snapshots of History," 34.

the sailors and attendants (just as the attendants united with their masters in gazing at them). The solemn attitude of the attendants contaminates his own attitude and marks the passage as a whole. Identifying with the attendants in the picture, Blumfeld seems to find dignity and a cause.

We could thus see the whole passage as a meditation on the role of the witness. While the war photograph depicts a political summit, with two top politicians in active roles, the passage describing it also pays attention to the role of the witnesses in sanctioning the political event. It depicts a ring of gazes performing the role of witnesses: the attendants in the photograph looking at the masters, the photograph (or the camera gaze) looking at the political scene, and the magazine reader looking at the photograph. This circle of silent gazes is part of the process of creating history, but without any active interference. Indeed, a war picture becomes iconic by virtue of the many gazes that have dwelled upon it and the emotional impact it has had on the viewers. Such pictures create silent witnesses; they know something about the brutal realities of war, but not necessarily how to speak about them. A gap is thus created between the visible and speech.[45]

Pursuing this question further, one could ask if a form of visual education takes place in this passage. Previously, we have seen how Kafka describes the sealed-off world of the photograph and the helplessness of the viewer with respect to what they see—that is, their inability to respond to the realities of the photograph. In this passage, however, we see how Blumfeld learns to behave as a spectator. He engages physically with the photograph and looks at the photograph with blinking eyes, but then he so to speak takes his cue from the attendants. On the one hand, he is immersed in the photograph; on the other hand, he adopts the same distance from the situation as the attendants. No sense of helplessness is uttered; the relation between who sees and who is seen is apparently as it should be. As Blumfeld sits safely in his home, he seems to take pleasure is his role as a beholder, lining up among the witnesses in the photograph.[46]

---

45. Jacques Rancière's view of the "intolerable image" is pertinent here: He points out that an image cannot be assessed merely based on its motif, for it is not a duplicate of a thing. Rather, an image is "a complex set of relations between the visible and the invisible, the visible and speech, the said and the unsaid." Rancière, "The Intolerable Image," 93.

46. In a similar way, Hannah Arendt stresses how K. in *The Trial* is "educated and transformed until he is fit to assume the role forced upon him [. . .] It is his way of adapting to the existing conditions." The education of the protagonist is in our context carried out through the media. See Arendt, "Franz Kafka," 97.

The Blumfeld passage thus raises questions regarding the act of looking at media images, and more particularly about what it means to witness photographs from the war in the illustrated press. Whereas this fictive passage offers a reflection on the response of the witness, the passage on the Montenegrin soldiers and the *Trial* passage based on it show a more emotional response and a sense of helplessness. Indeed, witnessing events that are mediated through photographs affects the beholders emotionally, but at the same time requires them to keep their distance, and this creates a mixed message. The beholders' responses to such mixed messages span widely: from immersion to detachment; from a feeling of helplessness to mere indifference.

Reading Kafka's comments in hindsight, we could ask to what degree the audience in his day was trained to process disturbing war photographs. We know that the twentieth century would soon provide crucial lessons in this domain, but early in the century such photographs were not yet commonplace. We could actually see "Blumfeld" as depicting the moment when such a picture becomes a commonplace to an ordinary beholder. He addresses the media shift when the press started to print photographs, thus documenting world events and wars through images. Ordinary newspaper readers were in this manner turned into witnesses of violent world events and were emotionally affected by what they saw. Today, as the ethics of beholding war photographs is fervently debated, Kafka's meditation on the topic is illuminating because it reflects upon the beholder's degree of involvement, reveals his profound ambivalence and uncovers the power of such photographs.[47]

Thus, we may conclude that Kafka was concerned with the circulation of photographs in the wider public sphere, and especially with disturbing pictures. We should further observe that Kafka often paid attention to similar issues with respect to private and public photographs: He addressed the effect such pictures had on their beholders and raised questions regarding absorption and detachment, submission and liberation. In this manner, Kafka invites the reader to reflect upon on the subtle powers of photographs. The impact of such images is connected, on the one hand, to the ways in which they act directly on the beholder and, on the other, to a set of discursive practices that reinforce their power. When Kafka lets Rossmann and Blumfeld adopt certain "naïve" ways of speaking about photographs, he exposes some of the clichés surrounding such pictures. Moreover,

---

47. Cf. Susan Sontag's discussions on the ethics of war photographs. Sontag, *Regarding the Pain of Others*.

Kafka's way of deploying the lynching photograph and the Lincoln photograph in the Oklahoma fragment speaks loudly about the ways in which these pictures circulate and suggest that such photographs gain their power from the discursive formations they are part of.

Creating Identity and Anonymity

Let us now consider the deeper issues at stake in Kafka's engagement with photography and try to identify a few characterizing features. Even if his writings on the topic are quite diverse (he comments on the photographs of Felice and himself, on family photographs, and on politically charged photographs), we may recognize an underlying issue uniting his various perspectives: the relation between identity and anonymity. Kafka has a sharp eye for the ways in which the photographed subject is inscribed in a set of power relations that pull toward identity or anonymity, and he saw how the use of photographs reinforces this dynamic. Reading Kafka, we recognize the precarious aspects of photography.

It is well known that portrait photographs buttressed bourgeois identity construction in the decades before and after 1900; they confirmed one's place in the nuclear family as well as one's role in society, while also limiting one's freedom and possibility space. Further, the increasing use of photographs in police archives and registration offices reinforced the link between photographs and identity; the authorities documented the identity of the citizens through their names and pictures, thus strengthening their control over the population.[48] Two photographic systems thus worked in tandem to bolster identity construction in this period.[49] However, the flipside of bourgeois "identity" is not simply a leap into "freedom"; it could also amount to anonymity. What, then, is anonymity, and what is the role of photographs in creating it? Often, anonymity refers to authors whose *names* are unknown, but it encompasses also *faces* whose names are unknown.[50] Indeed,

48. Alphonse Bertillon's system of identification or "signalment" from 1896 was important in this respect and marked a more systematic approach to the question of criminal identification: "*Signalment* is the description of one whom it is desired to identify." Bertillon, "Selections from Theoretical Study of Signalment."
49. Hamilton and Hargreaves, *The Beautiful and the Damned.*
50. Anonymous (from ancient Greek *anōnumos*, from *an*, without + *ōnoma*, name) means "without name." Merriam-Webster's dictionary lists both "namelessness" and "facelessness" as synonyms of "anonymity." *Merriam-Webster Dictionary*, s.v. "anonymity," accessed March 3, 2022, https://www.merriam-webster.com/dictionary/anonymity.

anonymous faces were one of the novelties of urban life and a key feature of the modern mass society.[51]

With the rise of the illustrated press in the decades after 1900, pictures of unnamed faces started to proliferate, and the notion of anonymity was given a new valence. In the age of the illustrated media, the notion of anonymity pertained to a larger degree to *mediated faces* that were without names but exposed to the public. A split was thus created between those who were ascribed an identity (a name) in a photograph and those who would be conferred to anonymity. Where family photographs, celebrity photographs, and photographs of politicians, prominently featured the names of the photographed subject, other kinds of photographs would leave the names of the subjects in the dark.[52] Of course, some groups were likely to fall into this category: the anonymous people representing a profession, anonymous people in the city crowd, and the anonymous outcasts that were not assigned any significant role in society.[53] In a certain way, photographic technology form an alliance with the anonymous. Insofar as it is an indexical art, it treats all subjects in an equal manner without raising questions about identity.

There is probably a connection between this development in the illustrated press and a new vogue in portrait photography emerging in the late 1920s: German photographers started to show an interest in anonymous faces as representing types rather than individualities.[54] In August Sander's photobook *Face of Our Time* [*Anlitz der Zeit*, 1929], ordinary people occupying various professions are portrayed, such as cook, clerk, or accountant, with captions stating their professions, not their names.[55]

51. Following Baudelaire, Benjamin reflected upon the possibility for being *incognito* in the city. Benjamin, "The Paris of the Second Empire in Baudelaire," 74; 79.

52. When Peter Tausk describes the uses of photographic portraits in the press in the period 1880–1914, he stresses that the genre was already popular at the time of engravings, as the audience liked to study the faces of famous people: "The portrait was popular in illustrated magazines already when it had to be engraved. The public was interested in characteristic features of the faces of the members of ruling families, politicians, actors, writers, musicians, and other famous personalities." Yet his selection of press photographs from the period shows that they also depicted anonymous people, taken by photographers such as Alfred Steglitz and Eugène Atget. See Tausk, *A Short History of Press Photography*, 44; 49–56.

53. A well-known example is David Octavius Hill's social documentary series on the Newhaven fishwives, which spurred Benjamin's thoughts about photography and remembrance. See Benjamin, "Little History," 276.

54. See Pepper Stetler's book on the Weimar photobook: Stetler, *Stop Reading! Look!*

55. Sander, *Anlitz der Zeit*.

Further, Herman Lerski published *Everyday Faces* [*Köpfe des Alltags*, 1931], portraits of anonymous working-class figures, combining sharp light and extreme close-up to achieve an aesthetic effect.[56] In this manner, he showed the beauty and vulnerability of everyday faces—albeit without their consent.

Photographic pictures of unknown persons were thus becoming a feature of everyday life in this period, and in my view, this notion of anonymity is important to understand Kafka's engagement with photographs. He not only addresses the ways in which portrait photographs bolstered bourgeois conceptions of identity, but also acknowledged that anonymity was the flipside of identity. In fact, the association of photographs and bourgeois identity was well established in Kafka's day, as it stemmed from nineteenth-century conceptions of photography, whereas the question of anonymity was much more urgent in the emerging visual and political culture of this period. The illustrated press endowed the anonymous masses with faces; publicities gave faces to the "everyman" and the "everywoman" as spokespersons of a modern lifestyle, and pictures of soldiers gave faces to the war industry marking the period. Through such pictures, the audience was gradually trained to look at anonymous faces.[57]

Looking closely at Kafka's writings, we see that the relation between identity and anonymity is constantly in play. Anonymity seems to be the condition of many of his characters, such as K. in *The Trial*, K. in *The Castle*, and "Negro" in the last part of *The Man Who Disappeared*, and, at the same time, questions about identity and identity papers are recurrent in his fiction. The novel *The Man Who Disappeared* is a case in point; this is a story about a man's fall from identity into anonymity.[58]

56. Lerski, *Köpfe des Alltags*.
57. According to photographic historian Gisèle Freund, the press photographs expanded the outlook of the readers: "The introduction of newspaper photography was a phenomenon of immense importance, one that changed the outlook of the masses. Before the first press pictures, the ordinary man could visualize only those events that took place near him, on his street, or in his village. Photography opened a window, as it were. [. . .] The individual, commissioned portrait in the reader's home in a sense gave way to the collective press portrait." According to Freund, press pictures were introduced in the newspapers during the two first decades of the twentieth century, whereas the weekly and monthly magazines printed photographs from 1885 onward. Freund, *Photography and Society*, 103.
58. Recognizing the importance of anonymity in Kafka's novels, Hannah Arendt speaks of his protagonists' "tantalizing anonymity." She mainly discusses *The*

Karl breaks with his family, is forced to live as a vagrant, and ends up at the enigmatic Oklahama Theater, registered as "Negro," and then virtually disappears. The photograph of his parents indicates his previous identity within the bourgeois family in Europe, whereas the reference to the lynching photograph from Holitscher's book suggests his leap into anonymity; now he becomes a "nobody" without rights. These two photographs thus embody the fall from identity to anonymity, and the power relations in both of them are suggested to the reader. Whereas the act of assuming an identity appears to be a trap for Karl, anonymity, too, appears to be a dangerous and risky condition.

Further, as we have seen, we find a recurrent fascination with pictures of anonymous persons in Kafka's fiction, especially soldiers: Montenegrin soldiers, a marching soldier, sailors on a ship, and a laughing soldier. These soldiers seem both powerful and unapproachable, and the pictures of them have a strong impact on the beholders. The description of the summit picture in "Blumfeld, the Bachelor" highlights the role of the anonymous soldiers as witnesses. Only the politicians and the highest-ranked officers are named, whereas rows of anonymous soldiers witness the event. In this manner, he suggests that there is a split between those who are attributed a name and an identity and those who remain nameless, as parts of the masses, as soldiers, or as outcasts. Further, the portrait of the laughing soldier seems to undermine the genre of portraiture as it gives individuality and passion to someone whose job it is to be "uniform." Dwelling on such pictures, Kafka addresses their ambivalence; they give a face to the military forces, but the soldiers remain anonymous, and the men in these pictures are both empowered and restricted by their roles

Overall, Kafka seems to acknowledge that the relation between identity and anonymity is key to the political paradigm of his day. From today's perspective, we may see this as a sensitivity to the biopolitical paradigm of modernity, as it has been described by Agamben. As he explains, the secret threat of sovereign power is that, once a person's identity and rights are granted (and confirmed through identity papers), they may be taken away, and this leaves the subject in an extremely vulnerable position. Thus, the hidden foundation of

Trial and *The Castle* (where the protagonists are referred to only as "K.") but she also refers briefly to *The Man Who Disappeared* (where the protagonist does have a name, Karl Rossmann) as a contrast, pointing to its "happy ending." She thus sides with Benjamin's optimistic reading of the novel and does not acknowledge its negative spiraling toward anonymity and death. See Arendt, "Franz Kafka," 102; 108.

modern democracies is this possibility of exclusion, which produces "bare life"; bodies without protection, without rights, and potentially exposed to violence.[59] The notion of "bare life" in many respects corresponds to the condition of anonymity as it is described by Kafka. We could thus see Kafka as exploring the hidden foundation of this political paradigm as it emerges in the modern period. As he shrewdly suggests in his writings, the relation between identity and anonymity is intimately connected with questions regarding freedom and violence, or life and death.

However, Kafka also offers a different take on the question of identity and anonymity: His careful description of Felice Bauer's photographs shows that he cannot pin her down and starts to look for something that goes *beyond identity*. Referring to the host of details in the pictures, he acknowledges that they are inexhaustible. Wishing to move beyond the surface, he refers to that which is invisible in them, and hinting at a knowledge that is immanent in them, he implies that pictures cannot easily be translated into words. This shows that, for Kafka, these photographs transcend the narrow confinements of the bourgeois portrait. As he comments on them, he depicts something that could be called true anonymity; a person's inscrutable ways of being, which always leaves something in the dark.

One could say that Kafka depicted a phase in the history of photography when the act of looking at portrait photographs was still an emotional and captivating affair, but at the same time envisioned a more critical role for the beholder. As we have seen, Kafka's responses to photographs—fictive and real—are marked with both strong emotion and critical reflection, both absorption and detachment, and this creates an ambivalence in the viewing situation. This emotional ambivalence prompts a nascent consciousness in the beholder with respect to the impact a picture may have on him. Depicting these processes, Kafka paves the way for critical views on photography while at the same time showing how pictures can inspire love.

---

59. Agamben, *Homo Sacer*. As he examines the biopolitical paradigm, Agamben several times refers to Kafka.

Chapter 3

Sympathy in Photographs: Virginia Woolf

Virginia Woolf's study of photographs, portraits, and faces is part of her investigations of the enigma of character and the ungraspable something surrounding each human being.[1] Critical of the biographical paradigm of the Victorian era, she attempted to depict an aspect of human life that is not about action or dialogue, but rather about emotional, thoughtful, and imaginary life. While she gave prevalence to the inner worlds of her characters, she also explored the role of visual communication. Using the technique of "showing seeing," she dwells on situations when action and dialogue stop and a visual activity takes over. The reading of faces, with their gestures, miens, and often unreturned gazes, is a key activity in her novels, although often carried out discreetly, in scenes involving portrait photographs and painted portraits, as well as the "natural" faces of her characters. It could indeed be argued that her contribution to modernist literature is not merely her exploration of the isolated "thought worlds" of each human being, but also her reflection upon the limited access we have to other "thought worlds" and our perpetual effort to connect with others. Indeed, Woolf's brilliancy was her ability to describe the distance between people and unfold the problem of communication. She understood that in a situation where people do not understand each other and partly have lost faith in words, they are more than ever confronted with each other's faces and with unspoken feelings of sympathy, reserve, or dismay.

1. As Diane F. Gillespie observes, photographs are "parts of the environments and consciousnesses of the characters in Woolf's fiction." See Gillespie, "Her Kodak Pointed at His Head," 113.

This fascination with faces marked numerous aesthetic endeavors in Woolf's day. Vanessa Bell's painted portrait of her sister in a deckchair (1912) can be seen as a manifestation of the uncertain status of the face in modernist painting: her face is just a featureless flesh tone block of color and appears as a "blank" space in the picture. Likewise, a portrait of the sister in an armchair (1912) shows an almost featureless face and no eyes. A similar effect is achieved through Woolf's verbal study of faces: when faces are looked at, transparency is often blocked and the beholder's gaze is not returned. In Woolf's fiction, the face thus becomes an outside that cannot be transgressed, but it is still a place where one abides, hoping to reach some kind of understanding. There is something in the face that requires the beholder to look at it: an enigma, striking beauty, or ambivalence, which suggests a person's contemplative life. At the same time, Woolf shows how the sitter suffers the gaze of the other, be it a photographer, a painter, or a beholder, and she explores the interplay between posing and sincerity, between self-consciousness and self-absorption. Faces and portraits thus come to represent a different mode of communication, one that relies on gazes and gestures rather than language, and that involves

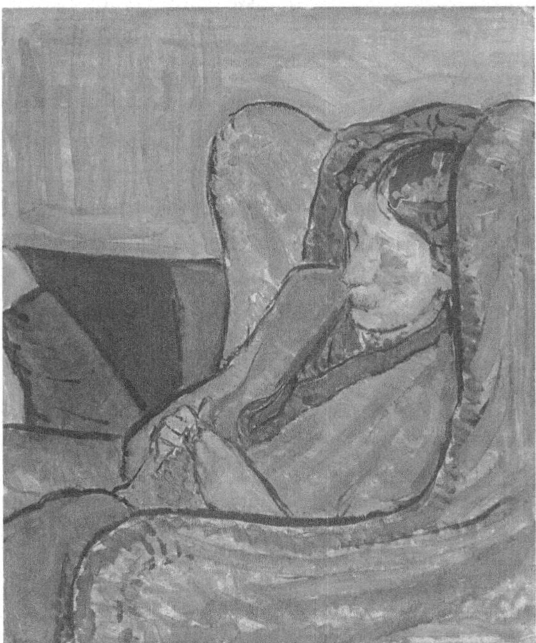

Figure 3.1   Painted portrait of Virginia Woolf by Vanessa Bell, 1912.
© National Portrait Gallery, London.

the conventions of posing pertaining both to photography and to social settings.[2] This communication is extremely complex; surely, the expression of a face can never be adequately translated into words.

As is well known, Woolf lived in an environment that spurred her interest in the visual arts.[3] There was a keen interest for the art of painting in the Bloomsbury Group, especially through the work of the painter and art critic Roger Fry, who introduced postimpressionist and modern painting in London, and through Woolf's older sister, Vanessa Bell, who was deeply interested in portraiture and abstraction. Further, Woolf's great-aunt was Julia Margaret Cameron (1815–79), the Victorian photographer whose legacy was very much kept alive in the family.[4] As many women of their generation, Virginia and Vanessa were familiar with the technique of photography and took numerous photographs of family members and friends themselves.[5] Woolf also kept photograph albums (as well as scrapbooks) and exchanged photographs with relatives, friends, and lovers. She was part of a photographic culture marked by the strong participation of women, and, in this respect, her outlook differs from that of Proust and Kafka.

Woolf's views on the role of photographs in everyday life communication can be indicated by an example from a crucial moment of her life: After Leonard has proposed to her in 1912, Virginia writes a touching letter to him, trying to explain her mixed emotions. Closing the letter, she implores the difficulty of communicating through a letter and refers to a photograph of herself, which she encloses: "One doesn't get much said in a letter, does one? I haven't touched upon the enormous variety of things that have been happening here – but they can wait. // D'you like this photograph? – rather too noble I think." According to Hermione Lee, the picture shows her "looking self-contained, demanding, and apprehensive."[6] It seems that Woolf here

2. Elizabeth Hirsch comments on Woolf's subversive use of the conventions of portraiture, making a similar point; she asserts that "the play of speech, silence, and image" is important both for Virginia's and Vanessa's views of portraiture. See Hirsch, "Virginia Woolf and Portraiture," 161. Kamilla Pawlikowska, too, stresses Woolf's subversive use of portraits, seeing Woolf as taking issue with physiognomy. Pawlikowska, *Anti-Portraits*.
3. Humm, *The Edinburgh Companion to Virginia Woolf and the Arts*; Marcus, *The Tenth Muse*; Gillespie, *The Multiple Muses of Virginia Woolf*; Spalding, *Virginia Woolf: Art, Life, Vision*.
4. Dell, *Virginia Woolf's Influential Forebears*.
5. Humm, *Modernist Women and Visual Cultures*.
6. Lee, *Virginia Woolf*, 311.

relies on the photograph to communicate something that she cannot so easily translate into words. As I will attempt to show, a similar function is granted to photographs in her novels; scenes involving portrait photographs are marked by quiet contemplation and feelings of sympathy, and yet the study of portrait photographs also leads to confrontations with otherness.

Yet what kind of emotional understanding could emerge from beholding photographed faces? Here, a debate on the differences between sympathy and empathy emerges. Although this topic cannot be discussed in full here, it is worth noticing that the word "empathy" was introduced into the English vocabulary in 1909 as a translation of the Romantic concept of *Einfühlung*.[7] *Sympathy*, by contrast, has a much longer history and does not carry with it the same idealistic aspirations. It denotes (more modestly) the ability to "feel for" another person, without fusing with this person, and it involves the use of the imagination, without intrusive tendencies. Seeing sympathy as an all but naïve "process for sharing feeling," Rae Greier has argued that it was of great importance to the realist novel.[8] In my view, the notion of sympathy also fits well with a modernist paradigm that acknowledges the difference of the other. Here I side with Kirsty Martin's view that "sympathy was central to modernism."[9] As she explains, Woolf never uses the word "empathy", whereas "sympathy" appears numerous times.[10] Yet, I will add, Woolf never takes sympathy for granted; rather she questions its possibilities in the modern world, and she explores how feelings of sympathy may emerge from the study of faces and photographs. Woolf observed how family portraits often supported conventional notions of identity, while at the same time appeared to transcend the familiar. At the same time, she saw how portrait photographs started to circulate in a global world, training the beholders to acknowledge otherness. Taking issue with narrow

7. As a translation of the Romantic-hermeneutic notion of *Einfühlung*, the word "empathy" carries the idea of deeply "feeling with" another person in such a way that the boundary between subject and object tends to collapse. See Greiner, "Thinking of Me Thinking of You," 417; Selboe, "Situations of Sympathy," 152–3. Admittedly, the notion of sympathy has been associated with a position of superiority, for which the modern notion of empathy seemed a democratic replacement. But, as Greiner argues, the distance that is posited in the case of sympathy represents a resistance to the somewhat naïve idea of fusing with the other.
8. Greiner, "Thinking of Me Thinking of You."
9. Martin, *Modernism and the Rhythms of Sympathy*, 10.
10. Martin, *Modernism and the Rhythms of Sympathy*, 9.

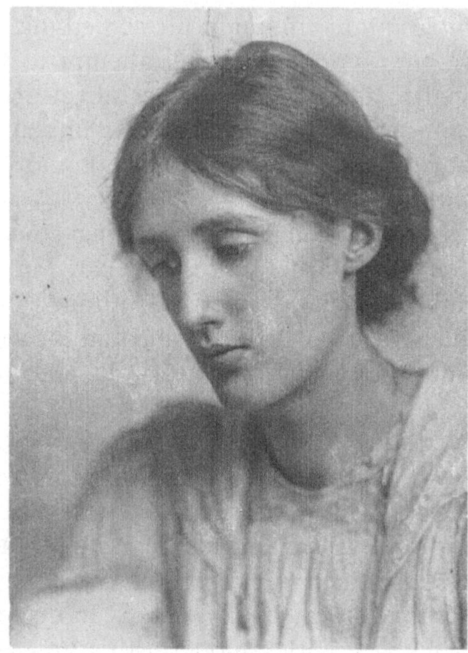

Figure 3.2   Portrait photograph of Virginia Woolf by George Charles Beresford, 1902. © National Portrait Gallery, London.

conceptions of identity, she understood how photographs allow us to see the other as a complex being, enigmatic and unknowable, and still develop feelings of sympathy for him or her.

In this chapter, I argue that Woolf uses portrait photographs in her writings to investigate the problems of sympathy, communication, and understanding. Although she explores these issues throughout her books, her take on them changes as her literary oeuvre evolves and her literary techniques develop. I first focus on her early novels *The Voyage Out* (1915) and *Night and Day* (1919), where these issues are explored within the framework of a love story. I show how she allows her characters to indulge in the contemplation of faces and portraits and thus exposes the traffic of gazes that takes place in human communication. This, I suggest, is a way of exploring the characters' confrontation with otherness and is part of the learning process depicted in the novels. In a second section, I study Woolf's mock biography *Orlando* (1928), where Woolf plays with genre conventions of biography and portraiture. My discussion centers on the series of photographs that are inserted into the novel and the portrait gallery that is depicted in it; these are seen as opposite takes on identity, representing the bourgeois album and the aristocratic ancestors' gallery, respectively. I suggest that the insertion of portrait photographs into the novel introduces zones of silence into the written discourse, inviting the reader to contemplate pictures. A similar assignment to the reader is given in Woolf's renowned essay on war, "Three Guineas" (1938), which is the subject of the third section. Here her imperative is "Look!" and the reader is brought to engage with the role of photographs in relation to war. With this essay, Woolf moves from a small-scale perspective—in love stories and in biography—to a large-scale perspective, entering the world scene. I argue that Woolf in this essay tries out how a "cosmopolitan gaze" could allow sympathy to extend to a world scale.

Concluding the chapter, I discuss Woolf's engagement with photographs in light of the processes of globalization in her day. Whereas photography had previously been associated with family photographs and was linked to Victorian ideas about identity, genealogy, and nationality, newspapers and magazines now showed pictures of foreigners living far away. Rather than depicting familiar faces, such photographs depicted foreign faces whose background and situation one did not know. This change to a global visual culture opened up for reflection on otherness and accustomed the audience to sympathize with strangers. One could thus venture to say that the globalization of photographs bolstered a transformation of the relation between the familiar and the foreign, as the foreign became more familiar and the familiar, in return, became more foreign. I argue that Woolf's views on photographs should be understood in light of this shift to a global visual culture.

Showing Seeing

In *The Voyage Out*, we follow young Rachel Vinrace's journey from her secluded home in London to a fictitious place named Santa Marina in South America, a journey that represents her attempt to reach out from her own "bubble," relate to others, and open up to the external world. Rachel's inwardness is never fully accounted for and appears as the enigma of the novel. On the one hand, it seems to be a result of her protected upbringing and thus of a lifestyle imposed upon her; after the death of her mother, her father left her in the care of her maiden aunts. On the other hand, it seems to be part of her personality, which includes a love of music and literature; in this sense, it represents her preference for inwardness and contemplative life. However, her inwardness is also depicted as exemplary of human loneliness generally, and this is accentuated through the novel's numerous comments on the problem of communication. "[H]ow communicate?" (71) one of the characters asks, while Rachel states elsewhere that it is "very difficult to know what people are like" (88). Rachel could thus be seen as embodying the problems of communication and shared understanding.[11]

However, communication for Woolf is not only about language; she persistently connects the shortcomings of verbal communication with an exploration of visual communication. In *The Voyage Out*, a number of scenes highlight the visual activity that takes place when the characters engage in the study of faces or portrait photographs.[12] Among these, two scenes that describe the contemplation of mothers' portraits are important. The first takes place in the London office of Rachel's father before she goes on board the ship. At its center is Rachel's deceased mother, Theresa, who is made present through a photographic portrait hanging on the wall behind her father's desk. The third-person narrator's description of it makes it clear that she still holds sway over them:

> Above him hung a photograph of a woman's head. The need of sitting absolutely still before a Cockney photographer had given her lips a queer little pucker, and her eyes for the same reason looked as though she thought the whole situation ridiculous. Nevertheless it was the head of an individual and interesting woman, who would no doubt have turned and laughed at Willoughby if she could have caught his eye; but when he looked up at her he sighed profoundly. (VO, 91)[13]

11. Rachel's introvert nature has been interpreted in various ways. Suzanne Raitt points out that Woolf in her early novels struggles with "the relation between voice and identity, between speech and silence." See Raitt, "Virginia Woolf's Early Novels," 30. This perspective is valuable, yet Raitt's overall reading differs from mine. For Raitt, the novels are about finding a voice and an identity, whereas I see them rather as meditations on the shortcomings of verbal and visual communication and as depicting learning processes in which the protagonists attempt to grapple with the difficulty of communication. According to Cristina Froula's feminist reading of *The Voyage Out*, Rachel's silence stems from her struggle with patriarchic structures. See Froula, "Out of the Chrysalis." This is certainly one aspect of the novel, but in my view, the deeper issue is existential loneliness and the problem of communication.
12. As Colin Dickey observes, photographs in Woolf's early fiction fall largely into three groups: photographs of dead loved ones and historical figures, haunting the lives of her characters; photographic prints of Greek and Roman ruins, kept by men who see themselves as inheritors of England's empire; and casual snapshots taken by women. Dickey, "Virginia Woolf and Photography," 376.
13. References are to the following edition, abbreviated as shown: VO: Virginia Woolf, *The Voyage Out*. Oxford: Oxford University Press, 2001.

Woolf's narrator brings attention to the uncomfortable situation of the sitter in front of the camera and highlights the little gesture in her face as well as the expression in her eyes, parts of a micro-physiognomy captured by the camera. The class conflict marking the photography session is also highlighted: a Cockney photographer imploring a bourgeois woman to sit still. This may be the cause of the "queer pucker" in her lips: she feels the gaze of the Cockney photographer portraying her as a typical bourgeois woman. She poses, but ironically, thus hiding her true emotions. However, her husband does not see that his wife is uncomfortable in the position where she has been placed, but rather idealized her in that very role. When he talks about Rachel's "educational journey," he looks at the portrait, as if asking for her approval: "'making a woman of her, the kind of woman her mother would have liked her to be,' he ended, jerking his head at the photograph" (VO, 93). Seemingly conscious of her husband's way of seeing her, Theresa appears to be ready to laugh at him "if she could have caught his eye," the narrator surmises, but she is—obviously—incapable of catching his gaze. There is thus an ambivalence and a latent laughter in the portrait that destabilizes it and makes it stand out from ordinary family portraits. One could say that the scene stages a play between the said and the unsaid, the visible and invisible, making it all apparent to the reader.

Rachel's aunt, Helen, is also affected by the portrait, but she is inclined to mockery: "Helen looked at Theresa pursing up her lips before the Cockney photographer. It suggested her in an absurd human way, and she felt an intense desire to share some joke" (VO, 92). Helen clearly wishes to break with the spell that Theresa has put on the living, and instead, she dwells on her sister's expression of awkwardness, which make her "real" to her. We may see this as an indication that she perceives a self-relation in the picture: Whereas Theresa's husband sees merely his ideal wife, Helen sees that Theresa struggles with the camera's gaze and understands that the portrait reflects an inner drama. Further, an additional aspect is made known to the reader at a later point the novel. Helen says about Theresa that "[m]ore people were in love with her than with any one I've ever known" (VO, 209). This suggests that she was attractive in a way that perhaps comes across also in the photograph, and that beholding her picture may also be a way of studying attraction and love.

This scene is put in perspective through a second scene in which characters study a mother's portrait. At their destination in Latin America, Rachel and Helen meet a company of English travelers at a hotel, and among them is Evelyn, a young woman whose situation in many respects resembles Rachel's. In an important scene, the two of them talk about love and life commitments, discussing how one should live one's life: marry, do social work, or play the piano. When Evelyn asks Rachel if she believes in anything, Rachel responds with vehemence: "'In everything!'" she exclaims, starting to finger objects in front of her, "'I believe in the bed, in the photographs, in the pot. [. . .] But I don't believe in God, I don't believe in Mr. Bax, I don't believe in the hospital nurse'" (VO, 290). Then suddenly, the sight of a photographic frame lying on the bed interrupts Rachel's speech, and when Evelyn informs her that it represents her mother, the following interchange takes place:

> Rachel considered the portrait. "Well I don't much believe in her," she remarked after a time in a low tone of voice.
>
> Mrs. Murgatroyd looked indeed as if the life had been crushed out of her; she knelt on a chair, gazing piteously from behind the body of a Pomeranian dog which she clasped to her cheek, as if for protection.
>
> "And that's my dad," said Evelyn, for there were two photographs in one frame. The second photograph represented a handsome soldier with high regular features and a heavy black moustache; his hand rested on the hilt of his sword; there was a decided likeness between him and Evelyn. (VO, 291)

Why doesn't Rachel believe in Evelyn's mother, and why is she still captured by the photograph? The pose is conventional and feminine, but Evelyn's mother is described as a subjugated woman—she looks crushed and is kneeling and clasping as if in need of protection. Paradoxically, her protection is a Pomeranian, a small toy dog. What makes the picture interesting is precisely this ambivalence: she is both posing before the camera and protecting herself from its gaze. This may also be the reason why Rachel does not believe in her. By contrast, Evelyn's father fully assumes his role; he is portrayed in an official manner, as a soldier with his sword. Both photographs represent Victorian conventions for portraiture and reflect the narrow social roles allotted to them, but only the mother displays ambivalence. Yet no latent laughter is present in her picture; rather, it expresses fear.

There are both gender and generational issues at play in this scene. As Marion Dell points out, Woolf often employs photographs as "signifiers of gender and as transgenerational link."[14] However, the scenes in which Woolf is "showing seeing" focus on the characters'

14. Dell, *Virginia Woolf's Influential Forebears*, 93.

attention to photographs rather than the photographs themselves. In the scene above, Rachel is so captivated by the photographs that she appears to forget about Evelyn's presence. Part of her attraction is due to Evelyn's claim that her mother and father loved each other, even if they were not married, and thus represent an unconventional form of love:

> Rachel sat down on the bed, with the two pictures in her hand, and compared them—the man and the woman who had, so Evelyn said, loved each other. That fact interested her more than the campaign on behalf of unfortunate women. [. . .] She looked again from one to the other.
>
> "What d'you think it's like," she asked, as Evelyn paused for a minute, "being in love?" (VO, 291)

But the couple's love for each other is not visible to Rachel in the photograph, and it is somewhat ironic that they are not photographed together, but instead joined in a twin-frame. It may be precisely the invisible and *inaccessible* nature of their love that pulls Rachel toward the images. Evelyn, for her part, wants to connect with Rachel, but is unable to do so: "When she looked at Rachel, who was still looking at the photographs on the bed, she could not help seeing that Rachel was not thinking about her. What was she thinking of, then? [. . .] Falling silent she looked at her visitor." Then Rachel offers a concluding remark, as she puts down the photographs and walks to the window: "'It's odd. People talk as much about love as they do about religion'" (VO, 292).

This scene presents a curious play on presence and absence, on connection and distance. Rachel is captivated by those who are not there and fascinated by the alleged love of the couple in the twin-frame. Evelyn, by contrast, seems (or pretends) not to care much for her parents and instead seeks intimacy with Rachel, yet she is frustrated by Rachel's absentmindedness and is almost jealous of the photographs (just like Helen is in the scene above). Rachel's casual remark about people's interest in love and religion in fact hits the nail on the head: The key theme in this scene is the possibility of connecting, relating, and communicating with someone or something who is essentially out of reach. Rather than making present those who are absent, the photographs give access to an absence, and this creates attraction as well as feelings of frustration.

Both these scenes involving parental photographs make visible a series of inscrutable gazes and an array of wordless emotions. They bring attention to the gender conflict between the idealized or subdued women in the photographs and a conventional male gaze on these women. Further, they make visible the generational conflict between the Victorian parents and their young daughters, who are in a position to choose differently. Woolf's scenes are thus preoccupied with "showing seeing," and this becomes a way of orchestrating unspoken emotions and giving weight to the unsaid. Nothing about the characters' emotions is *spoken* about in the scenes; the descriptions are offered to us by the narrator, who adopts the characters' perspective, and they gain emphasis through the various characters' persistent gazing at the photographs. The reading of portrait photographs thus appears as a silent, semiprivate, and highly emotional activity, even if it takes place in the company of others. We should notice that the photographs are not deciphered; they remain enigmatic, but in different ways open up emotional spaces in the characters.

Further, both scenes raise the question of love and its possibilities in relation to photography. Love thus comes across as the mystery of both photographs and marks the various attempts at "reading" them. Rachel's association of love and religion is particularly telling in light of a previous scene, taking place the same morning: There, she visits the church, and during the sermon she listens critically to the priest while at the same time engaging in face studies. What she discovers is that the faces surrounding her are full of lies; people are "pretending to feel what they did not feel" (VO, 264). The narrator relates that she "fixed her eyes on the face of a woman near her, a hospital nurse, whose expression of devout attention seemed to prove that she was at any rate receiving satisfaction. But looking at her carefully she came to the conclusion that the hospital nurse was only slavishly acquiescent [. . .] She was adoring something shallow" (VO, 265). Through this "revelation" Rachel becomes aware of a widespread human capacity to fake deep emotions and how the Church in fact encourages this kind of pretense. This scene is crucial as it leads Rachel to lose her faith and reject "all that she had implicitly believed" (VO, 265). Rachel thus goes out of the church as a truly modern human being.

Rachel's discovery of people's ability to pretend in religious matters seems to be a bad omen for the continuation of her love story and could be seen as deepening her disbelief in the possibility of communication and understanding. Yet the man she falls in love with, Terence, shares the same insight about the solitude of each human being, and this becomes the common ground on which their relationship is built. His remark to a friend at the hotel in Santa Marina is revealing in this regard: "You can't see my bubble; I can't see yours; all we see of each other is a speck, like the wick in the middle of that flame" (VO, 119). Even if Terence is more sociable than Rachel, he recognizes the difficulty of communication, and this shared insight is also what unites them. Toward the end of the novel, when Terence has started to get close to Rachel, an intimate scene occurs between them where they discuss the conditions of love and study each other's faces. Whereas Rachel "looked straight at him," Terence "examined her curiously" (VO, 347). Then he comments explicitly on the difficulty of penetrating beyond her face: "'You're not beautiful,' he began, 'but I like your face. I like the way your hair grows down in a point, and your eyes too – they never see anything." He continues: "But what I like about your face is that it makes one wonder what the devil you're thinking about" (VO, 347). Terence is thus aware that he does not have access to Rachel's thoughts, but has to stop at her face, and he observes that her eyes are often turned inward. Eyes that see without seeing are not directed toward the external world and do not seek to be met by someone else's eyes. They separate attention from perception, withholding something. The look on Rachel's face, which Terence studies carefully, thus appears to be a version of the "photographic look" that Barthes comments on. It is a look that intrigues Terence, who appears to accept her way of being and her contemplative mind.

The Voyage Out can be described as a novel about loneliness, love, and attempts of communication, and for a while it seems that love has won through all the difficulties and that Rachel and Terence have learned to accept the gap that separates them. But Woolf's first take on love stories does not include a happy ending; what eventually triumphs is not love, but the loneliness of illness and death. The novel ends with Rachel catching a disease, slowly disappearing in fever and eventually dying. Woolf describes in detail how she is slowly cut off from the outer world: "at intervals she made an effort to cross over into the ordinary world, but she found that her heat and discomfort had put a gulf between her world and the ordinary world" (VO, 383). Terence sits at her deathbed, studying her face. Sometimes her eyes are shut, but he also observes how they are "looking past him," appearing to be "looking at a vase on the shelf opposite" (VO, 388). This is a dreadful version of the unreturned gaze; Terence experiences Rachel simply not seeing him as she drifts away to a different world. The novel's ending reveals that Rachel does not succeed in her "voyage out," but is condemned to the isolation of her body, her fever-struck mind, and – ultimately – the solitude of death.

Woolf continues to explore the topics of love, distance, and communication in her next novel, *Night and Day*, and there, too, the study of photographs, portraits, and faces play a central role. The main character of the novel is Katharine Hilbery, a well-bred young woman from a respected family who is known for her beauty, manners, and quietness. She slowly realizes that she does not love the man she is expected to marry, William Rodney, and becomes convinced that she must follow her own emotions rather than succumbing to the conventions of the past and the expectations of her family. This is difficult because her mother practically lives in the past, cultivating Kathrine's grandfather, the great Victorian poet Richard Alardyce, whose biography she is writing and whose painted portrait she adores. Conventions thus forcefully clash with true feeling, and the past (the Victorian age) with the present.

In the opening scene, young Ralph Denham, a potential rival to William, visits Katharine's home and is soon taken to the room where the family keeps the Alardyce "relics." The center of attention is a painted portrait of Alardyce, "a square picture above the table, to which special illumination was accorded" (ND, 9).[15] It has a strong impact on Ralph (who is here referred to by his last name):

> Denham found himself looked down upon by the eyes of the great poet, Richard Alardyce, and suffered a little shock which would have led him, had he been wearing a hat, to remove it. The eyes looked at him out of the mellow pinks and yellows of the paint with divine friendliness, which embraced him, and passed on to contemplate the entire world. The paint had so faded that very little but the beautiful large eyes were left, dark in the surrounding dimness. (ND, 9)

We should observe that the ordinary roles of spectatorship are here reversed: It is the image that looks down on Ralph, not the other way around. Ralph suffers a little shock when he discovers the Victorian poet's gaze upon him, and it instills respect in him. Interestingly, he first feels embraced by this gaze, as if it surrounded him completely, but then the gaze passes beyond him on to the world, in an almost divine way. This suggests a reach that surpasses his individual existence and extends to history or eternity. Other scenes create similar feelings of being watched by a superior gaze, such as in the following remark:

15. References are to the following edition, abbreviated as shown: ND: Virginia Woolf, *Night and Day*. Oxford: Oxford University Press, 2009.

"From the surrounding walls the heads of three famous Victorian writers surveyed this entertainment" (ND, 97). Here, too, the pictures are granted agency, and the characters are reminded of the authority and "divine" perspective of their Victorian predecessors.

Ralph must in the opening scene suffer comparison with the men on the wall. Noticing his reluctance to compliment the Alardyce portrait, Katharine remembers that her mother had compared him with Mr. Ruskin, the great art critic, in order to connect him with "the great dead." The narrator relates that this leads Katharine to be more critical toward him than was fair, "for a young man paying a call in a tail-coat is in a different element altogether from a head seized at its climax of expressiveness, gazing immutably from behind a sheet of glass" (ND, 11). Studying Ralph's face, Katharine finds that he does not quite reach up to her ideals, that is, the male faces on the walls:

> He had a singular face—a face built for swiftness and decision rather than for massive contemplation. [. . .] Katharine only looked at him to wonder whether his face would not have come nearer the standard of her dead heroes if it had been adorned with side-whiskers. (ND, 11).

Ralph, for his part, expresses his hatred of "great men" and the "worship of greatness in the nineteenth century" (ND, 15), and thus pinpoints the prevailing atmosphere in the Hilbery house. The reader understands that the novel stages a revolt against Victorian conventions and ideals, which are represented by portraits. This theme is underlined when Kathrine in these opening pages looks up at the portrait of her grandfather with reverence and admiration:

> [S]he glanced up at her grandfather, and, for the thousandth time, fell into a pleasant dreamy state in which she seemed to be the companion of those giant men, of their own lineage, at any rate, and the insignificant present moment was put to shame. That magnificent ghostly head on the canvas, surely, never beheld all the trivialities of a Sunday afternoon, and it did not seem to matter what she and this young man said to each other, for they were only small people. (ND, 10)

Katharine here appears to succumb to the female Victorian role of being the companion of great men, and we may thus perceive a subtle irony in the way she is described. Yet it may be that she also dreams of being their equal, thus escaping the everyday trivialities that come with her position as a middle-class woman. The narrator brings attention to Katharine's subdued appearance, studying her as if she were a portrait. She "shrank from expressing herself" (ND, 40), the narrator observes and continues: "Her gestures seemed to have a certain purpose; the muscles round eyes and lips were set rather firmly, as though the senses had undergone some discipline" (ND, 44). Yet, the reader should expect that her self-esteem may well change during the course of this 500-page novel.

It is Katharine's mother, Mrs. Hilbery, who has compelled her family to live under the sway of the past. Her daily life is dedicated to writing her father's biography and caring for "relics" from the past. A scene in which she browses through a series of old photographs from that era reveals the way she idealizes the past and judges the present from its standards:

> Mrs. Hilbery had emptied a portfolio containing old photographs over her table, and was looking from one to another.
> "Surely, Katharine," she said, "the men were far handsomer in those days than they are now, in spite of their odious whiskers? Look at old John Graham, in his white waistcoat—look at Uncle Harley." [. . .]
> "What is nobler," she mused, turning over the photographs, "than to be a woman to whom everyone turns, in sorrow or difficulty? [. . .] They *were*, and that's better than doing. They seem to me like ships, like majestic ships." (ND, 116–17)

The scene describes how Mrs. Hilbery browses through the photographs, admiring them and commenting on their beauty and graciousness. She also implores Katharine to *look* and beseeches her to assume the role of an "angel in the house." For her part, Katharine is partly reluctant to follow her mother's gaze and partly drawn to the old photographs:

> [S]he could not forbear to turn over the pages of the album in which the old photographs were stored. The faces of these men and women shone forth wonderfully after the hubbub of living faces, and seemed, as her mother had said, to wear a marvelous dignity and calm, as if they had ruled their kingdoms justly and deserved great love. Some were of almost incredible beauty, others were ugly enough in a forcible way, but none were dull or bored or insignificant. The superb stiff folds of the crinolines suited the women; the cloaks and the hats of the gentlemen seemed full of character. (ND, 117–18)

What kind of beauty does Katharine perceive in these photographs? The reader is informed that they belong to her grandfather's days and thus to an early phase in the history of photography. Apparently,

Woolf based the pictures in the Hilbery family album on Julia Margaret Cameron and her sisters, frequently photographed by Cameron herself in ways that brought out their translucent beauty.[16] The photographic style in Mrs. Hilbery's portfolio is in some sense reminiscent of Cameron's style; both are marked by an enigmatic beauty. The sitters are described as being remarkably certain of themselves, calmly and majestically meeting the gaze of the camera, as if accepting the beholder's love without fear, ambivalence, or uncertainty. With Benjamin, we may see these photographs as a product of the early days of photography, when the photographed faces would still have an "aura" about them.

In keeping with this, Katharine appears to perceive an enigmatic beauty in these portraits, commanding love and devotion. The majestic portrait photographs contrast sharply with the "hubbub of living faces" and make her realize that the faces she is surrounded by in real life are shifting, multifaceted, and ungraspable. In this manner, she pinpoints the difficulty associated with the reading of faces in the modernist period. The old photographic portraits thus appear as sanctuaries for a troubled modern woman who cannot fully understand the people surrounding her. The old photographs welcome her gaze and invite her love, without requirements. They offer both distance and revelation, appearing to be remote and close at the same time.

The trouble with faces in daily life is also brought to the fore in an emotional scene between Katharine and William Rodney, her fiancé. As they discuss their relationship, Katharine tells him that she does not love him, and never has, whereas William pleads with her, incapable of understanding this. In the middle of their exchange, the narrator informs us that Katharine had yet to learn the "art of subduing her expression" and describes her in the following manner: "Her eyes fixed upon the ground, her brows drawn together, gave William a very fair picture of the resentment that she was forcing herself to control" (ND, 256). A few lines later, William's attention to appearances is contrasted with Katharine's self-forgetfulness:

> [H]e became suddenly aware of their situation, sitting upon the ground, among the dead leaves, not fifty yards from the main road, so that it was quite possible for someone passing to see and recognize them. He brushed off his face any trace that might remain of that unseemly exhibition of emotion. But he was more troubled by

16. Dell, *Virginia Woolf's Influential Forebears*, x.

> Katharine's appearance, as she sat rapt in thought upon the ground, than by his own; there was something improper to him in her self-forgetfulness. [. . .] She sat there, seeming unconscious of everything. (ND, 256–7)

This is a scene where Woolf is "showing seeing" and thereby exposes the silent micro-level of human intercourse. Paradoxically, they are both "out of reach" for one another, but for different reasons: Katharine is lost in inward contemplation, looking without seeing, whereas William has covered up his inner feeling with an appropriate expression. She is not attentive to him at all, whereas he is controlling the way he appears to her. At a later point in the novel, however, Katharine reaches some kind of understanding of William, and when she studies his face in this new light, he appears to her as a stranger:

> She looked at him attentively as if this discovery of hers must show traces in his face. Never had she seen so much to respect in his appearance, so much that attracted her by its sensitiveness and intelligence, although she saw these qualities as if they were those one responds to, dumbly, in the face of a stranger. The head bent over the paper, thoughtful as usual, had now a composure which seemed somehow to place it at a distance, like a face seen talking to someone else behind glass. (ND, 297)

What Katharine has discovered at this point is William's otherness, his way of being that differs radically from hers. This discovery is followed by a more general insight about "the infinite loneliness of human beings" (ND, 297). When the two of them start to confront their own feelings, however, there is a moment where William lets down his guard and Katharine thinks that "she saw him for the first time without disguise" (ND, 341).

The relationship between Katharine and Ralph Denham, the young contender, is also described through their various attempts at reading each other's faces. As they begin to get to know each other, Ralph still perceives a strangeness in her: "There was an emotion in her face which lent it an expression he had never seen there" (ND, 308). Katharine thus appears to him as someone he does not fully know or has access to. Observing her absentmindedness at a later point, he wonders whether he should leave her alone:

> [H]e looked at her taking in one strange shape after another with the contemplative, considering gaze of a person who sees not exactly

what is before him, but gropes in regions that lie beyond it. The far-away look entirely lacked self-consciousness. Denham doubted whether she remembered his presence. He could recall himself, of course, by a word or a movement – but why? She was happier thus. (ND, 349)

Again, Katharine is depicted as looking without seeing, immersing herself in her own thoughts. This scene raises the question of whether loneliness is the logical condition of modern man and casts doubts upon the possibility of love between two human beings. At the same time, it displays Katharine's awareness of Ralph's awkward situation; the narrator discloses that she "had an uneasy sense that silence on her part was selfishness" (ND, 349). Ambiguity and vague feelings of sympathy thus mark the silent exchange between them.

Yet Ralph also struggles with the fact that his inner image of Katharine must constantly be adjusted when he sees her, and Katharine also objects that he idealizes her and does not truly know her (ND, 401). The novel seems to mock Ralph's idealized vision of Katharine in a passage where Ralph reflects upon Katharine's beauty: "He possessed a book of photographs from the Greek statues; the head of a goddess [. . .] had often given him the ecstasy of being in Katharine's presence. He took it down from the shelf and found the picture" (ND, 405–6). Ralph's way of associating Katharine with a photograph of a Greek goddess recalls a similar passage in Proust, where Swann, associating Odette with Botticelli's Zipporah, holds a photograph of Zipporah against his chest and imagines that he embraces Odette. Both scenes seem to mock this way of idealizing a woman, but Woolf is undoubtedly firmer than Proust in her critique of such attitudes.

Mockery also characterizes some of the remarks related to the reading of faces, which implicitly refers to physiognomic thought. For instance, Ralph proves to be a character who is not fully capable of hiding his emotions, and the narrator thus remarks that "[h]is face was no bad index to what went on within him" (ND, 345). Even more clearly ironic is Mrs. Hilbery's self-description: "'I always judge by the expression of the eyes,' Mrs. Hilbery continued. ('The windows of the soul,' she added parenthetically)" (ND, 448). As Woolf shows us throughout the novel, however, there is no direct way of accessing someone's inner world, even if the face and especially the eyes may seem promising points of entry.

At this point in the novel, it becomes clear that Katharine has begun a learning process, where she realizes that she has not been true to herself but has lived according to other's expectations. But she does not yet understand her own emotions and does not yet know what to do. A scene where she once more studies the portrait of her grandfather reveals how her relation to the family patriarch has changed. Where she previously had immersed herself in the pictures of men of the past, forgetful of her own life and full of naïve sympathy for the life they had lived (ND, 10; 114), she now starts to see this picture in a new light:

> Katharine glanced at the portrait of her grandfather, as if to ask his opinion. The artist who had painted it was now out of fashion, and by dint of showing it to visitors, Katharine had almost ceased to see anything but a glow of faintly pleasing pink and brown tints, enclosed within a circular scroll of gilt laurel-leaves. The young man who was her grandfather looked vaguely over her head. The sensual lips were slightly parted, and gave the face an expression of beholding something lovely or miraculous vanishing or just rising upon the rim of the distance. The expression repeated itself curiously upon Katharine's face as she gazed up into his. They were the same age, or very nearly so. She wondered what he was looking for; were there waves beating upon a shore for him, too, she wondered, and heroes riding through the leaf-hung forests? For perhaps the first time in her life she thought of him as a man, young, unhappy, tempestuous, full of desires and faults; for the first time she realized him for herself, and not from her mother's memory. (ND, 335–6)

Katharine is puzzled by her grandfather's gaze, which is directed at something that she cannot see. What she perceives for the first time is something withheld in him; he appears to be immersed in a secret, an inner emotion, just like her. She thus realizes that a self-relation is at play in the picture, and in this manner he becomes real to her. As she becomes aware of his contemplative gaze, his facial expression is transposed to her; it is as if they connect in their thoughtfulness. Further, as the scene continues, Kathrine understands that they are "akin" and imagines that he "would have understood." Rather than paying tribute to him, she decides to address him with her own being: "she brought him her own perplexities," the narrator relates. Further, she understands the portrait's agency in a new way, thinking that "the dead asked neither flowers nor regrets, but a share in the life which they had given her" (ND, 336). The situation is thus altered as Katharine's contemplation of the portrait shifts to an inquiry and a conversation, and in this manner a feeling of sympathy and connectedness is created. What was previously perceived as a divine gaze now appears as a profane gaze that mediates human sympathy. When Kathrine at last looks at the portrait with her own eyes, it speaks to her, and, moreover, she appears to speak back, putting herself on a par with the family patriarch and finally expressing herself.

Just like *The Voyage Out, Night and Day* explores the problem of communication at both a visual and a verbal level. By "showing seeing," the novel reflects upon the reading of faces and the unspoken emotions involved in this endeavor. It offers no quick fix to the communication issue, nor does it end in a scene of total understanding, yet it describes how Katharine and Ralph learn to break the silence, begin to cope with their differences, and connect across the distance that separates them. The novel in many respects deals with the same difficulties as *The Voyage Out*, that is, love, distance, and communication, but where Woolf's first love story ended tragically with Rachel disappearing into her own world, *Night and Day* ends on a happier note, with sincere attempts at communication between Katharine and Ralph.

To summarize, we may say that Woolf's early novels use the technique of showing seeing to reveal the gap that exists between the characters, while at the same time displaying all the emotions that are involved in the attempt to read faces. The scenes in which the characters engage in faces studies serve to orchestrate different emotions, but also bring attention to the face as a medium in its own right. In Woolf's meditation on faces, portraits play an important part as they draw attention to faces, both framing them and revealing them. In this manner, the study of portraits prepares for close-up studies of faces and the silent communication that takes place between them. Writing in the era of photography and psychological inquiry, Woolf puts her characters in front of portraits and faces, showing how they attempt to mine the psychological depths underneath other people's surfaces. They try to figure out what others are like, but what they observe is ambivalence, pretense, and withdrawal. This contemplation of faces and portraits brings attention to the paradox of the human face; it exposes, but it also hides, and full access can never be granted.

Yet for Woolf, the face is not merely deceit or mask; it is a threshold and a point of contact through which unspoken feelings of sympathy can be established. Moreover, for Woolf's female protagonists, the study of portraits and faces is educational and offers subtle lessons in other people's self-relations and modes of being. In the course of these two novels, the characters learn to act more independently and to accept other people's otherness. Yet for both Rachel and Katharine, increased autonomy comes at a cost and opens up for profound feelings of existential loneliness. They are repeatedly described as being absorbed in their own thoughts and out of reach for the men courting them. They see without seeing, retaining something within themselves. Still, this is not depicted in a negative light, for these scenes foreground their capacity for contemplative life. Woolf's close-up studies of the young women's faces show that they in fact have a room of their own.

Orlando's Photograph Album

Already in *Jacob's Room* (1922), Woolf discussed the notion of "character" as something fleeting and manifold that cannot be given a definite form. Taking issue with various forms of "character mongering," including novels and biographies, she brought attention to something characteristic of human life that cannot be fully grasped: "They say that the novelists never catch it; that it goes hurtling through their nets and leaves them torn to ribbons. This, they say, is what we live by—this unseizable force."[17] It is this unseizable force that remains Woolf's central motif and literary obsession throughout her literary life.[18] Yet after *Mrs Dalloway* (1925) and *To the Lighthouse* (1927), *Orlando* (1928) offers a new take on this topic.

In *Orlando*, Woolf not only challenges the writing conventions attempting to capture "life," that is, the biographical paradigm, but she also questions the genre of portraiture. As she plays with the genre conventions of biography, Woolf inserts a series of portraits in the novel. These portraits are commonly seen as supporting the genre of mock-biography; just like the narrative, they undermine the idea of a true identity. If we look beyond the mockery, however, we may discover a more serious concern which is persistent in Woolf's oeuvre: a concern with visual communication, genre conventions, and the reading of faces. We may also discover a keen consciousness about a new visual regime, opening up new possibilities for the study of others. In this section, I discuss the use of photographs in *Orlando*, suggesting that the insertion of portrait photographs into the novel introduces zones of silence into the written discourse and invites the reader to engage in face studies. In this manner, Woolf

17. Woolf, *Jacob's Room*, 217.
18. Her essay "Modern Novels" (1918), revised as "Modern Fiction" (1925), explicates this, arguing that "life is a luminous halo, a semi-transparent envelope surrounding us." See Woolf, "Modern Fiction," 9. Her critical essays on biography, published shortly before *Orlando*, pursues the same project.

leaves to the reader the assignment that she gave to her female protagonists in her early novels.

Before I address *Orlando* and its innovative use of portrait photographs, however, I wish to bring attention to her early views on photography. This will allow us to acknowledge that Woolf early on connected the medium to a play with identity and thus see *Orlando* as part of an ongoing reflection on photography. Presumably, Woolf was inspired by her great-aunt Julia Margaret Cameron, who often dressed up her models to make them represent mythical and heroic figures, thus making them transcend their own identity. Two years before the publication of *Orlando*, Woolf coedited (with Roger Fry) a book of Cameron's photographs, *Victorian Photographs of Famous Men and Fair Women*. This was in fact two whole decades before Cameron was recognized as a major Victorian photographer. Further, Woolf's fascination with Cameron's photographic projects was expressed also in *Freshwater*, a comedy she wrote on her great-aunt and her artistic circle. Although it was written in 1923, it was never published, and it was followed by a second, elaborated version for a Bloomsbury performance in 1934. Neither of them is a masterpiece, but especially the original represents an interesting source with respect to Woolf's early views on photography.

The play is set at Cameron's home in Freshwater, and it depicts her as a person who treats everyone as a photographic model; she entreats people to stand still, to pose, and to do it for the sake of art. Desperately searching for a model suited to pose as the Arthurian knight Sir Galahad, she eventually finds "him" in a woman, Ellen Terry, and makes her wear men's clothes. Up to this point, Ellen has posed as "Modesty" for George Watts, the symbolist painter, although he is in despair because he has misinterpreted an important symbol and "made Modesty symbolize the fertility of Fish."[19] Posing as a man, Ellen likes wearing trousers so much that she declares that she will never wear anything else. When she states that she cannot understand the babble about symbols and wants to go to a place where people talk sense, Watts then replies: "Go to Bloomsbury. In that polluted atmosphere spread your doctrines, propagate your race, wear your trousers."[20] When Ellen sets off to Bloomsbury with Mr. Craig, whom she intends to marry, Mrs. Cameron offers Ellen her camera as a wedding present: "It is my wedding gift, Ellen. Take my lens. I bequeath

19. Woolf, *Freshwater*, 65.
20. Woolf, *Freshwater*, 72.

it to my descendants. See that it is always slightly out of focus."[21] The play obviously mocks the complex symbolism typical of both Watts and Cameron and refers to Bloomsbury as a contrast. How, then, should we understand the legacy that Mrs. Cameron bequeaths to her descendants? Is the camera "slightly out of focus" pure mockery, or did Woolf capture an aspect of her own aesthetics in this phrase? It is certainly an antirealist statement, expressed shortly after the publication of her first experimental novel (*Jacob's Room*, in 1922), so perhaps it is permissible to read a little of both into it.

It is also interesting to observe that *Freshwater* represents an early instance of crossdressing in Woolf's work, and that this is related to posing before a camera. Indeed, one may wonder if Cameron's portrayal of her contemporaries as heroic and historical figures may have inspired Woolf's transgender and trans-history experiments in *Orlando*, as well as her decision to include a number of photographic portraits in the novel. Further, it is noteworthy that Woolf had a curious experience with crossdressing before a camera as early as in 1910, when she participated in a practical joke organized by her brother's friends and referred to as the "*Dreadnought* hoax." They fooled the crew of the British battleship HMS *Dreadnought* into receiving a fake Abyssinian delegation, disguising themselves with turbans and "foreign" outfits. A group photograph was taken of the delegation, in which Virginia poses as one of its male members, with a turban on her head. Playing with identities was thus not a new idea to Woolf when she started to write *Orlando*, and it seems likely that she also associated photographs with this kind of identity play.

In *Orlando*, Woolf thus plays with the concept of identity, giving photographs a central role. Rather than being an easily recognizable person living in a defined span of time, Orlando is transhistorical and transgendered, with a lifespan that reaches from the sixteenth century to early twentieth century and a gender that is first masculine, later feminine, but which remains "mixed." "Same, but different" is the credo of this novel as it mocks the expectations of the reader. A series of photographs inserted in the novel testify to this paradox. They depict various versions of Orlando and a few close relations: four painted portraits and four portrait photographs. With these pictures, Woolf raises the question of how portraits can convey something important about a person's life, well aware that pictures communicate in a different way than language.

21. Woolf, *Freshwater*, 73.

Orlando's uncertain status is also due her being a fictive character whose life is inspired by real-life events. As is well known, Woolf's lover Vita Sackville-West served as a model for Orlando, and their love affair must have stirred Woolf's reflection on androgyny and gender. Moreover, the majestic history and ancestral lineage of the Sackville-Wests' impressive fifteenth-century estate, named Knole, inspired Woolf's description of Orlando's home and ancestors. Sackville-West's book *Knole and the Sackvilles* (1922) served as a source, and the painted portraits Woolf inserted into the book were taken from the Knole galleries.[22] It is significant that, in Woolf's day, the estate's proud history had been tainted by a lawsuit dating from 1910 regarding the rights of heritance, which featured in the newspapers and revealed illegitimate family relations. The case also demonstrated how the privilege of male bloodlines worked; apparently, Vita might have inherited the property if she had been a man. Woolf was thus playing with a British inheritance that had already started to fall apart; the pure bloodlines of the family tree were already known to be fiction, and the male privilege was being questioned. Identity, heritage, and history did not line up as easily as in the Victorian era.

Yet *Orlando* plays not merely with the genre of biography, but also with the genre of portraiture and its historical manifestations. A contrast is established between the traditional portrait gallery in Orlando's estate and the modern portraits inserted into the book. Whereas the former upholds the ideas of identity and heritage, the latter make all such notions unstable. To understand how this contrast plays out, let us first look into the description of the portrait gallery, which is a recurrent motif in the novel. The first time we are presented with this motif, young Orlando has withdrawn to his estate, having been disappointed in love and started to relish thoughts of death and decay. The narrator describes how Orlando, "after pacing the long galleries and ballrooms with a taper in his hand, looking at picture after picture as if he sought the likeness of somebody whom he did not find, would mount into the family pew and sit for hours watching the banners stir."[23] On the next page, a similar phrase creates repetition: "[H]e returned to that curious moody pacing down the galleries, looking for something among the pictures" (O, 68–9). Orlando's walk in the gallery is thus marked by unrest and has the character of

22. Elizabeth Hirsch describes this context in more detail; see Hirsch, "Virginia Woolf and Portraiture," 171–5.
23. References are to the following edition, abbreviated as shown: O: Virginia Woolf, *Orlando: A Biography*. Oxford: Oxford University Press, 2008.

a search. As the ancestor's gallery typically symbolizes heritage, family identity, and tradition, Orlando's contemplative musings, restless walk, and feelings of deception suggest a gap between the gallery and Orlando's modern "self." He seems not to identify with these ancient portraits and cannot see himself reflected in their stoic gazes from the wall. Orlando thus tries to merge with his family history through its "relics" (first portraits, and then also banners, and coffins), but he cannot quite find what he searches for.

At a later point in the novel, the centuries have passed, Orlando's gender has changed, and she returns to England as a woman after a long journey abroad. There she finds that she is nonexistent and is no longer in possession of her titles and properties. Several lawsuits are filed against her, the accusation being that she is dead *and* that she is a woman, and consequently, the court sets out to decide whether she is alive or dead, a man or a woman. This, in turn, will decide whether she has the right to her titles and her properties. Here we hear the echo of the court case in the Sackville-West family and the disputed right to inherit Knole. In Woolf's novel, the narrator relates that Orlando is permitted to reside in her family estate in a "state of incognito or incognita," pending the legal judgment (O, 161). With this comment, the narrator cunningly demonstrates that grammar will not grant full anonymity to a person; it requires Orlando to have a gender. One could say that Woolf's novel thus puts language conventions on trial, accusing them of upholding narrow conceptions of life.

It is in this state of nonexistence that Orlando returns to her estate, enters the gallery, and once more feels the gaze of her ancestors: "Orlando took a silver candle in her hand and roamed once more through the halls, the galleries, the courts, the bedrooms; saw loom down at her again the dark visage of this Lord Keeper, that Lord Chamberlain, among her ancestors" (O, 164). Going through several phases of reflection she finds herself disenchanted with great men with their great houses: "'I am growing up,' she thought, taking her taper at last. 'I am losing some illusions,' she said, shutting Queen Mary's book, 'perhaps to acquire others'" (O, 166). The phrase expressing her disillusion is repeated on the next page, thus underlining the message: "'I am growing up,' she thought, taking her taper. 'I am losing my illusions, perhaps to acquire new ones,' and she paced down the long gallery to her bedroom." Leaving the gallery and her ancestors, Orlando is conscious that the process she is going through is disagreeable but also "amazingly" interesting, the narrator explains (O, 167). But what kind of process is taking place here? It seems that Orlando is losing her illusions about the old regime of representation, in which solemn portraits served to limit the possibility space of the subjects, ascribing them a fixed identity within the family history. Indeed, the portrait gallery is described as "out of sync" with Orlando. Feeling that the portraits no longer hold sway over her, Orlando is free to explore other possibilities.

Orlando is thus a written narrative where the role of ancestors, portrait galleries, and family relics is central, and this is key to the understanding of the book's pictures. For the truly innovative part of this book is the insertion of photographic pictures into it, eight altogether. These pictures make up an alternative portrait gallery, or, rather, a modern and eclectic *photograph album*, put before the eyes of the reader. Whereas the painted portraits we *read* about represent male aristocracy and inheritance, the portrait photographs we *look* at represent a playful and modern approach to identity, with ambiguous gender associations. The photographs showcase a modern medium that easily lends itself to play and deception, while at the same time establishing a more intimate relation to the beholder.

This way of inserting photographs into a novel was original, but also very timely in 1928. Photographs had at this point become an integrated part of everyday life, and people were used to handling, organizing, and manipulating photograph collections in displays and albums. This is also the period in which the first photobooks were being published, so the association of photographs and books was about to be established: Woolf and Fry's *Victorian Men and Fair Women* by Julia Margaret Cameron had been published a few years earlier, and Germany saw a boom of photobooks around 1930.[24] Further, André Breton published his experimental novel *Nadja* the same year, which just like Orlando included photographs. Indeed, Woolf's idea to insert portrait photographs in a mock-biography was clever, but in retrospect we see that it was also somewhat near at hand.

Looking more closely at the eight pictures in *Orlando*, we find that four are photographs and four are photographs of paintings, all

24. Julia Margaret Cameron allegedly created the first photobook to illustrate a literary work, an illustrated edition of Tennyson's *Idylls of the King*, which contained twelve images that Cameron had created specifically for the book. In the first edition of the book (1874), the photographs were reproduced as wood engravings, but Cameron then sought a new publisher and created her own version of *Idylls of the King*, containing her original photographs as albumen prints, which came out shortly after (volume 1 in December 1874 and volume 2 in 1875). See Tennyson, *Tennyson's Idylls of the King.*

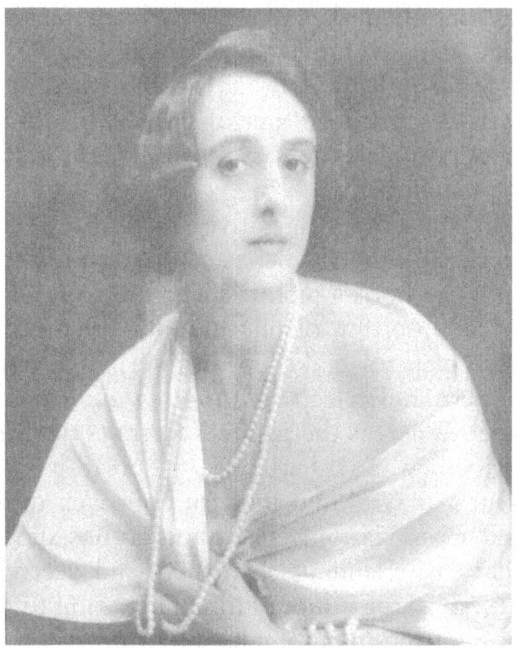

Figure 3.3   Portrait photograph from Virginia Woolf's book *Orlando: A Biography*, 1928. The model is Vita Sackville-West, and the photographer may have been Lenare.

of them in black and white with captions.[25] In the original edition, they were dispersed throughout the text, but more recent publications have often collected all eight in an image section in the middle of the book (and some have simply omitted the pictures, thus overlooking an important part of the novel). Whereas the paintings and the drawing were taken from Knole (all of them from the seventeenth century), the four photographs were all staged and taken for the occasion, with Vita Sackville-West posing as Orlando in three of them and Vanessa Bell's daughter Angelica posing as a Russian princess in one.

The first picture we encounter is a Renaissance-style full-length painting of "Orlando as a boy," with a characteristic use of perspective leading the beholder's gaze deep into the background of the picture. The second is an odd photograph of "The Russian Princess

25. For details about the pictures (mostly referential details), see the notes to the Cambridge edition of *Orlando*, edited by Suzanne Raitt and Ian Blyth. Woolf, *Orlando*, 305; 323–6.

as a child," which looks more than a photomontage than a realist photograph. The awkward position of the model's head (Angelica), with an upward gaze, and the sharp contrast between her head and the abstract background undermine any idea of a "natural" style (the bottom section of the portrait has in fact been painted over). Her innocent face, in combination with her over-posed style (two shawls and several chains of pearls), reminds one of Cameron's allegorical photographs, only with more artifice. The third picture is presented as a painting of another character in the novel, "The Archduchess Harriet." It is a three-quarter-length portrait, also in Renaissance style, but more "flat," without depth and perspective and with more emphasis on geometrical forms. The forth image is a painted head-and-shoulder portrait that allegedly represents "Orlando as ambassador." This picture, too, is from the seventeenth century, but its lines are softer than the other ones, and it is more approachable.

The fifth picture is perhaps the most intriguing; it is a head-and-shoulder photograph of "Orlando on her return to England," an occasion that in the narrative is set in the early eighteenth century. Yet the photograph depicts Orlando as a modern woman with fairly short hair—a style that was fashionable in the 1920s. Its model, Vita Sackville-West, presents herself in a candid way; with her right chin slightly turned towards the camera, she looks sideways at the beholder, and her gaze is open, but also watchful. She wears a long chain of pearls around her neck and a shawl around her shoulders, which she carefully holds together with her left hand. The sixth image is a three-quarter-length photograph of "Orlando about the year 1840," depicting her sitting on a chair with a voluminous blouse with flower embroidery and a flat hat, resting her head in her hands and looking the camera confidently in the eye. It has been claimed that her costume is anachronistic for a picture that allegedly dates from 1840, but it could in fact be seen as reminiscent of Julia Margaret Cameron's rather voluminous outfits. The seventh image claims to represent "Marmaduke Bonthrop Shelmerdine, Esquire," the man Orlando marries. He is represented as an elegant young gentleman with a feminine face and soft, curly hair. The "real" portrait painting is from 1820 and has very soft lines, but the caption in the novel does not date the picture. The eighth and last image is a photograph of "Orlando at the present time." It is a snapshot photograph taken outdoors at a few meters' distance, showing Orlando standing in a field before a gate with her two dogs, surrounded by leaves and grass. The features of her face are barely perceivable. This picture seems more casual and less staged than the other photographs of Vita as Orlando.

The album put together here is thus quite diverse and presents itself as a truly modern assemblage. Not only do the motifs differ, but also the techniques and styles. And even if the images appear in a chronological order, following Orlando and the other two characters through the novel's historical developments, the techniques and styles that are used do not fully correspond to the time of the narrative. A Russian Renaissance princess is depicted in a manipulated photograph, and Orlando returning to England around 1700 is depicted in a photographic portrait with hair and clothes suggesting that she belongs to the twentieth century.

How should the reader respond to these pictures? The captions offer some help in relating the pictures to the story, but at the same time they make allegations about the pictures that appear to play with the reader's expectations. The relation between text and images is thus not at all clear, as several researchers have noted. As for the prose narrative, it comments on the portraits only twice, and in both cases the narrator invites comparison and thus encourages the reader to scrutinize the pictures carefully. The first comment occurs shortly after Orlando has become a woman; at this point, the narrator claims that, even if she has become a woman, Orlando had "remained the same" in every other respect. Commenting on the two Orlandos, the former and the present, the narrator asserts that the change of gender did not "alter their identity." To prove this, the narrator refers to the portraits, but in a quite general way: "Their faces remained, as their portraits prove, practically the same" (O, 133). This passage is intriguing, for what does it mean to change *gender*, but remain the same in every other aspect? What does it mean to remain *practically* the same? How does the relation between identity and difference play out in this context? Yet the comment is not without truth: When we consider the painting of Orlando as ambassador (male) and the photograph of Orlando returning to England (female), androgynous features are perceivable in both. The male version has a soft look, an open gaze and lips that are slightly pouting in a rather feminine—and somewhat posed—way. The woman has an oval face with a large forehead that might also have belonged to a man, whereas her vulnerable and somewhat watchful gaze as well as her sensual mouth suggest femininity. The images thus evoke the idea of androgyny that the novel is premised upon, and they invite the reader to judge for herself whether Orlando has remained the same or not.

The second reference to the images occurs some fifty pages later in the novel, and this time the different ways of posing are highlighted.

A connection is here assumed between clothing, gender, and ways of behaving and posing:

> So, having now worn skirts for a considerable time, a certain change was visible in Orlando, which is to be found if the reader will look at plate 5, even in her face. If we compare the picture of Orlando as a man with that of Orlando as a woman we shall see that though both are undoubtedly one and the same person, there are certain changes. The man has his hand free to seize his sword, the woman must use hers to keep the satins from slipping from her shoulders. The man looks the world full in the face, as if it were made for his uses and fashioned to his liking. The woman takes a sidelong glance at it, full of subtlety, even of suspicion. Had they both worn the same clothes, it is possible that their outlook might have been the same. That is the view of some philosophers and wise ones, but on the whole, we incline to another. The difference between the sexes is, happily, one of great profundity. Clothes are but a symbol of something hid deep beneath. (O, 180)

Once more, the reader is invited to look carefully at the images and compare them, but this time the narrator's description guides the reader's gaze. In fact, this is the only attempt in the novel at describing the images, that is, to use ekphrasis as a literary technique. Surprisingly, however, the narrator is specific only with respect to image 5 of Orlando as a woman and does not tell the reader which male portrait it should be compared to, so the reader must therefore handle this by herself. Yet the narrator may simply be referring to the frontispiece of the first edition of *Orlando* (which is not always reproduced in modern editions), a painting of a nobleman facing the beholder, his right arm holding a sword raised up in the air, his left arm holding a shield with a heraldic design in front of him. This picture combines portraiture and heraldic imagery in a way that is typical of British family portrait galleries, where a heraldic design is seen as the property of the individual or the family.

What the narrator assert is that the man and the woman have different attitudes to the world and that this can be seen through the way they use their hands, or through the way they are "naturally" inclined to use their hands. A man's hand is free, but for a purpose— for the purpose of fighting, and this seems to give him rather limited options. A woman, on the other hand, is not free; she "must" use her hands to attend to her appearance, making sure that she looks well and decent at the same time. A man is thus inclined to action, whereas a woman is inclined to take care of her appearance. In keeping with this, the narrator stresses the way their gazes differ, the man looking directly at the outer world, ready to "face" it, whereas the woman is looking obliquely, distrustfully, without revealing fully what she thinks. Looking closely at image 5, we see that Orlando's gesture, her way of wrapping her satin shawl around her, makes her look as if she is protecting herself from the camera's gaze. She presents herself to its gaze, but she also hides behind the shawl, withholding something in her oblique and suspicious gaze. Indeed, this is what makes the photograph interesting to look at; it hints at that which is invisible.

Having inspected the eight pictures as well as the text–image relations in the novel, we should inquire into the role the images play in the novel as a whole. A comparison with Woolf's use of photographs in the early novels is helpful here: As we have seen, she there created scenes in which the characters contemplate portraits or faces, in this manner introducing zones of silence into the novels. In *Orlando*, Woolf takes this endeavor a giant step further: She uses real images—real portraits—instead of describing them verbally, and she places the reader in the situation in which she had previously placed her characters. She bypasses words altogether, allowing the portraits to speak for themselves. The narrative technique of "showing seeing" is thus replaced by an invitation to contemplate "real" portraits.

Thus, in order to grasp what the images in the novel actually convey, one should acknowledge that they stop the flow of words and open up a contemplative and silent zone where emotions are allowed to grow forth without relying on words, concepts, and ideas. The pictures are thus entrusted to the reader without detailed instructions. Contemplating the pictures, the reader must do without the narrator's "insider" voice and is left at the outside, so to speak. As the images introduce a different modality, they invite a different receptivity in the reader. They allow the reader to try for herself to meet the sitter's gazes, to read their faces, and to try to come to terms with the enigma of another person. Looking at the pictures, the reader must ponder the question of identity and the transhistorical, transgendered life of Orlando. What does it mean to be the "same, but different"? Yet the effect of the pictures depends upon the reader's readiness to become attuned to the atmospheres they create. Not all readers will be prepared for the reading of photographs (without guidance), and some of them will probably not take this opportunity to contemplate pictures but will instead look instinctively for the next paragraph to continue their reading. Others will perhaps see pure mockery in the pictures and not be attentive to their enigmatic beauty. Indeed, reader conventions matter with respect to text–image relations and innovative books such as *Orlando*.

Woolf thus uses a new media regime to challenge the mindset of the reader. She plays with the Victorian idea of portraiture as reflecting identity, character, and inheritance and introduces instead an instable notion of identity, closely related to the medium of photography and the eclectic assemblage of the photograph album. The various portraits inserted in *Orlando* incite the reader to reflect upon the question of what life really is and how it can be adequately represented. Further, in this endeavor, Woolf makes use of the evidentiary function of photographs. The photographs of Orlando's life serve to document her life and appear to prove the narrator's claim that she has lived for centuries. In this manner, her being is inscribed in the archives of history through an "objective" point of view. For a novel—and a mock-biography—this makes a great difference; Orlando is not merely depicted through the narrator's rendering of her subjective consciousness, but also through an external view: photography. Woolf's use of photography thus places the reader at the outside trying to look in, trying to ponder the meaning—and the age and gender—of a face.

As the novel moves toward its ending, the question of what life really is dominates the narrative, and here it takes a new turn: The life of individuals is here contrasted with something infinitely vaster—history, or life beyond the individual. Building up to this perspective, Woolf makes sure to mock the biographer's and the novelist's interest in the life of action as opposed the life of thought and imagination.[26] As Orlando sits down by a desk and immerses herself in a writing process, the narrator expresses the frustration a biographer or a novelist feels when the action stops and their protagonists "disappear" for a while to indulge in a subjective world (O, 254–6). Yet, as a contrast, the reader is offered a view that goes beyond the individual: Orlando suddenly rises from her writing desk and looks out of the window at the life that has continued while she was "away" in her thoughts and that would have continued if she were dead, she assumes. She understands that the "external" world exists independent of her and

26. The same issue was addressed in the essay "The New Biography" (1927), published a year before *Orlando*. Discussing the history and development of biography, Woolf there asserted that before Boswell, there was no room in biography for "the inner life of thought and emotion" because it was dedicated to action. This was also a main concern in "Modern Fiction," where Woolf took issue with realist and plot-based novels.

realizes that she belongs to history and to time. She thus reaches an understanding of life that transcends her own being. This means that she considers the world not from a subjective perspective, not filtered through her subjective consciousness, but as tentatively seen through an external and impersonal point of view.

What kind of viewpoint is this? The medium that may best captures this external point of view is photography. The camera makes it possible to represent life without the mediation of subjective consciousness, allowing us to see the world represented without us, as it exists by and for itself. In this manner it gives us a fresh and often alienating view of the familiar world. In Woolf's day, the spread of photography made this a fascinating experience accessible to more and more people. As we have seen, Proust and Kafka both reflected upon such experiences, the former stressing the feeling of alienation prompted by the external look of the camera, the latter highlighting the uncanny feeling it incited. In Woolf's essay on the cinema, published two years before *Orlando*, we find an explicit reflection on this experience of the exterior world. There, Woolf asserts that the cinema allows us to "see life as it is when we have no part in it. As we gaze we seem to be removed from the pettiness of actual existence."[27] It could thus be suggested that Woolf's reflections upon life as belonging to history and as transcending individual experience were in some sense related to her experience of photography and film. This should not, of course, be seen as a direct and causal relation; rather, the invention of the camera's external viewpoint should be seen as part of the cultural premises that allowed Woolf to conceive of life in that manner at that point in history.

In the last pages of the novel, Woolf lets Orlando return to the portrait gallery, this time seeing it in a new light. Walking down the gallery, she realizes that the house "was no longer hers entirely. [. . .] It belonged to time now; to history; was past the touch and control of the living" (O, 304). A corollary of this new insight into the workings of history and time is that Orlando's status in the novel changes; from being the main character of a (mock) biography, she is now turned into a witness standing at the outside of the events, "a very indifferent witness to the truth of what was before her" (O, 307). Orlando thus steps out of the novel's center of action, acknowledging the impersonal force of history and leaving the biographical paradigm behind her. This "Copernican turn" may be understood in the context of the new visual media, making possible Orlando's new outlook.

27. Woolf, "The Cinema," 173.

Cosmopolitan Vision

In the essay "Three Guineas," Woolf takes a step out of the private sphere of love stories and the semiprivate sphere of biographies, and discusses the question of human understanding on a larger scale. She addresses two questions that were urgent in 1938: war and education for women.[28] In this manner, she enters the world scene, concerned with the problem of universal understanding, cosmopolitan ideals, and the furthering of "humanity." What will interest us in this section is the fact that a main line of her argument revolves around photographs and the role they might have in the prevention of war. In vogue with the ideological currents in her day, Woolf sees photography as instrumental in creating "global" sympathy. Woolf thus continues her exploration of the ways in which pictures excite emotions while also contributing to the ongoing discussions about the uses of photography in a world perspective.

Woolf's starting point in the essay is that complete understanding is impossible and "could only be achieved by blood transfusion and memory transfusion" (TG, 121).[29] Yet she dryly points out that the substitute for blood and memory transfusion in her day is biography and autobiography, and as usual she mocks the illusion conveyed by these genres. Her general point is that we have various resources to help us achieve an understanding of others and need not rely merely on experience; in addition to biographies, there are newspapers ("history in the raw") and photographs (TG, 121), she asserts. The latter category proves to be significant in her discussion of war and how it can be prevented.

The context of war looms large in the essay: As is well known, it was written during the Spanish Civil War between the elected Republican government and General Franco's Nationalist rebels (1936–9), with a growing awareness of the rise of fascism in Germany and the danger of a catastrophic new world war. The essay is shaped as a response to a male lawyer who has written to her and asked what "we" could do to prevent war. It builds upon the argument that the "we" he assumes is illegitimate insofar as women's and men's perspectives differ. This is due to their different rights and roles in

28. For an overview of the reception history of "Three Guineas," as well as the existing research on the essay, see Jane Marcus's "Introduction" to the Harcourt edition of the essay.
29. References are to the following edition, abbreviated as shown: TG: "Three Guineas," in *A Room of One's Own & Three Guineas*. London: Penguin Books, 2000,

society, and more precisely to the fact that women do not have (full) access to education or the professions. "[T]hough we look at the same things, we see them differently," she asserts (TG, 119). Woolf's consideration of the gap between the sexes is important because she sees war as a result of a patriarchal culture favoring competition rather than compassion. Consequently, she argues that women must get unfettered access to education and the workforce to counter the warmongering culture they live in.

When she addresses the role of photography in this context, she first takes issue with a genre of photographs that were frequently seen in the newspapers in her day: "official" photographs of men in pompous uniforms, which, according to Woolf, contributed to upholding and endorsing war. A series of photographs integrated into the essay showing a judge, a scholar, a soldier, and similar figures demonstrate the pomp and circumstance of this kind of picture and serve as placeholders for patriarchal society.[30] As Alice Staveley has demonstrated, these photographs refer to men that would be recognized in Woolf's day, men that were in various ways responsible for the current politics of war.[31] Some of the men even appeared on cigarette cards, which circulated widely.[32] Pointing to these images, Woolf shows the reader what the world of men looks like to women, that is, what public and professional life looks like from the private home: "Let us then by way of a very elementary beginning lay before you a photograph—a crudely coloured photograph—of your world as it appears to us who see it from the threshold of the private house" (TG, 133). Woolf asserts that these photographs at first look impressive, but then she assumes a connection between them and the photographs from the war. She argues that men in such roles and costumes stress their superiority over others and in that manner stir up competition and jealousy, thus encouraging a disposition toward war. To counter this logic, she implies, it is necessary to reveal the ridiculousness of such appearances and "discourage the feelings that lead to war" (TG, 138).

As a contrast to these "official" photographs representing patriarchal society, Woolf addresses a different kind of picture: "raw"

30. For a discussion of the performative power of clothes in "Three Guineas," see Randi Koppen's article, which asserts that the essay presents "a gendered analysis of the relation between dressed bodies and social order." Koppen, "Re-thinking the 'Performative Turn,'" 178.
31. Staveley, "Name that Face."
32. Wisor, "About Face," 2.

war photographs. Whereas education for women is a long-term goal that can prevent the growth of a warmongering culture, such photographs are a more direct means to foster antiwar attitudes, Woolf suggests. She calls upon her interlocutor to look at a series of photographs from the Spanish Civil War depicting dead bodies and ruined houses and carefully starts to lay out her argument regarding photographs and emotions:

> Photographs, of course, are not arguments addressed to the reason; they are simply statements of fact addressed to the eye. But in that very simplicity there may be some help. Let us see then whether when we look at the same photographs we feel the same things. Here then on the table before us are photographs. The Spanish Government sends them with patient pertinacity about twice a week. They are not pleasant photographs to look upon. They are photographs of dead bodies for the most part. This morning's collection contains the photograph of what might be a man's body, or a woman's; it is so mutilated that it might, on the other hand, be the body of a pig. But those certainly are dead children, and that undoubtedly is the section of a house. A bomb has torn open the side; there is still a birdcage hanging in what was presumably the sitting-room, but the rest of the house looks like nothing so much as a bunch of spillikins suspended in mid air. (TG, 125)

Woolf here asserts that photographs convince us because of their evidential (indexical) function and suggests that men and women's emotional response is the same because they see the same thing. Her depiction of a photograph that she appears to hold before her highlights its matter-of-factness: it gives visual proof of the destructive power of war in the shape of dead bodies and ruined houses. She stresses the direct impact such photographs have on the senses, and how men and women respond to such "raw" impressions in the same way:

> Those photographs are not an argument; they are simply a crude statement of fact addressed to the eye. But the eye is connected with the brain; the brain with the nervous system. That system sends its messages in a flash through every past memory and present feeling. When we look at those photographs some fusion takes place within us; however different the education, the traditions behind us, our sensations are the same; and they are violent. You, Sir, call them "horror and disgust". We also call them horror and disgust. And the same words rise to our lips. War, you say, is an abomination; a barbarity;

war must be stopped at whatever cost. And we echo your words. War is an abomination; a barbarity; war must be stopped. For now at last we are looking at the same picture; we are seeing with you the same dead bodies, the same ruined houses. (TG, 125)

Woolf thus asserts that in looking at such images "our sensations are the same," and "raw" photographs from the war may thus serve to bridge the gap between men and women. Moreover, Woolf claims that such photographs require something from the beholder; not merely speeches and formalities, but a more active response:

> Here it is enough to say that though the three measures you suggest seem plausible, yet it also seems that, if we did what you ask, the emotion caused by the photographs would still remain unappeased. That emotion, that very positive emotion, demands something more positive than a name written on a sheet of paper; an hour spent listening to speeches; a cheque written for whatever sum we can afford—say one guinea. Some more energetic, some more active method of expressing our belief that war is barbarous. (TG, 126)

Woolf here underlines the emotional force of photographs and implies that they have some kind of agency. Her claim is that war photographs can prompt the beholders to express their resistance to war because of their emotional impact. Indeed, Woolf's line of argument leads the reader to believe that the war images she received were themselves instrumental to her decision to write the essay, and that one of her aims is to highlight the effect photographs may have on the beholder. Seeing photographs as instrumental in fostering human understanding, she wants the readers to take these photographs seriously, so to be able to respond emotionally and actively to war.

Yet men in official positions have cut themselves off from such emotional responses, Woolf argues. Aiming to understand the roots of patriarchal culture, she suggests that it is necessary to inquire into the social forces (education and social structures) that made these men who they are. Her argument reaches a crucial stage when she asserts that men in patriarchal society are trained to disregard their senses:

> [I]f people are highly successful in their professions they lose their senses. Sight goes. They have no time to look at pictures. Sound goes. They have no time to listen to music. Speech goes. They have no time for conversation. They lose their sense of proportion—the relations between one thing and another. Humanity goes. [. . .] What then remains of a human being who has lost sight, and sound, and sense of proportion? Only a cripple in a cave. (TG, 197)

When people's senses are dulled, they no longer have time to look at pictures, Woolf claims, and she thereby implies that "pictures" can make a difference, exciting both compassion and feelings of responsibility. Here we are at the core of Woolf's argument: She believes in humanity and sympathy as universal capacities; it is something that may unite people if they remain in touch with their senses, but it is also something that they may lose or repress, and the consequences may be fatal. Indeed, humanity and sympathy cannot be taken for granted in modern society, Woolf claims, and proper education—of men as well as women—is therefore crucial.

Yet Woolf was not the only one in her day to see photographs as fostering human understanding, and to see her stance more clearly, some context may be helpful. Woolf's political agenda was very much in line with important social currents in the first half of the twentieth century, notably the peace movement, internationalism, and cosmopolitanism. Even before the advent of the First World War, the vogue for cosmopolitanism was thriving, and a series of initiatives were taken that involved collaboration and communication between countries, such as the League of Nations (founded in 1920). During this period, there was a growing belief that the medium of photography could serve to bridge linguistic and cultural barriers and thus represented a means to promote global understanding. A key example is the undertakings of the French philanthropist Albert Kahn, who organized an immense photographic project: a world tour to provide "local" photographs of people from all corners of the world, followed by a series of public photographic exhibitions (1909–31). Photography was in this project seen as a world language, an ally of the liberal idea of internationalism, and the explicit intention was to further global understanding.[33]

Cosmopolitanism in many respects agreed with the liberal mindsets of the Bloomsbury Group. It represented a different vision of politics than the one taking place at the level of political institutions and was thus more compatible with writers' belief in the autonomy of aesthetic matters. Moreover, Leonard Woolf was involved in the work leading up to the creation of the League of Nations and thus formed a link to the new institutions working to promote peace.[34] Even if Virginia Woolf did not usually commit to political issues, preferring aesthetic matters to remain uncorrupted, "Three Guineas" is

33. A wealthy and well-connected philanthropist, Kahn was not without political influence; his circle played a role in establishing the League of Nations. See Bjorli and Jakobsen's Introduction to *Cosmopolitics of the Camera*.
34. Wilson, "Leonard Woolf, the League of Nations, and Peace between the Wars."

part of a political and cultural movement. The cosmopolitan spirit is explicitly referred to in the essay and seems to underlie Woolf's belief in the possibility of human understanding and sympathy. Woolf quotes a biography that refers to the "League of Nations" and the prospects of peace and disarmament, as well as Wilfred Owen, the British poet who more than any represented an antiwar stance after the First World War ("war is inhuman, as Wilfred Owen said," TG 162). And importantly for our context, Woolf expresses a cosmopolitan belief in photographs as a global language at the service of humanism and pacifism. Her claim that in looking at war photographs "our sensations are the same" addresses the possibility of global sympathy.

Still, Woolf's perspective breaks with the cosmopolitan view of photography in a crucial way: Where the cosmopolitan tradition placed its hopes in portrait photographs of ordinary people in everyday contexts, Woolf placed her beliefs in war photographs depicting suffering and dead bodies. The difference is staggering: A portrait photograph offers itself for the reading of faces, and the beholder easily recognizes a degree of agency in the sitter. By contrast, in war photographs of dead bodies, the depicted persons have lost all agency, and there is no question of "reading faces." Far worse than the unreturned gaze and an avoidant look is a body that is no longer animated and that has lost the capacity of responding completely. Yet Woolf's view is that the horror we feel in witnessing such photographs comes from the senses and must necessarily lead to feelings of compassion—without passing through reason. We here recognize the association of photographs and emotional responses that we saw in Woolf's novels, but in the case of war photographs, the "soft" feelings of sympathy are replaced by "raw" feelings of horror.

To fully understand Woolf's stress on the emotional impact of the war photographs from Spain, we should keep in mind that in 1938 "raw" war photographs represented something new and that Woolf is here describing a novel phase in the history of photography. Previously, war photographs had a certain decency to them, partly because of the censorship exercised by various governments and presses, and partly because technological shortcomings made action images from the war impossible. During the Spanish Civil War, however, photojournalists would enter the battlefield with their mobile cameras and capture the effects of a fatal gunshot with precision (as demonstrated in Robert Capa's iconic and hotly debated photograph *Falling Soldier* from 1936). They would also take photographs of dead victims and ruins that were left behind after the fighting had ended. Still, British newspapers rarely printed photographs from the

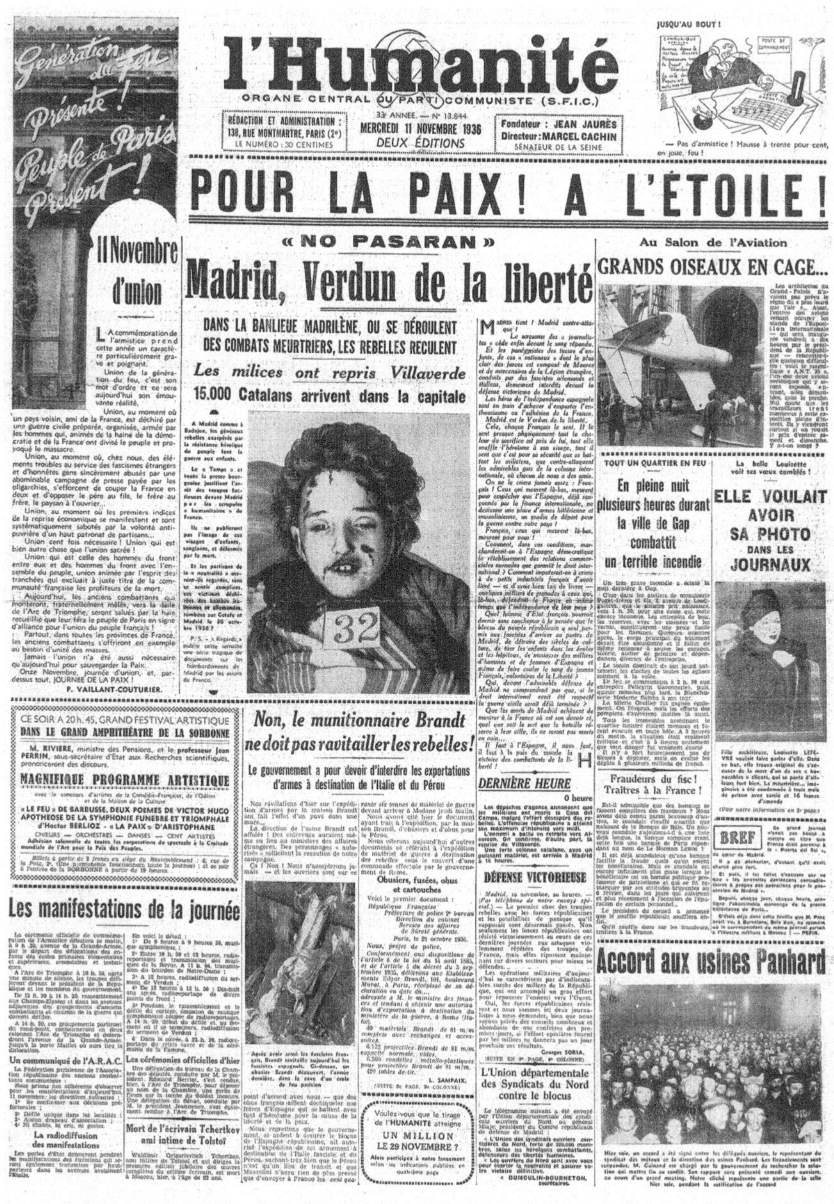

l'Humanité

ORGANE CENTRAL DU PARTI COMMUNISTE (S.F.I.C.)

RÉDACTION ET ADMINISTRATION :
138, RUE MONTMARTRE, PARIS (2e)
LE NUMÉRO : 30 CENTIMES

33e ANNÉE. — N° 13.844
MERCREDI 11 NOVEMBRE 1936
DEUX ÉDITIONS

Fondateur : JEAN JAURÈS
Directeur : MARCEL CACHIN
SÉNATEUR DE LA SEINE

POUR LA PAIX ! A L'ÉTOILE !

11 Novembre d'union

« NO PASARAN »

Madrid, Verdun de la liberté

DANS LA BANLIEUE MADRILÈNE, OU SE DÉROULENT DES COMBATS MEURTRIERS, LES REBELLES RECULENT

Les milices ont repris Villaverde

15.000 Catalans arrivent dans la capitale

Au Salon de l'Aviation

GRANDS OISEAUX EN CAGE...

TOUT UN QUARTIER EN FEU

En pleine nuit plusieurs heures durant la ville de Gap combattit un terrible incendie

ELLE VOULAIT AVOIR SA PHOTO DANS LES JOURNAUX

La belle Louisette voit ses vœux comblés !

Non, le munitionnaire Brandt ne doit pas ravitailler les rebelles !

Le gouvernement a pour devoir d'interdire les exportations d'armes à destination de l'Italie et du Pérou

DERNIÈRE HEURE

0 heure

DÉFENSE VICTORIEUSE

Traîtres à la France !

CE SOIR A 20 h. 45, GRAND FESTIVAL ARTISTIQUE DANS LE GRAND AMPHITHÉÂTRE DE LA SORBONNE

MAGNIFIQUE PROGRAMME ARTISTIQUE

Les manifestations de la journée

L'Union départementale des Syndicats du Nord contre le blocus

Accord aux usines Panhard

Figure 3.4   The front page of the French newspaper *L'Humanité* on November 11, 1936. Source: Bibliothèque nationale de France (BnF).

Spanish Civil War, as they practiced a certain censorship or caution with respect to war photographs in general. Thus, the photographs in question in "Three Guineas" could not be seen in the British newspapers; they were allegedly sent to Woolf by the Republican Spanish government (which undertook such dispatches to potential sympathizers on a regular basis). By contrast, the French press was far less squeamish, printing photographs of dead bodies on their front pages, including a series of close-up images of dead children.[35] These "portraits" of dead children showed the young faces bereft of any expression, but marked by the brutality of their death. The effect of these photographs on the beholders must have been staggering: They provoke horror, but also an extreme sadness. There is reason to believe that Woolf saw some of these disturbing front pages during her visit to France in May 1937. Woolf, who during the 1930s collected newspaper cuttings on the war in scrapbooks and notebooks, must have paid attention to such horrifying pictures.

When uncensored war photographs were made known to the public, the brutality of war was presented to the eyes of ordinary citizens who might never before have imagined that this was what war looked like. Uncensored photographs made war's reality visible and reduced the level of abstraction in the debates about war. When Woolf discusses the impact of war photographs, she in fact addresses a new regime of images, whose emotional impact was extreme. In this perspective, her view of photographs in "Three Guineas" could be seen as bridging the "old" cosmopolitan belief in portrait photographs as fostering global sympathy and a new emotional response to war photographs. Her argument could be seen as premised upon a new phase in the history of visual media, where suffering and dead bodies in foreign countries were made visible to ordinary citizens.

Today, Woolf's belief in human sympathy and her cosmopolitan view of photography may easily be criticized as representing a naïve universalism. Yet such a critique would in my view be simplistic. Woolf tries to come to terms with the conditions of sympathy and compassion in the age of globalization, seeing the circulation of war photographs as a game changer; they create feelings of horror and compassion, thus bypassing abstract language, which truly invites ideas of universalism. Woolf thus gestured toward something that lies deeper than cultural and national specificities: the human capacity for

---

35. See Emily Dalgarno's valuable study of Woolf's reading of the news, which stresses the difference between the British and the French media coverage of the civil war and describes photographs of dead children in one of the French newspapers, *L'Humanité*. Dalgarno, *Virginia Woolf and the Visible World*, 157–61. Jane Marcus, too, asserts that Woolf's publication of "Three Guineas" was "sparked by her horror at photographs of children killed by Franco's bombs in Spain." See Marcus, "Introduction."

suffering. This does not mean that she bypasses the question of differences, but rather that she cared about the shared condition of human beings. This position also made her eager to defend universal rights: not only women's rights, but the rights of all.

Indeed, the question of rights was urgent in 1938. What made Woolf's feminist agenda especially pressing was the fact that women were not completely excluded from society anymore; they were about to get access to it and had to decide how to contribute. A limited number of women were included in the suffrage in 1918 (women over thirty who met a property qualification), and another decade passed before all women over twenty-one were included in the universal suffrage, in 1928. In 1938, after years of striving for women's liberation, women had thus been granted political rights and Woolf asks how they can start to make a difference without adopting patriarchal values. The question was timely, for in 1938 universal suffrage was still recent and not something that could be taken for granted. With the rise of fascism in Germany, women saw their rights (obtained in the Weimar Republic) taken away because a more traditional role for women was prepared in the fascist vision of the national state. With the outbreak of the Spanish Civil War, war started to become a reality, and Woolf saw the need to engage in politics – in her own manner.[36]

Important is also the fact that Woolf not merely advocated women's rights in this essay but joined a broader fight for civil rights that characterizes this period and culminated in the UN's Universal Declaration of Human Rights ten years later, in 1948. The abolition of slavery and the question of rights for African Americans were still sensitive topics in 1938, and Woolf compares the women's movement with the Society for the Abolition of Slavery (TG, 167). She asserts "that any woman who enters any profession shall in no way hinder any other human being, whether man or woman, white or black, provided that he or she

---

36. As a writer, Woolf had previously expressed an intention to "fight intellectually" rather than engaging directly in political matters, and "Three Guineas" thus represents a more explicit way of addressing political issues than before, even if the form is literary. Generally, the threat of fascism represented by Hitler, Mussolini, and Franco created a split between those who remained in pacifist positions and those who, seeing pacifism as irresponsible, supported the war. Leonard Woolf advocated rearmament and action, whereas Virginia was persistent in her pacifist stance, resolute to "fight intellectually." Despite Woolf's reluctant attitude to politics and activism, she had a strong engagement on the level of ideas, which became stronger with the rise of fascism. See Lee, *Virginia Woolf*, 678–98.

is qualified to enter that profession, from entering it; but shall do all in her power to help them" (TG, 191). She also calls upon her interlocutor to recognize the discrimination against both Jews and women ("The dictatorship [. . .] against Jews or against women [. . .] is now apparent to you") and she implores him to assert "'the rights of all'—men and women" (TG, 228). Being married to a Jew, Woolf certainly felt the growing anti-Semitism in Europe. So even if she argues specifically for women's rights, she more broadly defends "the rights of all," and she underscores that the fight for democracy is ultimately the same fight as the fight against tyranny, against the patriarchal state, and against the fascist state (TG, 226–7; 272).

To be sure, fighting for universal rights is something entirely different from promoting a "universalist" view of humankind. In her discussion, Woolf explicitly acknowledges differences and speaks in favor of preserving them. Moreover, recognizing the value of the outsider's position, she puts forward the idea of an "Outsider's Society" (TG, 231–2) as an alternative to a patriotic community. "What does 'our country' mean to me an outsider?" she asks (TG, 233). Woolf stresses that the outsider's position is near at hand for a woman, who is not included in power in the first place. She recommends that women should step into society as outsiders, and, moreover, that everyone should step into society as an outsider (rather than becoming part of a general "we" supporting the nation). Woolf also shows that the boundaries between a citizen and a foreigner are in fact fluid and somewhat absurd. A woman's nationality is decided by her husband, so by marrying a foreigner a British woman becomes a "foreigner" herself. This leads to her renowned proclamation: "as a woman, I have no country. As a woman I want no country. As a woman my country is the whole world" (TG, 234).

These reflections are very much in line with cosmopolitan ways of thinking in the interwar period, attempting to overcome patriotism and to find new ways of relating to one another, beyond the national state. They are also in line with the spirit of the Bloomsbury Group, whose worldview was liberal and open-minded and never in service of the nation. Indeed, they show that Woolf, to a greater extent than many of her contemporaries, advocated a *critical* cosmopolitanism that did not seek to erase the difference of others, but to grant others *equality* and civil rights. It is also intriguing to see to what extent Woolf's views anticipate the deconstruction of metaphysical ideas about community and the postcolonial critique of the idea of nationhood. Woolf's "outsider's society" is in line with contemporary philosophical discussions on how to conceive of community without the constraints of the national state and without a metaphysical idea of nationhood, with important contributions from Jean-Luc Nancy and Giorgio Agamben.[37] Unlike these contemporary philosophers, however, Woolf argues that the medium of photography is capable of bridging differences between people insofar as it shows us reality through an external (quasi-objective) gaze. In an "outsider's society," we may assume, photography could play an instrumental role in establishing a shared reality and a shared understanding.

In "Three Guineas," Woolf thus weaves together a series of questions that were urgent in her day, discussing them with critical awareness and emotional receptivity: the danger of war, the discrimination of women, and the spread of new visual media. Yet her deeper concern is that of the difficulty of communication and human understanding, and her argument thus ties in with the key topics of her novels. Whereas she had previously explored the role of visual communication in the private and semiprivate sphere, she now explicitly discusses how a new genre of photographs communicates: war photographs. The thrust of her argument is that war photographs have an evidential function (objectivity) bypassing debates about what the facts are, and that this matter-of-factness creates emotional responses in the beholders (subjectivity), who see and feel the same things (intersubjectivity). Her hope and belief is that war photographs—as visual documents—may serve to bridge the gap between men and women, and, by extension, can create sympathy and understanding between people with different educations and backgrounds. Further, she contends that the emotions spurred by war photographs require an active response from the beholders, and thus implies that the photographs in themselves—placed in the right context—may have some kind of agency.

However, Woolf's argument becomes more complicated toward the end of the essay. What she now pretends to put before us is not a picture of suffering fellow beings, but a photograph of the Führer, and she denounces any simplistic response to it, such as antipathy or hatred. Instead, she stresses the way we as humans respond to photographs of other human figures:

> But we have not laid that picture before you in order to excite once more the sterile emotion of hate. On the contrary it is in order to

37. Jean-Luc Nancy, *The Inoperative Community*; Agamben, *The Coming Community*. Chantal Delourme discusses Woolf's essay in this context in his article "Three Guineas."

> release other emotions such as the human figure, even thus crudely
> in a colored photograph, arouses in us who are human beings. For
> it suggests [. . .] that the public and the private worlds are insepa-
> rably connected; that the tyrannies and servilities of the one are the
> tyrannies and servilities of the other. But the human figure even in a
> photograph suggests other and more complex emotions. It suggests
> that we cannot dissociate ourselves from that figure but are ourselves
> that figure. It suggests that we are not passive spectators doomed to
> unresisting obedience but by our thoughts and actions can ourselves
> change that figure. (TG, 270)

Woolf's claim here is that a photograph of a human figure prompts feeling of identification in the beholder. A photograph of the Führer—instead of the mere mention of his name—thus turns him into a human body resembling us. This may remind us that the people acting on the world stage are humans, too, and that there is a connection between the public and the private spheres. Photographs in a certain sense put people in power at the same level as the beholders (on the same eye-level, so to speak), making ordinary citizens realize that they need not be passive observers but can themselves contribute to change. Indeed, photographs serve an important role by reducing the level of abstraction, and may change the ways in which people look at war. Of course, this part of Woolf's argument—related to pictures of the Führer—was risky and probably worked best at a theoretical level. Presumably, it did not sit well with readers facing the fascist threat in 1938, who surely looked at photographs of Hitler with feelings of hatred, and it is easy to imagine that these passages were partly responsible for the tepid response the essay received.

Also problematic is Woolf's unwavering belief in photographs as "evidential" documents whose signification cannot be contested and whose emotional impact is unanimous. At this point, her argument may be vulnerable to criticism from a generation that has learned to what degree technical images can be manipulative and deceitful and cause various responses. Where the early phase of "raw" war photography was seen as brutally honest and considered by Woolf as transforming the public attitude toward war, more recent views on the role of images in war are more critical. Two contributions are particularly relevant for a discussion of Woolf's essay: those by Susan Sontag and Jacques Rancière.

In her essay *Regarding the Pain of Others* (2003), Susan Sontag famously takes issue with Woolf's stance in "Three Guineas." Although she respectfully praises Woolf for her "brave, unwelcomed reflections on the roots of war," she criticizes her naïve belief in the universality of emotions, arguing that it matters "who is killed by whom."[38] Sontag's claim is that war for Woolf is generic and that she dismisses historical and political specificity.[39] These objections are certainly important and point to the difficulty of handling photographs in today's media-saturated society. Yet it could be argued that Sontag's critique of Woolf is not entirely fair, for her so-called "universalism" was not naïve or without constraints. In my view, her essay should be assessed within a greater historical context: it was part of a mid-war vision of a peaceful society, promoting international collaboration and communication, including communication through photographs. Moreover, Woolf wrote in the early days of war photographs, at a time when it was not clear how the role of photographs would develop. Sontag, by contrast, wrote in the age of television and photojournalism, when pictures from conflict zones were spreading in volumes that were unheard of in the interwar years. In Woolf's day, war photographs allowed a glimpse into a world that had previously remained unseen; in fact, such pictures changed the premises of visibility.

In the essay "The Intolerable Image," Jacques Rancière appears to have learned something from Woolf as well as from Sontag. Just as Sontag, he discusses the media's use of photographs from massacres and photographs of nameless bodies, but he asserts that such images are in fact carefully selected and in no way dominate the news. What dominates the media images, he argues, is the "talking heads" of politicians, experts, and journalists: "We do not see too many suffering bodies on the screen. But we do see too many nameless bodies, too many bodies incapable of returning the gaze that we direct at them, too many bodies that are an object of speech without themselves having a chance to speak." This, Rancière claims, teaches us that "not just anyone is capable of seeing and speaking" and we should therefore overturn "the dominant logic that makes the visual the lot of multitudes and the verbal the privilege of a few."[40] Rancière thus raises the question of agency and argues that it is too often attributed to people who are already in power. If the media would give agency to so-called victims or ordinary people, the power balance would change. By contrast, photographs of nameless, dead bodies only bolster the existent power relations. Rancière thus argues in favor of a

38. Sontag, *Regarding the Pain of Others*, 3; 9.
39. Sontag, *Regarding the Pain of Others*, 8.
40. Rancière, "The Intolerable Image," 96–7.

more ethically conscious journalism: It should not merely document silent witnesses but show victims capable of speaking, capable of presenting themselves, and returning one's gaze.

If we look at "Three Guineas" in this light, we see that Woolf in fact highlights the contrast between the two categories of photographs described by Rancière: on the one hand, the highly visible men practicing their professions wearing uniforms that make their power manifest; on the other hand, the invisible photographs of dead bodies—photographs that are *not* reproduced in the essay. Woolf implores the reader to pay attention to the victims who are usually overlooked or reduced to numbers in news articles. Her imperative is "Look!" but she takes care not to actually show the pictures of dead and suffering bodies.[41] She thus attempts to grant visibility to the victims of war, while protecting them from excessive exposure. Woolf commented on the first generation of uncensored war photographs, certain that they would make a difference, and she made it her business to make people look and feel. In this manner, she demonstrated her longstanding concern with the problem of communication, but this time on a world scale.

Sympathy for Strangers

We have seen that Woolf's writings are marked by a persistent concern with photographs as a way of relating to others. From the early novels, where her characters find themselves studying photographs and faces, via her experiments with portrait photographs in *Orlando*, to her discussion of war photographs in "Three Guineas," Woolf is interested in the emotional impact of photographs on the beholder. Where her broader concern is the problem of understanding, her subtle reflection on photography addresses the role of visual communication as opposed to words. Yet there is a development in Woolf's engagement with photographs: She goes from exploring soft feelings of sympathy in response to portrait photographs to discussing feelings of horror in response to war photographs. How, then, can this development be accounted for? In my opinion, Woolf's views on photography may be better understood if we consider it in light of one of the main currents in the modernist period: The onset of

41. Printing the photographs might have been problematic for several reasons: Probably she did not have access to the negatives, and the pictures would anyhow have broken with the code of decency in the British press.

globalization and the spread of cosmopolitan and internationalist ideas after the First World War. This current went hand in hand with the growth of a new visual culture diffusing photographs worldwide. Woolf responded to both these currents and thus came to link her reflection on photography to a cosmopolitan outlook.

In the nineteenth century, photography had largely been associated with family photographs and linked to Victorian ideas about identity, genealogy, and nationality, most explicitly manifested in the National Portrait Gallery in London, glorifying British "personalities." Early in the twentieth century, however, photographs increasingly circulated worldwide, beyond the private sphere and beyond the boundaries of the nation. Newspapers, magazines, and various international exhibitions featured pictures of people from other countries, accustoming the audience to behold the faces of foreigners and making possible a sympathy for strangers. Rejecting the family and the nation as the sole foundations of identity, more and more people indulged in cosmopolitan and internationalist ideas in relation to photography. They would no longer see photographs merely as representing a Victorian singularity, individuality, or "character," but rather see them as representing humanity and a common ground. At the same time, the strangeness of the "other" was being acknowledged, and the spread of photographs worldwide prompted new reflections on similarities and differences across cultures.

Curiously, these efforts to create a cosmopolitan outlook and global understanding paralleled a major tendency in modernist art and literature that seemingly went in the opposite direction: a commitment to mining the depths of the individual psyche. The discovery of unconscious mental processes created a growing awareness of the strangeness of any other person, including one's closest relations. One could venture to say that the circulation of photographs in this period contributed to a transformation of the relation between the familiar and the foreign, as the foreign became more familiar and the familiar became more foreign. There is thus a paradox at the core of modernism: the period saw both a pull toward exploring the singular human being (in art and literature) and a pull toward establishing common ground between human beings on a global scale (in intellectual and political life). Both the singular and the common were sought after in this period, as if the one necessitated the other.

In the years after the First World War, cosmopolitan and internationalist ideas were thriving. Already in the nineteenth century, the world exhibitions had created a global outlook, and various communist, socialist, and liberalist societies looked beyond the nation for other ways of belonging and connecting. The anti-imperialist voices at the turn of the century and the antiwar declarations after the First World War were part of a vogue of cosmopolitan ideas, internationalist perspectives, and a search for a common ground on which humanity could build. The period saw the birth of numerous institutions and intellectual programs to create global understanding and peace: among them the Red Cross (1863), the first book on Esperanto as a universal language (1887), the League of Nations (1920), the International Broadcasting Union (1925), and the Geneva Conventions (1929).

Narrowing the scope to Great Britain, we see how such tendencies were thriving also in Woolf's closest environment, especially in the form of pacifism. Clive Bell wrote antiwar pamphlets in 1915, Bertrand Russell gave lectures on pacifism in 1916, and other people in Woolf's circle, such as Lady Ottoline Morrell, represented the pacifist stance. Leonard Woolf, on his part, was not a pacifist, but the war spurred his commitment to political work and international relations.[42] His political and social engagement contributed to the policy of the League of Nations. The cultural counterpart to this internationalist vogue in political life was *cosmopolitanism*, expressed as a growth in cultural networks promoting exchange between nations, a cosmopolitan outlook marking literature, the arts, and the media, and, not least, a cosmopolitan way of thinking about photographs.

Even if Woolf is firmly situated in a European tradition, her writings reflect the global outlook of the period and build up to the cosmopolitan engagement in "Three Guineas." In her first novel, Rachel's "voyage out" goes to a nonspecific place in Latin America and is all but successful. More independence is granted to Orlando, who voyages to Istanbul and returns to London transformed. Important is also Woolf's reference in "A Room of One's Own" (1929) to Aphra Behn, the notorious eighteenth-century female writer who wrote *Oroonoko* (1688), allegedly the autobiography of a slave. *Oroonoko* was one of the inspirations for Woolf's mock-biography *Orlando*, and Woolf discussed Aphra Behn with Vita Sackville-West, who wrote a book on this remarkable author (1927).[43] Further, as a citizen of the Commonwealth, Woolf

42. Leonard Woolf joined the Labour Party and the Fabian Society (a socialist society led by intellectuals), playing important roles in both, and he published a number of books on international politics, such as *International Government* (1916) and *The Framework of a Lasting Peace* (1917).
43. For a study of Woolf's relation to Vita Sackville-West generally and their discussion of Aphra Behn specifically, see Sproles, *Desiring Women*, 112.

was of course sensitive to the colonial heritage of Great Britain, and her great-aunt Julia Margaret Cameron had stayed in India for many years with her husband. Leonard Woolf's first novel, *The Village in the Jungle* (1913), was based on experience and critical of imperialism, as was E. M. Forster's *A Passage to India* (1924). Accordingly, we may situate Woolf in a literary context where global issues were discussed and reflected upon.[44]

Yet cosmopolitanism was not limited to the field of literature. All these internationalist and cosmopolitan ideas found resonance in a new visual language that allowed people to connect at a global scale: photography. It could indeed be argued that the processes of globalization were primed by the spread of this media technology. By many, photography was considered a world language, making communication possible in new ways; photographs could bridge the cultural and linguistic boundaries and connect people across traditional dividing lines. As photographed faces were spread worldwide, this helped create a global awareness and a sense of sharing one's human condition with people living in other countries. Arguably, this sense of belonging to a community and a shared humanity was less abstract than the one created through words. Beholding pictures of foreign faces, one could acknowledge that they, too, had at their disposal a rich repertoire of emotions and carried with them vast inner worlds. Photographs thus helped make foreign faces more familiar.

To understand how globalization processes, media, and emotions intersect, the perspectives of the German sociologist Ulrich Beck are helpful. In *Cosmopolitan Vision* (2007), he discusses globalization processes after the Second World War, highlighting the important role played by television. Watching televised images of people from other parts of the world, we develop empathy with strangers and feel that we live in a globalized community, and this again leads to the *globalization of emotions* and to *cosmopolitan empathy*, he asserts.[45] This line of reasoning also sheds light on the modernist period, where the dominating visual media were photography and film, not televised images. It allows us to see that the globalization of emotions and the development of cosmopolitan empathy were already starting to become a reality during this period, when photographs were

44. For a study of Woolf as a "world writer," see Caughie and Swanson, *Virginia Woolf: Writing the World*, a collection of essays that offers numerous perspectives on the topic.
45. Beck, *The Cosmopolitan Vision*, 7. It should be pointed out that Beck's interest lies not in vision as such but rather in the cosmopolitan outlook in a more general sense.

spread in newspapers, magazines, and photobooks. A "cosmopolitan vision" was created through the global spread of photographs, inciting the audience to feel empathy with strangers. [46]

In this perspective, Woolf's essay "Three Guineas" can be seen as an early reflection on media and globalization, the globalization of emotions, and cosmopolitan sympathy. Just like a number of other modernists, Woolf seems to have recognized photography as an emotional language capable of creating a form of understanding without words. In her essay on film, "The Cinema" (1926), she had already highlighted the connection between seeing and feeling, stressing the emotional impact of cinema, and in *Orlando* (1928), she had explored the emotional impact of photographs on the beholder.[47] In her essay on war from the critical year 1938, Woolf tried to come to terms with a new media situation in which photographs circulated worldwide, discussing how photographs can create sympathy and understanding. In this context, our capacity for feeling sympathy with others is presented as an alternative to strained forms of community. Denouncing the idea of nationhood, Woolf claims to be moved "not by forced fraternity, but by human sympathy" (TG, 233). Yet it is important to see this belief in human sympathy in the light of her acknowledgment of differences. To be sure, Woolf's take on sympathy is marked by her concern with "otherness," and her attention to faces as "outsides." In this perspective, feelings of sympathy would always be tantamount to "sympathy for strangers" and correspond to a cosmopolitan outlook.

In 1938, the same year as "Three Guineas" was published, Woolf contributed to a magazine's inquiry into cosmopolitanism, in which she expanded on her views on the topic. Responding to the question "What interests you most in this cosmopolitan world of today?",[48] she offered the following title: "America, WHICH I HAVE NEVER SEEN, interests me the most in this cosmopolitan world of today." In this playful piece of writing, Woolf sends the Imagination to America to see what it is like, and the Imagination reports back on its modern features such as traffic and speed, but also comments on the houses in which people live. She exclaims that "there is no privacy" and adds that there are "no dark family portraits hanging in shadowy recesses." She thus depicts a contrast to Woolf's England, which is

46. Cf. Benedict Anderson's notion of "imagined communities." Anderson, *Imagined Communities*.
47. Woolf, "The Cinema," 175.
48. *Hearst's International*, April 1938.

burdened by Victorian privacy and family portraits. Free from tradition, America is turned toward the future rather than the past, and this provides the ideal conditions for a democracy where everyone is equal. As the Imagination puts it: "From this extraordinary combination and collaboration of all cultures, of all civilizations will spring the future." The cosmopolitan idealism in the article is striking, although Woolf is cunningly speaking through the voice of the Imagination, which, she warns, "is not always strictly accurate."[49]

As we have seen, however, Victorian paintings loom large in Woolf's novels, full of British tradition and imposing personalities. Yet they appear to have receded into the background, to give way to a modern era dominated by new visual media and a new global outlook. Her characters contemplate photographs; photographs find their way into the experimental novel *Orlando*, and they play a key role in her outlook in "Three Guineas." We may thus see Woolf as testifying to a new media situation: Victorian family portraiture, reflecting character and identity, are replaced by pictures of strangers, whose name and situation one does not know.

At the same time, Woolf advocates a view of other people as "strangers," whose inner worlds are largely inaccessible, even if they are one's closest relations. More than Proust and Kafka, Woolf seems to acknowledge the face of the other as an outside. Yet, in her fiction, Woolf makes visible all that takes place on the micro-level of communication, without the use of words. As she lets her characters engage in faces and photographs, she shows all the emotions involved in the study of others, and she suggests that faces and photographs may foster feelings of sympathy. This view of photographs as capable of fostering "sympathy for strangers" can be seen in terms of a cosmopolitan outlook, open to new forms of community. Moreover, Woolf's work can be seen in light of the globalization processes in the modernist period, reconfiguring the relationship between the familiar and the foreign.

49. Woolf, "America."

Chapter 4

Conclusions: Living with Mediated Faces

In the decades before and after 1900, portrait photographs offered new ways of studying and perceiving the human face. As we have seen, Proust, Kafka, and Woolf all took an interest in the medium and depicted how their characters engaged in the reading of portrait photographs. Yet this literary attention to the medium should be correctly understood. When Proust, Kafka, and Woolf describe the cultural and affective practices surrounding portrait photographs, these scenes are not merely representations of a set of trivial media habits, subordinated to the respective novel's course of action. Rather, such scenes serve as fictive laboratories for the study of portrait photographs and their relation to the beholder. They could be described as modernist media labs, exploring the attraction of portrait photographs and the uncertain status of the mediated face. Even if such scenes are usually not in the foreground, they are of great significance. Reading them attentively, we see that Proust, Kafka, and Woolf took the impact of portrait photographs seriously and explored the ways in which such pictures work on the beholder.

When literary texts reflect on the media situation, this allows us to consider the media as part of a lived environment and to comprehend the emotional and relational implications of media change. As media theorist Friedrich Kittler states, modernist literature was highly sensitive to the new media technology:

> [I]n the founding age of technological media the terror of their novelty was so overwhelming that literature registered it more acutely than in today's alleged media pluralism [. . .] What writers astonished by gramophones, films, and typewriters – the first technological

media – committed to paper between 1880 and 1920 amounts, therefore, to a ghostly image of our present as future.[1]

The modernists testify both to the terror of the new media and to the love of those media, and above all to the "mediated life" of the modernists.[2] Indeed, literary texts are capable of capturing the complexity of media change. As we have seen, Proust, Kafka, and Woolf depict ambivalences and hesitation in the beholder as well as the variety of situations and contexts involving such pictures. To be sure, no single media theory could encompass this complexity. The three writers make visible an array of details and nuances and allow us to study that which is on the edge of semantic availability. They also depict the historical-material conditions of the media situation and reveal how media practices are liable to historical change. This literary attention to portrait photographs conveys a sense of what it was like to live with technical images and mediated faces early in the twentieth century.

So, what do Proust, Kafka, and Woolf teach us about the role of portrait photographs in their day? Above all, they depict the *emotional* and *relational* implications of such pictures. They stress the characters' affective investment in such pictures and the wide range of emotions elicited by them. They describe a longing for connectedness and ways of physically engaging with the photographs. Attempts at reading and interpreting the pictures are thus embedded in a variety of emotions and relational issues, and the hermeneutical activity often comes to a halt.

One could say that these writers offer *phenomenological* and *affective* approaches to photographs, while also offering *critical* reflection on the power of such pictures. Further, in Lacanian terms, we could say that the reading of photographs involves *the imaginary* (often associated with portrait photographs): the characters dream about the persons in the photographs and cherish the pictures as visual "doubles." Yet it also involves *the real* (as captured by the camera eye): The characters are concerned with the inassimilable nature of such photographs and seem to recognize how such pictures testify to an "external" world. What is more, these writers are sensitive to the *aesthetic quality* of portrait photographs and the way they can create visibility, discovery, and revelation. And, not least, they are

1.   Kittler, *Gramophone, Film, Typewriter*, xl.
2.   Cf. Goble, *Beautiful Circuits*.

attentive to the *materiality* of such photographs and how analog pictures invite physical interaction. This literary reflection on portrait photographs offers a variety of ways of thinking about the medium and captures ambivalent views and coexistent tendencies, as well as historical tensions.

In this concluding chapter, I summarize the main findings in the book's three chapters, while drawing a line from the modernist media culture to today's digital culture. I first discuss the key features characterizing the modernists' engagement with faces and portrait photographs. Next, I look at the boundaries between the private and the public, between identity and anonymity, and between the familiar and the foreign. Finally, I consider how we look at photographs today, suggesting that we may have something to learn from the analog era.

Modernist Faces

When film actress Gloria Swanson (a star in the days of silent film) portraying film actress Norma Desmond in Billy Wilder's *Sunset Boulevard* (1950) looks back at the days of silent film, she claims, "We had faces. There just aren't any faces like that anymore." This remark suggests an era that has passed; the time when expressive faces were essential to film. As the "talkies" took over (the first sound movie premiered in 1928), verbal communication made the expressivity of faces superfluous, or at least less essential. Yet the era of silent film that Swanson looks back upon is also the age of portrait photographs; this is the period in which portrait photographs starts to coexist with silent film and their expressive close-ups. Thus, during a short interval, two media coexisted that explored *silent faces* and their expression. Indeed, the prominent role of faces in portrait photographs and silent film in this specific period is important to understanding how modernist literature engaged with the motif of faces.

Acknowledging the modernists' profound concern with portrait photographs and mediated faces allows us to reconsider the dominant view of modernist literature as preoccupied mainly with the face as a mask and the face as marked by a blasé attitude.[3] Undoubtedly, the mask and the blasé attitude are crucial in modernist literature, but the modernist ways of engaging with faces go beyond this well-worn

---

3. Cf. Simmel, "The Metropolis and Mental Life."

formula. When the modernists reflect on the "crisis of the face," this includes a probing of the problem of mediated faces and the array of emotions they elicit. The modernists understood that the medium of photography offered new ways of seeing the human face and of relating to others.

Moreover, the modernists' study of portrait photographs allows us to reconsider the question of the unreturned gaze, which has almost become a shorthand for alienation in modernist studies. To be sure, Proust, Kafka, and Woolf often describe the unreturned gaze in a photograph as disturbing, but it also allows the characters to reflect on the strangeness of the other. The unreturned gaze marks a threshold signaling both distance and proximity, creating hope and longing, on the one hand, and confusion and bewilderment, on the other. Thus, the unreturned gaze in a photograph is not just a source of distress; it can also be perceived as revealing someone's singular way of being. In a photograph, the beholder can contemplate the expressivity of a face. As it makes visible a gaze that reaches out into the world, the photograph exposes a self-relation and a way of appearing to others.

This view of photographs as creating new forms of visibility and insight is key to the modernist fascination with them. As I have shown, the engagement with portrait photographs in Proust, Kafka, and Woolf is often marked by a cautious belief in them as sites of revelation and communication. Photographs make visible inscrutable gazes, intimate gestures, and ways of being in the world. Insofar as they expose that which *appears* rather than that which *exists*, photographs could be understood in terms of a modal ontology.[4] Setting aside the question of essence, this philosophical outlook may help us move beyond the interiority/exteriority and the mind/body dichotomies. Thinking in terms of modalities allows us to acknowledge that there is always something in play in a portrait photograph—a play between presence and absence, showing and hiding, revelation and opacity.

Portrait photographs could even be seen as "visiting cards" from others, objects that invite reflection on the sitter's way of being. They serve as meditation objects, as relational tools, or as spaces of revelation, endlessly fascinating for the viewer. Through its silent gestures, a portrait photograph offers a way of sharing the life of thought and

---

4.   Cf. Agamben's writings on a modal ontology and Silverman's writings on photography in terms of revelation. See Agamben, *The Use of Bodies*; Silverman, *The Miracle of Analogy*.

emotion with others. Indeed, this visual language was crucial in a period marked by a suspicion of language and verbal communication. As Proust, Kafka, and Woolf dwell on scenes involving portrait photographs, they create an awareness about this form of communication. What may appear as "soft" and trivial media devices from today's perspective thus seem to have had a much greater impact.

However, what Proust, Kafka, and Woolf give us is not theories of photography, but literary ways of exploring the phenomenon. Using the technique of "showing seeing" in combination with close-ups and ekphrastic descriptions, they make visible the emotional and relational implications of photographic pictures. Yet this is also a way of exploring the epistemological foundations of the characters. While it is well known that the modernists experimented with voice to depict the subjective worlds of their characters (interior monologue and stream-of-consciousness) and used various techniques to depict their feelings of alienation (such as the topos of the face as a mask), we could single out yet another characteristic of their writings: They let their characters indulge in the study of photographs, highlighting the face as a threshold toward the other and the portrait photograph as a site where the self is put into play. The contemplation of portrait photographs thus invites reflection on the possibilities for contact and communication in the modernist age.

Emotion and Reflection

From today's perspective, the emotions connected to analog media practices may seem excessive and strange, even silly. We are used to handling various digital platforms on a daily basis without effort or emotional commitment. Yet the practices surrounding portrait photographs in the analog age may show us a different way of relating to pictures. Let us look at the key features that distinguish the ways the modernists' used this literary motif.

We have seen that Proust, Kafka, and Woolf describe *the attraction of portrait photographs*. They describe their characters as drawn to photographs, stressing the active quality of the picture and its strong tendency to work on the beholder. There is something in the picture that speaks to them, creating hope and enchantment on the one hand, and disappointment and distress on the other. This view of photographs as acting on the beholder speaks to their performative power. With W. J. T. Mitchell, we may speak about "the lives and loves of images," acknowledging that they have desires and drives of their own.[5] At the same time, we should acknowledge that the power of photographs is bound up with social energies that stem from the discursive networks surrounding them. When Proust, Kafka, and Woolf depict the relation between picture and beholder, they show that portrait photographs are not merely dull pastime devices or blank screens for projection of a person's fantasies; such pictures are active and create a variety of responses in the beholder.

A key issue in this regard is that portrait photographs, as described by Proust, Kafka, and Woolf, create *emotional ambivalence* in the beholder. As I have shown, the affective register involved is broad: On the one hand, we find quiet moments of contemplation marked by reflection, where photographs arouse joy, gratification, and feelings of connectedness. To some extent, this can be seen as an attempt to renegotiate Romantic aspirations on modernist terms; the beholder must here acknowledge the distance that separates us from others. On the other hand, we find moments where the emotions are more intense and border on *affect*. In this case, the act of looking at photographs seems to destabilize the beholder, pulling them out of their ordinary patterns of thought and behavior. However, almost all the scenes involving portrait photographs, both those characterized by quiet emotions and those involving more intense feelings, are marked by ambivalence, and many of them develop through several stages.

In many respects, the modernists' experiences with portrait photographs are a precursor to their more radical experiences with film. The moving image and the cinematic apparatus transform viewers' perceptions, their frames of mind, and their ways of situating themselves in the world. This is why film is often analyzed in terms of affect. A quick look at Deleuze's writings on the close-up in early film is helpful here: Deleuze outlines what he sees as the two poles of the close-up: In D. W. Griffith's films, the emotional faces of the characters unfold a drama that is integrated in the film's course of action. For Deleuze, this is the "reflexive face," whereas Sergei Eisenstein's close-ups work in a different manner. In his montages, the enlarged face is cut off from the narrative and becomes abstract, devoid of any signification. For Deleuze, this is the "intensive face", the face of pure intensity, pure affect.[6]

5. Mitchell, *What Do Pictures Want?*
6. Deleuze discusses the close-up as an "affection-image," occupying the interval between a troubling perception and a hesitant action. See Deleuze, *Cinema 1: The Movement-Image*, 87–101.

We may see a parallel between the two poles of the film close-up and the two poles of portrait photographs in Proust, Kafka, and Woolf, or, more precisely, the two poles of their beholders' *responses* to portrait photographs. In Proust, Kafka, and Woolf, some scenes involve reflection and "soft" emotions (which can be viewed as responses to "reflexive faces"), whereas some scenes are marked by greater intensity and distraction, bordering on affect (responses to more "intensive faces"). Yet the visual premises are different. Portrait photographs can be seen as less radical than film close-ups; they typically show more conventional poses and less expressivity. They are still images inviting prolonged acts of contemplation. But even if portrait photographs can legitimately bear comparison with film close-ups, the disruptive effects of looking at portrait photographs should not be underestimated; the confrontation with the external gaze of the camera and the feeling of alienation thereby created may potentially undermine the foundation of the subject and change the beholders' mindsets and ways of situating themselves in the world.

Moreover, the effect created by portrait photographs seems to be related to their *paradoxical* way of operating: they both show and hide, reveal and conceal. Proust, Kafka, and Woolf show how this paradox plays out: On the one hand, such photographs capture visible poses, gestures, and ways of being in the world; on the other hand, they are marked by silences, secrets, and an extensive array of details. Portrait photographs allow the beholder to study the sitter's self-relation, a self that is in play, but at the same time, the sitter appears unknowable to the beholder. In Proust, Kafka, and Woolf, such photographs thus present themselves as enigmas to contemplate rather than objects that can be mastered or exploited as means to personal ends.

This is also why portrait photographs serve as *lessons in otherness*. Proust, Kafka, and Woolf show how such pictures create an increased awareness of the relation between self and other. Depicting how the beholder indulges in the study of portrait photographs, they demonstrate the impossibility of penetrating the mind of the person in the photograph. The characters are thus left with a set of contingent and vulnerable relations, without the possibility of full transcendence. This can be understood as a learning process in which the characters start to relate to other human beings as "outsides." Rather than seeing the other as merely putting on a "mask" or as a "projection" of their own fantasies, they start to appreciate the strangeness of the other. Through such scenes, the modernists convey a profound insight into the epistemological conditions that characterize modern life.

Yet the modernist period spans many decades, and it would be wrong to assume that a single way of responding to photographs persisted for the entire period. Indeed, the ambivalence and hesitation that Proust, Kafka, and Woolf ascribe to their characters when viewing portrait photographs suggest that the response to such pictures was not static but dynamic and subject to change. We should recall that these three authors were writing at a specific time in history, after the early days of photography, but before the time when film started to dominate the visual scene. We can regard this as a transitional period during which several processes were at work simultaneously: We find attempts to renegotiate on modernist terms the Romantic aspiration to create transcendence and "correspondences" (as in "the gaze that is returned"); we find disruptive experiences with photographs that destabilize the beholder; and we find processes where the beholder starts to acquire *visual literacy* as they learn to accept a relation that is *close but distant*, and become acquainted with a level of intimacy that is *affective yet detached*. Such emotional and relational negotiations are depicted in detail in the writings of all three authors, suggesting that the status of photographs and mediated faces was still uncertain in their day.

However, even if a number of common features mark this engagement with photographs, there are, of course, important differences between these three writers, each of whom has their own signature. In this book, I have highlighted their singularity by using different frameworks for each chapter. Thus, I have argued that Proust addressed the question of truth, Kafka the question of power, and Woolf the question of sympathy. Yet a more general comparison allows us to notice some interesting tendencies.

Proust is more committed to a subjective viewpoint in contemplating photographs than Kafka or Woolf. Seeing truth as something that lies at a deeper level, he presupposes that it requires a process of subjective development. Yet Proust also recognizes the way in which a picture actively reveals something to the beholder; the facial gestures in a photograph may expose a person's way of being, and, more radically, the picture of a well-known person may prompt the beholder to see him or her as a stranger. It is with respect to this feature that *The Search* depicts a learning process: Marcel's confrontations with the gaze of the camera teach him the existence of different viewpoints, and he understands that his way of seeing the world differs from that of others. At the same time, there are indications that his fascination with portrait photographs begins to wane, although primarily, it would seem, in connection with commercial and "flat" photographs rather than exclusive and "deep" photographs.

Kafka is more concerned with the danger of being captivated by photographs, both as a beholder and as a sitter. He depicts responses to photographs that are even more violent and conflicted than those that Proust describes, and which seem to involve a greater degree of affect. Like Proust, he depicts a learning process in the beholder, but it is more explicitly related to the power of photographs. Kafka describes a nascent consciousness in the beholder, both in his account of the shift from absorption to detachment and when he inquires into the correct distance to pictures, and this seems to indicate that his characters are alert to the power of pictures. Yet the question of otherness seems to interest Kafka to a lesser degree, perhaps because the theme of subjectivity and otherness is played out in a different way in his writing. With respect to the pictures of Felice, he is ambivalent; he is tuned in on his own frustration, on the one hand, and shows concern for her situation and her way of appearing on the other. While he seems to acknowledge her as an enigma beyond his grasp, he does not offer explicit reflections on otherness.

Woolf depicts scenes of quiet contemplation and emotional unrest rather than scenes involving violent emotion. More than Proust and Kafka, she is interested in the ways in which the contemplation of photographs can entail confrontation with otherness, and contemplation in her case is marked by a respectful distance. Woolf seeks to transcend simplistic notions of identity in photographs and explores what it is that evokes feelings of sympathy. She depicts her characters undergoing a learning process in this respect; they learn to live with otherness and develop feelings of sympathy for "strangers." However, in relation to war photographs, the emotions Woolf describes are violent, and her position is no longer that of respectful distance; in this case, she is not discussing portrait photographs as vehicles for soft sympathy but rather raw war photographs as visual evidence that elicit horror in every beholder. Yet here, too, her overall concern is the possibility for sympathy with strangers at a time when the relation between the strange and the familiar is being reconfigured.

Comparing the three writers, we also see that Proust and Kafka stand out as male authors whose ways of writing about women can be analyzed in terms of the "male gaze": They depict a male desire for photographs of women and a tendency to objectify the women in the pictures. Applying this conceptual framework, we notice some differences between the two writers: Proust's narrator seems more assured in his belief in the prevalence of the subjective gaze and voluntarily engages his imagination when indulging in the pictures, whereas Kafka appears more naïve as he describes his desire and the way he sees Felice. Yet, as I have shown, there is much more going on with respect to Proust's and Kafka's preoccupation with photographs of women, and we should be careful not to allow the notion of the "male gaze" to reduce this complexity. Both Marcel, as he looks at pictures of Albertine, and Kafka, as he looks at pictures of Felice, perceive the respective women as enigmas they cannot grasp, and the study of these pictures leads to frustration just as much as satisfaction. In this manner, the contemplative act leads to reflection on the woman's strangeness as well as reflection on the nature of photographic pictures. Indeed, the combination of emotion and reflection is key to all three writers. They show us a situation in which the beholder strives to find the right distance to such pictures, balancing immersion and detachment, love and critique, fetishism and iconoclasm.

The Private and the Public

As we try to construct the bigger picture, it is important to acknowledge that the motif of studying portrait photographs is a device not merely for speaking about private emotions, but also one that discloses something important about emotions and affects on a societal level. This aspect is more difficult to grasp; it concerns the ways in which emotions and affects are structured and distributed according to certain boundaries that are defined socially and historically. In this book, I have argued that such boundaries were rearranged with the increased circulation of photographs. Whereas Proust saw how the boundaries between the private and the public spheres started to dissolve as photographs became more widespread, for Kafka portrait photographs bolstered the creation of both identity and anonymity. Woolf, for her part, observed how portrait photographs started to circulate in a global world, making the foreign more familiar and extending one's sense of community with others. These processes are obviously interrelated, and we could, in fact, speak of three ways of conceptualizing a threshold between self and others; of regulating one's interaction with others, one's way of appearing to others, and one's sense of commitment to others.

When established societal boundaries are reconfigured, they are revealed to be malleable and subject to historical change, and it is only at that point that we can truly recognize them. Thus, what becomes discernable through the reading of Proust, Kafka, and Woolf is that the boundaries in question were largely a set of bourgeois constructions that came under pressure through the encounter with a new media regime. Whereas the bourgeois era was based largely on written communication, the spread of photography and film created a new media situation, changing the relations between the private and the public, between identity and anonymity, and between the individual and the global. This paradigm shift started with the advent of the daguerreotype in 1839 and came to full completion after 1900, with the spread of cinema and the illustrated press. This caused a series of profound but subtle transformation processes that we have only started to come to terms with today. Although we may believe that the modernist era has passed, and that the digital era has restructured the premises for our lives, technical images and mediated faces are still central to our everyday practices. Looking back at the heyday of modernism, when these phenomena were keenly noticed and reflected upon, may help us understand some of these processes in our own day and age.

Let us first consider the relation between the private and public. If the boundaries between these realms were reconfigured in the modernist period, where are we today? I suggest that we can draw a line of continuity from Proust's skepticism about the social world and of the illustrated press to today's critique of Facebook and other social media. In today's media culture, people are constantly publishing pictures of themselves and their close contacts—on a variety of platforms. What used to be private seems to have leaked into the public sphere to such a degree that the very notion of "privacy" can seem outmoded. To discuss "privacy" today, it is helpful to consider the phenomenon against the backdrop of historical developments such as the history of portrait photography and the mediated face.

As we have seen, Proust seems to distinguish between public and private pictures, seeing the former as dull and masklike and the latter as possible sites where truth is revealed. Indeed, this divide resembles Benjamin's analysis of photographs a decade or two later, where he points out the difference between early portrait photographs emanating an "aura" (pre-1860 or so) and "industrial" portrait photographs, in which the sitters had learned to pose. But where Benjamin speaks of an "aura" and a photographic "industry," Proust speaks of truth and beauty and the illustrated press. Further, whereas Benjamin's "little history" is based on the technological availability of "auratic" and "industrial" photographs, Proust based his fictive history on the uses of portrait photography in everyday life—thereby pushing the clash between the two forms into the twentieth century. Thus, Proust's position on photography is rather complex. He was critical toward the "industrialization" of photographs in the illustrated press which led to a proliferation of mediated faces in public. For him, the world of society was a place for pretense. Nevertheless, he remained fascinated with photographs that possessed a certain exclusivity, pictures that seemed to give the beholder a privileged view and access to truth. Indeed, it could be argued that Proust was not opposed to the technological media as such, but rather critical toward a new regime of photographs specializing in the public display of faces *without truth.*

Yet Proust witnessed only the beginnings of a large-scale development. Whereas he observed private faces being rendered visible in the press, we have experienced the "explosion of the private into the public" on the World Wide Web and on platforms such as Facebook and Instagram. The intimate sphere that was once kept behind closed doors and restricted to one's family and close circle—in the *bourgeois home*—is now increasingly exhibited in the public through various media. Some embrace this as an opportunity to share or expose their "identities," "lifestyles," and preferences in more or less candid ways, using images to express who they want to be and how they feel, in an endless performative game. Others look for greater privacy, shying away from social media, with its proliferation of private images and its vast, largely anonymous audience. Obviously, these boundaries are negotiated and managed in different ways by different people, but the problem is that ever more frequently they are handled for us by addictive media platforms and complex algorithms. The processes at work are boxed, and we are left with no choice and no consciousness of alternatives. In this situation, the old idea of "private life" may seem almost irrelevant.

We may therefore need a new way of thinking of "private life," in order to fathom what it is all about. We should recall that private life is not merely about bourgeois discretion, social exclusivity, or legal rights. It comprises not merely our biological life, that is, nutrition, health, reproduction, sleep. Private life also includes our thoughts and emotions. It comprises that which borders on language; the threshold of speech. In my view, Proust's novel offers profound insight into the nature of this essential but evasive domain of life. In *The Search*, the life of thought and emotion is associated with intimacy and affection, and with silence and secrecy. Yet, in our day, the danger is that this zone in which imagination, thoughts, and emotions unfold is reduced to an exhibition gallery marked by the ideology of capitalist media.

The risk is that this space of appearing is reduced to a space for performance and branding.

Yet, in the modernist period, portrait photographs still represented a way of sharing the life of thought and emotion. What we lost with the passing of the analog age is this sense of photographs as sites of revelation in everyday life, allowing us to study a face that is intimate, yet distant; a gaze that reaches out, without quite meeting our own. A way of appearing, of showing and hiding; an enigma to contemplate. Instead, we have welcomed a constant flow of superficial pictures, immaterial and hard to relate to both physically and emotionally. True portrait photographs may still be possible, but in the supermarket of images, they are hard to find and not easy to engage with.

Identity and Anonymity

With respect to the relation between identity and anonymity, Kafka's writings may seem to be prophetic. It is hardly controversial to see a line of continuity between his exploration of this topic and today's debates on disciplinary processes, surveillance, and biopolitics. Indeed, the work of Foucault, Deleuze, and Agamben have offered theoretical tools to address the power issues that are at stake in Kafka's fiction. In ingenious ways, Kafka depicts how semi-invisible powers operate and require everyone to assume an identity. In this power game, the circulation of photographs plays an important role; depending on the genre, they ascribe someone an identity (in a portrait photograph or an identity photograph) or assign them anonymity (in a lynching photograph or a newspaper picture). In this situation, showing and hiding, surfacing and disappearing, are issues that are not primarily existential so much as deeply political; in this situation, a photograph can become a matter of freedom and violence, of life and death.

For us today, such photographs are increasingly associated with personal exposure on various media platforms. Today's digital media, such as Facebook and Instagram, have reinforced the identity game that started with the advent of portrait photography.[7] Moreover, surveillance capitalism—turning personal data into a commodity—pushes us toward sharing more and more personal data online.[8] At

---

7.   For a discussion of how selfies and blogs are used to shape identity, see Walker, *Seeing Ourselves through Technology*.
8.   The concept of surveillance capitalism refers to the commodification of personal data in the age of Google and Facebook. See Zuboff, *The Age of Surveillance Capitalism*.

the same time, governmental control of our identities has increased in recent decades, through various surveillance tools, and we are now used to biopolitical measures, such as requirements to submit identity photographs, fingerprints, and retina scans, and we usually accept that our bodies are made available for governmental identification. However, new "face technologies" are emerging today that make these issues even more urgent. Nowadays, facial recognition technology allows a face that would otherwise be anonymous in public to be matched against a submitted data set and thus identified without our knowing it. In countries with full democracy, the access to such data is restricted by law (albeit not in flawless ways), whereas other countries, such as China, use such data without democratic control. This means that our faces and bodies are politicized and our lives reduced to sets of data that are targeted and exploited.

In this light, anonymity seems to be an ambiguous condition, both attractive and suspect; both a privilege and a vulnerability. On the one hand, anonymity is conducive to private life and freedom in today's media society, beyond identity politics and surveillance capitalism. On the other hand, an anonymous person is more at risk; whereas facial identity and citizenship grant a person rights, a truly anonymous person is in danger of being treated as a nonhuman or even as nonexistent.

If the processes depicted by Kafka have accelerated in today's surveillance regimes, what have we lost? Clearly, we have lost freedom and agency, but also emotional breadth in relation to photographs: the practice of looking for more than an "identity" in a photograph; the habit of responding to images without critical alertness or emotional defense. In a world where photographs can expose us in ways that leave us in a precarious position, we may have exchanged some of our love of images for a well-founded suspicion of them.

Yet Kafka shows us an alternative way of engaging with portrait photographs in his private letters: He shows how they are central to a love affair. The pictures of Felice are studied with affection and puzzled amazement, and at times with suspicion and despair. The photographs here convey something that goes beyond identity and is hard to pin down in language; a self-relation, a way of being, an attitude to the world. For Kafka, they are the portal to an enigma that he contemplates but cannot solve. Perhaps this is what we could describe as true anonymity; that which remains unspoken in a photograph, but which may still draw us in. To confront the power of photographs in today's media society, we may need to develop a new appreciation of this kind of anonymity, haunting every mediated face.

The Familiar and the Foreign

Woolf's perspectives on photography are also highly relevant in our own day. We can trace a line of continuity from her concern with sympathy, cosmopolitanism, and the sense of community to today's debates on cultural differences, the conditions of community (beyond the nation), and globalization. Today we are acutely aware of these topics; the deconstructionist paradigm has taught us to acknowledge otherness as the premise of every relation, and postcolonial studies have increased our awareness of how we relate to other cultures. In a world that has become increasingly "global," we have learned to live without the constant comfort of the familiar and to form a relationship to that which may appear foreign. Yet even if the processes of globalization have extended our horizons, the relation between the familiar and the foreign still plays a very significant role in our everyday lives; it is a dynamic relation, marking our ways of being in the world.

Woolf was a pioneer insofar as she broke out of the Victorian bubble that cultivated identity and familiarity and began to explore the foreignness of the other. As we have seen, her persistent interest in the relation between the familiar and the foreign appears to go hand in hand with her concern with photography. Woolf observed how family portraits often supported conventional notions of identity, while at the same time appearing to transcend the familiar. She also observed how portrait photographs started to circulate in a global world, training the beholder to acknowledge otherness. Taking issue with narrow conceptions of identity, she understood how photographs allow us to see the other as a complex being, enigmatic and unknowable, while still leaving us scope to develop feelings of sympathy for the person concerned. For Woolf, the insight that each person represents an enigma to others entailed an understanding of fellow beings as strangers and, vice versa, of strangers as fellow beings. In this context, portrait photographs could be seen as a testing ground for one's capacity to relate to others.

If photographs were a major force in the globalization processes of the modernist period, their impact only increased in the course of the twentieth century: The media propagated pictures of people who lived in faraway places and invited audiences to relate to them. Institutions working for peace and international collaboration used photographs to create feelings of global sympathy and responsibility. Without such pictures, the world and its community of fellow citizens would be hard to imagine and relate to, and one could argue

that the worldwide circulation of photographs played a role in form-
ing an imagined *global* community. Where print culture was instrumental in establishing an "imagined community" for the emerging
bourgeois class, photographs as a "world language" played a key
role in establishing the idea of a "global community" in the decades
before and after 1900.[9] Yet how should we conceive of such a global
community? Here we may take our cue from Woolf's notion of an
"Outsider's Society," which acknowledges each person's status as an
outsider. With this concept, she anticipated post-metaphysical notions
of community, as reflected in the writings of Blanchot, Nancy, and
Agamben; this notion of community is based on difference rather
than identity and sameness.[10] To be sure, Woolf's "Outsider's Society" is still inspiring in a hyper-globalized world.

If Woolf was ahead of her time in observing the potential of new
media to bolster global currents, today we have seen a global explosion of pictures. The danger is that the overload of such images no
longer contributes to an integrated world, but rather fosters a fragmented outlook where the sheer quantity of such pictures makes us
indifferent to others rather than more sensitive. This situation puts a
lot of pressure on the beholder. As Sontag warned us, we risk "regarding the pain of others" without sensitivity or understanding.[11] As
war photographs have become more commonplace, the impact of
looking at them must be discussed in a new context. In fact, one may
need to consider when to follow Woolf's imperative "Look!" and
when to look away.

Today, it seems that we have partly lost Woolf's firm belief in the
emotional appeal of photographs, as well as the critical cosmopolitanism underpinning her way of looking. Well aware that images are
manipulated and manipulating, we are inclined to be critical of them.
Yet, as Woolf reminds us, portrait photographs transcend simple
notions of identity and nationality; they prompt us to become aware
of the strangeness of the other. As a corollary, they may also bring
about feelings of sympathy. In a frantic visual culture, the association of photographs and sympathy may in fact be educational: It may
encourage us to select the pictures we look at more carefully, to study
them more attentively, and to appreciate how they negotiate between
the familiar and the foreign.

9. Anderson, *Imagined Communities*.
10. See Blanchot, *The Unavowable Community*; Nancy; *The Inoperative Commu-
    nity*; Agamben, *The Coming Community*.
11. Sontag, *Regarding the Pain of Others*.

The Return of the Analog?

Today's media landscape is dominated by facial technologies that go well beyond mere portrait photographs, and this makes an enormous difference. We live in a screen culture where platforms such as Facebook, Instagram, Zoom, and Snapchat allow for contact and communication on a global scale. Through these platforms, mediated faces have become an integrated part of our everyday lives to a degree that was unthinkable in the modernist period. How do we relate to mediated faces today?

Whereas Proust, Kafka, and Woolf could ponder a limited number of carefully selected photographs, the virtual images that inundate us today are, to a large degree, not selected by us, but rather by the algorithms of global media companies. We engage with visual "doubles" on a daily basis and we have grown used to "unreturned gazes" and disembodied faces. Our relation to technical pictures is less tactile and emotional than it was in the modernist period; one could say that we have perfected "close but distant" as a visual formula. In the twenty-first century, the mystery of mediated presence seems to have worn out; what was once an almost magical form of appearing that created a new form of connectedness has become a pragmatic form of communication, often dull and uninspiring. Habit and speed today triumph over aesthetic sensibility and the impulse to deep thought. We readily accept that mediated faces are flat, lacking the fleshy and vibrant three-dimensionality of "real life." In an advanced media society, real-life meetings may actually seem demanding, slow, and risky, since they cannot be edited and preclude the comfort of a delayed response. Immersed in our media habits, we are not always aware of how media affects our lives. Yet studying the modernists may help us comprehend some of the key processes at work in the history of the mediated face and allow us to consider our own media culture in light of the media culture around 1900.

In our day, the flow of digital images has changed the way we relate to photographs; the sheer quantity of images devalues them individually, making them less likely to receive attention and love than those in a small collection of analog photographs. At the same time, the constant access to media networks intensifies our relation to the media. It would be legitimate to ask whether our emotions have transferred from the physical picture to the media device, that is, the device we hold in our hands that connects us to a vast network. Our relation to the smartphone is the obvious example here; it is the tactile portal to a sense of being connected. As we know, this kind of emotional investment can create addiction, an insatiable thirst to be online. These emotions are at the heart of the attention economy, which, in turn, creates forms of attention that are fragmented and frantic rather than focused and prolonged.

In a world dominated by virtual images, our bodily relation to images changes. The joy of touching disappears, or it is transformed into a new notion of the "haptic" (which implies that we "touch" the digital media in a different way). To be sure, the kissing and caressing associated with analog photographs has become a thing of the past. Even if people may still kiss the pictures on their phones, the taste is different, as is their relationship to digital photographs generally. We also lose the sense of how photographs are marked by time, as objects of attention for successive generations of beholders that succumb to processes of fading and decay. Instead, we have become used to flawless and "timeless" pictures stored in an infinite archive that allows constant availability. This in turn affects our sense of time and history; a worn analog picture stores experience in a different way than a digital picture might do.

In this media situation, discussions on faces and photographs seem to be dominated by critical perspectives rather than affective perspectives. Deleuze and Guattari's critique of "faciality" as a norm has had a strong impact, as has Susan Sontag's critique of our ways of looking at photographs. To be sure, a critical consciousness is necessary in order to understand how images seduce and lie and are programmed to do so within capitalist media networks. Yet after many decades of critical approaches to images, some of us may in fact be better trained to criticize and resist images than to appreciate them and to fathom their attraction. Fatigue and critical alertness seem to be common responses to the image flow of today's visual culture.

However, there may also be a countertendency: a craving for materiality, for physical bodies, for emotion, and for community, as reflected in the "affective turn" in the humanities. As Alexander Galloway has argued, analog themes are very much on the agenda in the digital age.[12] In this climate, we see a renewed interest in analog media, including analog cameras, photographs, and developing procedures. I believe that this is more than just nostalgia; it can be seen as an effort to create different premises for the production and contemplation of images; an attitude that appreciates a slower pace, imperfections, and opportunities to devote attention to that which

12. See Galloway, "Golden Age of Analog."

is unique. We may ask if the keen interest in emotions, materiality, bodies, and community in our own day might be symptoms of a media situation that creates distance and an emotional void. Does the digital media situation push us to look for forms that compensate for our abstract and mediated relations to others; to finding ways of nurturing our emotional, relational, and communal needs? Are we seeing the return of the analog? Insofar as our bodies are still analog, this should come as no surprise. After a few decades of digital media, we may need to find a new balance between the analog and the digital.

To be sure, the analog era is not over, and the contemporary interest in affective and relational issues may help us reappreciate the ways in which the modernists engaged with portrait photographs. What we learn from the modernists is that they cultivated an emotional way of engaging with portrait photographs combined with a critical reflection on our ways of relating to others. The modernists show us that a portrait photograph can be a site of revelation and a place where the self is put into play. This way of looking at photographs is still available to us, even if the terms are different.

To appreciate this possibility, we may also look to the realms of contemporary art and literature, where a number of writers and artists work with portrait photographs, employing more or less explicit references back to earlier media practices. A visual artist such as Fiona Tan explores the genre of portrait photography with allusions to the photograph album and the photographic archive. Evoking specific historical and cultural contexts, she explores a plastic notion of identity and questions how we look at images today. A writer such as Annie Ernaux makes extensive use of portrait photographs in her novels. As her narrators study pictures of themselves at various ages, they reflect upon time, history, and identity, expressing feelings of estrangement as well as affection. In their respective ways, Tan and Ernaux testify to a longstanding fascination for portrait photographs and their potential to confront us with the enigma of the human face.

Bibliography

Agamben, Giorgio. *The Coming Community*. Translated by Michael Hardt. Minneapolis: University of Minnesota Press, 1993.
—. "The Face." In *Means without End: Notes on Politics*, 91–100. Translated by Vincenzo Binetti and Cesare Casarino. Minneapolis: Minnesota Press, 2000.
—. *Homo Sacer: Sovereign Power and Bare Life*. Translated by Daniel Heller-Roazen. Stanford: Stanford University Press, 1998.
—. "Judgment Day." In *Profanations*, 23–7. Translated by Jeff Fort. New York: Zone, 2010.
—. "Kommerell, or on Gesture." In *Potentialities: Collected Essays in Philosophy*, 77–85. Translated by Daniel Heller-Roazen. Stanford: Stanford University Press, 1999.
—. *The Use of Bodies*. Vol. IV, 2 of *Homo Sacer*. Translated by Adam Kotsko. Stanford: Stanford University Press, 2016.
Allen, James. *Without Sanctuary: Lynching Photographs in Amerika*. Santa Fe: Twin Palms Publishers, 2000.
Amad, Paula. *Counter-archive: Film, the Everyday, and Albert Kahn's Archives de la Planète*. New York: Columbia University Press, 2010.
Anderson, Amanda, Rita Felski, and Toril Moi. *Character: Three Inquiries in Literary Studies*. Chicago: Chicago University Press, 2019.
Anderson, Benedict. *Imagined Communities: Reflections on the Origins and Spread of Nationalism*. London: Verso, 1983.
Andriopoulos, Stefan. "The Terror of Reproduction: Early Cinema's Ghostly Doubles and the Right to One's Own Image." *New German Critique* 33, no. 3 (Fall 2006): 151–70. https://doi.org/10.1215/0094033X–2006–014
Anz, Thomas. "Kafka, der Krieg und das größte Theater der Welt." *Neue Rundschau* 107, no. 3 (1996): 131–43.
Apel, Dora. *Imagery of Lynching: Black Men, White Women, and the Mob*. New Brunswick: Rutgers University Press, 2004.
Apel, Dora, and Michele Smith Shawn. *Lynching Photographs*. Berkeley: University of California Press, 2007.
Arendt, Hannah. "Franz Kafka, Appreciated Anew." In *Reflections on Literature and Culture*, edited by Susannah Young-Ah Gottlieb, 94–109. Stanford: Stanford University Press, 2007.

—. "The Jew as Pariah: A Hidden Tradition." In *Reflections on Literature and Culture*, edited by Susannah Young-Ah Gottlieb, 69–90. Stanford: Stanford University Press, 2007.

Bal, Mieke. *The Mottled Screen: Reading Proust Visually*. Stanford: Stanford University Press, 1997.

Balázs, Béla. *Early Film Theory: Visible Man and The Spirit of Film*. Translated by Rodney Livingstone. New York: Berghahn Books, 2010

Barthes, Roland. *Camera Lucida: Reflections on Photography*. Translated by Richard Howard. New York: Hill & Wang, 1981.

—. "The Face of Garbo." In *Mythologies*, 56–7. Translated by Anette Lavers. New York: Hill & Wang, 1972.

—. "Proust and Photography." In *The Preparation of the Novel: Lecture Courses and Seminars at the Collège de France (1978–1979 and 1979–1980)*, 305–15. Translated by Kate Briggs. New York: Columbia University Press, 2011.

Bataillard, Aloys J. "Un personnage de Marcel Proust: La Comtesse Greffulhe," *Gazette de Lausanne*, August 30–1, 1952.

Batchen, Geoffrey. *Forget Me Not: Photography and Remembrance*. New York: Princeton Architectural Press, 2004.

Beck, Ulrich. *Cosmopolitan Vision*. Translated by Ciaran Cronin. Cambridge: Polity Press, 2006

Belting, Hans. *Face and Mask: A Double History*. Translated by Thomas S. Hansen and Abby J. Hansen. Princeton: Princeton University Press, 2017.

Benhaïm, André. *Panim: Visages de Proust*. Villeneuve d'Ascq: Presses universitaires de Septrion, 2006.

Benjamin, Walter. "Franz Kafka: On the Tenth Anniversary of His Death." In vol. 2.2 of *Selected Writings*, edited by Michael W. Jennings, Howard Eiland, and Gary Smith and translated by Rodney Livingstone et al., 794–818. Cambridge, MA: Belknap Press of Harvard University Press, 1999.

—. "Little History of Photography." In *The Work of Art in the Age of Its Technological Reproducibility, and Other Writings on Media*, edited by Michael W. Jennings, Brigid Doherty, and Thomas Y. Levin and translated by Edmund Jephcott, Rodney Livingstone, Howard Eiland, and others, 274–98. Cambridge, MA: Belknap Press of Harvard University Press, 2008.

—. "On Some Motifs in Baudelaire." In *The Writer of Modern Life: Essays on Charles Baudelaire*, edited by Michael W. Jennings and translated by Howard Eiland, Edmund Jephcott, Rodney Livingstone, and Harry Zohn, 170–210. Cambridge, MA: Harvard University Press, 2006.

—. "The Paris of the Second Empire in Baudelaire." In *The Writer of Modern Life: Essays on Charles Baudelaire*, edited by Michael W. Jennings and translated by Howard Eiland, Edmund Jephcott, Rodney Livingstone, and Harry Zohn, 46–133. Cambridge, MA: Harvard University Press, 2006.

—. "The Work of Art in the Age of Its Technological Reproducibility." In *The Work of Art in the Age of Its Technological Reproducibility, and Other Writings on Media*, edited by Michael W. Jennings, Brigid Doherty, and Thomas Y. Levin and translated by Edmund Jephcott, Rodney Livingstone, Howard Eiland, and others, 19–55. Cambridge, MA: Belknap Press of Harvard University Press, 2008.

Bergstein, Mary. *In Looking Back One Learns to See: Marcel Proust and Photography*. Amsterdam: Rodopi, 2014.

Bernard, Anne-Marie, ed. *Le Monde de Proust vu par Paul Nadar*, Éditions du patrimoine. Paris: Centre des monuments nationaux, 1999.

Bertillon, Alphonse. "Theoretical Study of Signalment." In *Picture Industry: A Provisional History of the Technical Image 1844–2018*, edited by Walead Beshty, 179–93. Zürich: Luma, 2018.

Bjorli, Trond, and Kjetil Ansgar Jakobsen, eds. *Cosmopolitics of the Camera: Albert Kahn's Archives of the Planet*. Bristol: Intellect Books, 2020.

Blackwood, Sarah. *The Portrait's Subject: Inventing Inner Life in the Nineteenth-century United States*. Chapel Hill: The University of North Carolina Press, 2019.

Blanchot, Maurice. *The Disavowed Community*. Translated by Philip Armstrong. New York: Fordham University Press, 2016.

Boltanski, Luc. *Distant Suffering: Morality, Media, and Politics*. Cambridge: Cambridge University Press, 1999.

Borchard, Gregory, and David W. Bulla. *Lincoln Mediated: The President and the Press through Nineteenth-century Media*. New York: Routledge, 2015.

Bourdieu, Pierre. *Photography: A Middle-brow Art*. Translated by Shaun Whiteside. Stanford: Stanford University Press, 1996.

Brassaï. *Marcel Proust sous l'emprise de la photographie*. Paris: Gallimard, 1997.

Cadava, Eduardo, and Paola Cortés-Rocca. "Notes on Love and Photography." *October* 116 (2006): 3–34. http://www.jstor.org/stable/40368422.

Cameron, Julia Margaret. *Victorian Photographs of Famous Men & Fair Women*. With introductions by Virginia Woolf and Roger Fry. London: Hogarth Press, 1926.

—. *Julia Margaret Cameron: By herself, Virginia Woolf and Roger Fry*. London: Pallas Athene, 2016

Carroll, Noël. "Béla Balázs: The Face of Cinema." *October* 148 (May 2014): 53–62. https://doi.org/10.1162/OCTO_a_00174.

Caughie, Pamela L., and Diana L. Swanson. *Virginia Woolf, Writing the World*. Clemson: Clemson University Press, 2015.

Caygill, Howard. "The Fate of the Pariah: Arendt and Kafka's 'Nature Theater of Oklahoma.'" *College Literature* 38, no. 1 (2011): 1–14.

—. "Kafka and the Missing Photograph." *photographies* 4, no. 1 (2011): 89–103. DOI: 10.1080/17540763.2011.552756

Crary, Jonathan. *Suspensions of Perception: Attention, Spectacle, and Modern Culture*. Cambridge, MA: MIT Press, 1999.

Dalgarno, Emily. *Virginia Woolf and the Visual World*. Cambridge: Cambridge University Press, 2001.

Danius, Sara. *Proust – Benjamin: Om fotografin*. Stockholm: Moderna museet / Axl Books, 2011.

—. *Prousts Motor*. Stockholm: Bonnier, 2000.

—. *The Senses of Modernism: Technology, Perception, and Aesthetics*. Ithaca: Cornell University Press, 2002.

Deleuze, Gilles. *Cinema 1: The Movement-Image*. Translated by Hugh Tomlinson and Barbara Habberjam. Minneapolis: University of Minnesota Press, 1986.

—. *Proust and Signs*. Translated by Richard Howe. London: Continuum, 2008.

Deleuze, Gilles and Félix Guattari. *Kafka: Toward a Minor Literature*. Translated by Dana Polan. Minneapolis: University of Minnesota Press, 1986.

—. *A Thousand Plateaus: Capitalism and Schizophrenia*. Translated by Brian Massumi. London: Continuum, 2004.

—. *What is Philosophy?* Translated by Hugh Tomlinson and Graham Burchell. New York: Columbia University Press, 1986.

Dell, Marion. *Virginia Woolf's Influential Forebears: Julia Margaret Cameron, Anny Thackeray Richie, and Julia Presep Stephen*. New York: Springer, 2015.

Delourme, Chantal. "Three Guineas: Virginia Woolf's Poetics of Community." *L'Atelier* 2, no. 2 (2010): 1–17.

Dickey, Colin. "Virginia Woolf and Photography." In *The Edinburgh Companion to Virginia Woolf and the Arts*, edited by Maggie Humm, 375–91. Edinburgh: Edinburgh University Press, 2010.

Döveling, Katrin, and Elly A. Konijn. *Routledge International Handbook of Emotions and Media*. London: Routledge, 2021

Duttlinger, Carolin. *Kafka and Photography*. Oxford: Oxford University Press, 2008.

—. "Snapshots of History: Franz Kafka's 'Blumfeld ein älterer Junggeselle' and the First World War." *Modern Austrian Literature* 39, no. 1 (2006): 29–43.

Edwards, Elizabeth. *Raw Histories: Photographs, Anthropology and Museums*. Oxford: Berg, 2001.

Ekman, Paul. *Emotions Revealed: Recognizing Faces and Feelings to Improve Communication and Emotional Life*. New York: Times Books, 2003.

Emery, Elizabeth. *Photojournalism and the Origins of the French Writer House Museum (1881–1914): Privacy, Publicity, and Personality*. Farnham and Burlington: Ashgate Press, 2012.

Engel, Manfred, and Bernd Auerochs, eds. *Kafka Handbuch: Leben—Werk—Wirkung*. Stuttgart: Metzler, 2010.

Epstein, Jean. "On Certain Characteristics of *Photogénie*." In *French Film Theory and Criticism: A History/Anthology, 1907–1939, Volume 1:*

1907–1929, edited by Richard Abel, 314–18. Princeton: Princeton University Press, 1988.

Finn, Jonathan. *Capturing the Criminal Image: From Mug Shot to Surveillance Society*. Minneapolis: University of Minnesota Press, 2009.

Flusser, Vilém. *Into Immaterial Culture*. Translated by Rodrigo Maltez Novaes. Metaflux, 2015.

Freeland, Cynthia A. *Portraits and Persons: A Philosophical Inquiry*. Oxford: Oxford University Press, 2010.

Freund, Gisèle. *Photography and Society*. Boston, MA: David R. Godine, 1980.

Fried, Michael. *Absorption and Theatricality: Painting and Beholder in the Age of Diderot*. Chicago: University of Chicago Press, 1988.

Froula, Christine. "Out of the Chrysalis: Feminine Initiation and Female Authority in Virginia Woolf's *The Voyage Out*." *Tulsa Studies in Women's Literature* 5, no. 1 (1986): 63–90.

Galloway, Alexander R. "Golden Age of Analog." *Critical Inquiry* 48, no. 2 (Winter 2022): https://doi.org/10.1086/717324

Gillespie, Diane F. "'Her Kodak Pointed at His Head': Virginia Woolf and Photography." In *The Multiple Muses of Virginia Woolf*, edited by Diane F. Gillespie, 113–47. Columbia: University of Missouri Press, 1993.

Gillespie, Diane F., ed. *The Multiple Muses of Virginia Woolf*. Columbia: University of Missouri Press, 1993.

Goble, Mark. *Beautiful Circuits: Modernism and the Mediated Life*. New York: Columbia University Press, 2010.

Goebel, Rolf J. "Kafka and Postcolonial Critique: *Der Verschollene*, 'In der Strafkolonie,' 'Beim Bau der chinesischen Mauer.'" In *A Companion to the Works of Franz Kafka*, edited by James Rolleston, 187–212. Rochester: Camden House, 2003.

Goffman, Erving. "On Face-Work." *Psychiatry* 18, no. 3 (August 1, 1955): 213–31. https://doi.org/10.1080/00332747.1955.11023008.

Gray, Richard T. *About Face: German Physiognomic Thought from Lavater to Auschwitz*. Detroit: Wayne State University Press, 2004.

Greiner, Rae. "Thinking of Me Thinking of You: Sympathy Versus Empathy in the Realist Novel." *Victorian Studies* 53, no. 3 (2011): 417–26.

Grøtta, Marit. *Baudelaire's Media Aesthetics: The Gaze of the* Flâneur *and 19th-century Media*. New York: Bloomsbury, 2015.

—. "At the Door of the Theater: Kafka's Oklahama Theater and the Nature Theater Movement." *New German Critique* 48, no. 1 (2021): 103–23. DOI: https://doi.org/10.1215/0094033X–8809371

—. "Fotografi og følelser: Om Proust, portrettfotografier og lengselen etter å nå utover seg selv." *Agora: Journal for metafysisk spekulasjon* 34, no. 1 (2016):118–47.

—. "Showing Seeing: The Study of Faces and Portrait Photographs in Virginia Woolf's Early Novels." *Journal of Modern Literature* 45, no. 3 (2022): 3–20. muse.jhu.edu/article/860641.

Guerlac, Suzanne. *Proust, Photography, and the Time of Life: Ravaisson, Bergson, and Simmel*. London: Bloomsbury, 2021.

Gunning, Tom. "In Your Face: Physiognomy, Photography, and the Gnostic Mission of Early Film." *Modernism/Modernity* 4, no. 1 (January 1, 1997): 1–29. https://doi.org/10.1353/mod.1997.0003.

Hamilton, Peter, and Roger Hargreaves. *The Beautiful and the Damned: The Creation of Identity in Nineteenth-century Photography*. Aldershot, Hampshire: Lund Humphries, 2001.

Haustein, Katja. *Regarding Lost Time: Photography, Identity, and Affect in Proust, Benjamin, and Barthes*. London: Legenda, 2012.

Hegel, Georg Wilhelm Friedrich. *Aesthetics: Lectures on Fine Art : Vol. 2*. Translated by T. M. Knox. Oxford: Clarendon Press, 1998.

Heimböckel, Dieter. "'Amerika im Kopf': Franz Kafkas Roman *Der Verschollene* und der Amerika-Diskurs seiner Zeit." *Deutsche Vierteljahrsschrift für Literaturwissenschaft und Geistgeschichte* 77, no. 1 (2003): 130–47.

Hillis-Miller, J. *The Conflagration of Community: Fiction Before and After Auschwitz*. Chicago: University of Chicago Press, 2011.

Hirsch, Elizabeth. "Virginia Woolf and Portraiture." In *The Edinburgh Companion to Virginia Woolf and the Arts*, edited by Maggie Humm, 160–77. Edinburgh: Edinburgh University Press, 2010.

Hirsch, Marianne. *Family Frames: Photography, Narrative, and Postmemory*. Cambridge, MA: Harvard University Press, 1997.

Hitchmough, Wendy. *The Bloomsbury Look*. New Haven: Yale University Press, 2020.

Holitscher, Arthur. *Amerika heute und morgen*. Berlin: S. Fischer Verlag, 1912.

Hornby, Louise. *Still Modernism: Photography, Literature, Film*. Oxford: Oxford University Press, 2017

Humm, Maggie, ed. *The Edinburgh Companion to Virginia Woolf and the Arts*. Edinburgh University Press, 2010.

Humm, Maggie. *Modernist Women and Visual Cultures: Virginia Woolf, Vanessa Bell, Photography, and Cinema*. Rutgers University Press, 2003.

Kafka, Franz. "Blumfeld, ein älterer Junggeselle." Published online by Project Gutenberg. https://www.projekt–gutenberg.org/kafka/blumfeld/blumfeld.html.

—. "Blumfeld, the Bachelor." Translated by Willa and Edwin Muir. In *The Complete Stories*. New York: Schocken Books, 1971. Published online by Vanderbilt.edu. https://www.vanderbilt.edu/olli/class–materials/Franz_Kafka.pdf

—. *Briefe an Felice Bauer*, edited by Hans-Gerd Koch. Frankfurt am Main: Fischer, 2015.

—. *Letters to Felice*, edited by Erich Heller and Jürgen Born, translated by James Stern and Elisabeth Duckworth. New York: Schocken Books, 2016.

—. *The Man Who Disappeared*. Translated by Ritchie Robertson. Oxford: Oxford University Press. 2012.

—. *Der Process*. Berlin: Fischer, 2011.

—. *The Trial*. Translated by Mike Mitchell. Oxford: Oxford University Press, 2009.

—. *Der Verschollene*. Frankfurt am Main: Fischer Taschenbuch, 2008.

Kittler, Friedrich A. *Gramophone, Film, Typewriter*. Translated by Geoffrey Winthrop–Young and Michael Wutz. Stanford University Press, 1999.

Koppen, Randi. "Re-thinking the 'Performative Turn': Fashioned Bodies, Sartorial Semiotics and the Performance of Culture 1900–1930." In *Exploring Textual Action*, edited by Lars Sætre, Patrizia Lombardo, and Anders M. Gullestad. Aarhus: Aarhus University Press, 2010.

Kracauer, Sigfried. *Theory of Film: The Redemption of Physical Reality*. Princeton: Princeton University Press, 1997.

Langford, Martha. *Suspended Conversations: The Afterlife of Memory in Photographic Albums*. Montreal: McGill-Queen's University Press, 2001.

Larkin, Áine. *Proust Writing Photography: Fixing the Fugitive in* À la recherche du temps perdu. London: Legenda, 2011.

Lavater, Johann Caspar. *Essays on Physiognomy*. Translated by Thomas Holcroft. London: B. Blake, 1840.

Lee, Hermione. *Virginia Woolf*. London: Vintage Books, 1997.

Lerski, Helmar. *Köpfe des Alltags*. Berlin: Verlag Hermann Reckendorf, 1931.

Levinas, Emmanuel. *Totality and Infinity: An Essay on Exteriority*. Translated by Alphonso Lingis. Dordrecht: Kluwer Academic Publishers, 1991.

Lichtwark, Alfred. "Einleitung." In Fritz Matthies-Massuren, *Künstlerische Photographie: Entwicklung und Einfluss in Deutschland*, 8–18. Berlin: Marrquardt, 1907.

Lowry, Richard S. *The Photographer and the President: Abraham Lincoln, Alexander Gardner, and the Images That Made a Presidency*. New York: Rizzoli Ex Libris, 2015.

Marcus, Jane. "Introduction." In Virginia Woolf, *Three Guineas: A Biography*, xxxv–lxxii. New York: Hartcourt, 2006.

Marcus, Laura. *The Tenth Muse: Writing about Cinema in the Modernist Period*. Oxford University Press, 2007.

Marcus, Sharon. *The Drama of Celebrity*. Princeton, NJ: Princeton University Press, 2020.

Marien, Mary Warner. *Photography: A Cultural History*. Boston, MA: Pearson, 2015.

Martin, Kirsty. *Modernism and the Rhythms of Sympathy: Vernon Lee, Virginia Woolf, D. H. Lawrence*. Oxford: Oxford University Press, 2013.

Massumi, Brian. *Parables for the Virtual: Movement, Affect, Sensation*. Durham, NC: Duke University Press, 2002

Mathieu, Patrick. *Proust, une question de vision: Pulsion scopique, photographie et représentations littéraires*. Paris: L'Harmattan, 2009.

Mitchell, W. J. T. *Picture Theory: Essays on Verbal and Visual Representation*. Chicago: University of Chicago Press, 1995.

—. "Showing Seeing: A Critique of Visual Culture." *Journal of Visual Culture* 1, no. 2 (August 2002): 165–81. https://doi.org/10.1177/1470412 90200100202

Moholy-Nagy, László. *Malerei, Fotografie, Film*. Munich: Albert Langen Verlag, 1925.

Mulvey, Laura. "Visual Pleasure and Narrative Cinema." *Screen* 16, no. 3 (Autumn 1975): 6–18. https://doi.org/10.1093/screen/16.3.6

Nancy, Jean-Luc. *The Inoperative Community*. Translated by Peter Connor, Lisa Garbus, Michael Holland, and Simona Sawhney. Minneapolis: University of Minnesota Press, 1991.

—. *Portrait*. Translated by Sarah Clift and Simon Sparks. New York: Fordham University Press, 2018.

Ngai, Sianne. *Ugly Feelings*. Cambridge, MA: Harvard University Press, 2005.

Pawlikowska, Kamila. *Anti-Portraits: Poetics of the Face in Modern English, Polish and Russian Literature (1835–1965)*. Leiden: Brill, 2015.

Pearl, Sharrona. *About Faces: Physiognomy in Nineteenth-century Britain*. Cambridge, MA: Harvard University Press, 2010.

Peters, John Durham. *Speaking into the Air: A History of the Idea of Communication*. Chicago: University of Chicago Press, 1999.

Prendergast, Christopher. *Paris and the Nineteenth Century*. Oxford: Blackwell, 1995.

Prodger, Phillip. "Photography and the Expression of the Emotions." In Charles Darwin, *The Expression of the Emotions in Man and Animals*, edited by Paul Ekman. London: HarperCollins, 1998.

Proust, Marcel. *Against Sainte-Beuve and Other Essays*. Translated by John Sturrock. London: Penguin, 1988.

—. *À la recherche du temps perdu* I–IV, edited by Jean-Yves Tadié. Paris: Gallimard (Bibliothèque de la Pléiade), 1987–89.

—. *Contre Sainte-Beuve*, edited by Pierre Clarac. Paris: Gallimard (Bibliothèque de la Pléiade), 1971.

—. "John Ruskin." In *Écrits sur l'art*, edited by Jérôme Picon, 116–30. Paris: Flammarion, 1999.

—. *In Search of Lost Time 1–5*, edited by William C. Carter. Translated by C. K. Scott Moncrieff and William Carter. New Haven: Yale University Press, 2013–23.

—. *In Search of Lost Time 5–6*. Translated by C. K. Scott Moncrieff and Terence Kilmartin and revised by D. J. Enright. London: Vintage Books, 1992.

Rabaté, Jean-Michel. *The Pathos of Distance: Affects of the Moderns*. New York: Bloomsbury, 2016.

Raiford, Leigh. "The Consumption of Lynching Images." In *Only Skin Deep: Changing Visions of the American Self*, edited by Coco Fusco and Brian Wallis. New York: International Center of Photography, 2003.

Raitt, Suzanne. "Virginia Woolf's Early Novels: Finding a Voice." In *Cambridge Companion to Virginia Woolf*, edited by Susan Sellers, 29–48. Cambridge University Press, 2010.

Rancière, Jacques. "The Intolerable Image." In *The Emancipated Spectator*, 83–106. Translated by Gregory Elliott. London: Verso, 2011.

—. "Mechanical Arts and the Promotion of the Anonymous." In *The Politics of Aesthetics: The Distribution of the Sensible*, 31–4. Translated by Gabriel Rockhill. London: Continuum, 2004.

Rossetti, Dante Gabriel. "Stillborn Love." In *The House of Life*. Woodbridge: D. S. Brewer, 2007.

Rugg, Linda. *Picturing Ourselves: Photography and Autobiography*. Chicago: University of Chicago Press, 1997.

Sandbye, Mette. "Looking at the Family Photo Album." *Journal of Aesthetics and Culture* 6, no. 1 (2014): 1–17. DOI: 10.3402/jac.v6.25419

Sander, August. *Anlitz der Zeit: 60 Fotos deutscher Menschen*. Munich: Transmare Verlag, 1929.

—. "Lecture 5: Photography as a Universal Language." Translated by Anne Halley. *The Massachusetts Review* 19, no 4 (Winter 1978): 674–9.

Schillemeit, Jost. "Nachbemerkung." In Franz Kafka, *Der Verschollene*, 323–7. Frankfurt am Main: Fischer Taschenbuch, 2008.

Schneider, Gesa. *Das Andere schreiben: Kafkas Fotografische Poetik*. Würzburg: Königshausen & Neumann, 2008.

Sekula, Allan. "The Traffic in Photographs." *Art Journal* 41, no. 1 (1981): 15–25. https://doi.org/10.2307/776511.

Selboe, Tone. "Situations of Sympathy: Eroding Emotions and Everyday Life in the Realist Novel." *Landscapes of Realism: Rethinking Literary Realism in Contemporary Perspectives* 2, 151–67, edited by Svend Erik Larsen, Steen Bille Jørgensen, and Margaret R. Higonnet. Amsterdam: John Benjamins Publishing Company, 2022

Sentilles, Sarah. "The Photograph as Mystery: Theological Language and Ethical Looking in Roland Barthes's *Camera Lucida*." *The Journal of Religion* 90, no. 4, 2010: 507–29. https://www.journals.uchicago.edu/doi/abs/10.1086/654822?journalCode=jr

Silverman, Kaja. *The Miracle of Analogy, or, The History of Photography: Part 1*. Stanford: Stanford University Press, 2015.

Simmel, Georg. "The Metropolis and Mental Life." In *The Sociology of Georg Simmel*. Edited and translated by K. Wolff. New York: The Free Press, 1964.

Sirois-Trahan, Jean-Pierre. "Un spectre passa . . . Marcel Proust retrouvé." *Revue d'études proustiennes*, no. 4 (2016) 2, *Proust au temps du cinématographe: un écrivain face aux médias*, 19–30.

Sontag, Susan. *On Photography*. New York: Anchor Books, 1990.

—. *Regarding the Pain of Others*. London: Penguin Books, 2004.

Spalding, Frances. *Virginia Woolf: Art, Life and Vision*. London: National Portrait Gallery, 2014

Sproles, Karyn Z. *Desiring Women: The Partnership of Virginia Woolf and Vita Sackville-West*. Toronto: Toronto University Press, 2006.

Staveley, Alice. "Name that Face." *Virginia Woolf Miscellany* 51 (Spring 1998): 4–5.

Stach, Reiner. *Kafka: Die Jahre der Entscheidungen*. Frankfurt am Main: Fischer, 2014.

—. *Kafka: The Decisive Years*. Translated by Shelley Frisch. Orlando: Harcourt, 2005.

Steimatsky, Noa. *The Face on Film*. Oxford: Oxford University Press, 2017.

Stemmler, Joan K. "The Physiognomical Portraits of Johann Caspar Lavater." *The Art Bulletin* 75, no. 1 (1993): 151–68. https://doi.org/10.2307/3045936.

Stetler, Pepper. *Stop Reading! Look! Modern Vision and the Weimar Photographic Book*. Ann Arbor: University of Michigan Press, 2015.

Stierle, Karlheinz. *La Capitale des signes: Paris et son discours*. Paris: Édition de la Maison des sciences de l'homme, 2001.

Stoichita, Victor I. "Johann Caspar Lavater's 'Essays on Physiognomy' and the Hermeneutics of Shadow." *RES: Anthropology and Aesthetics*, no. 31 (1997): 128–38. http://www.jstor.org/stable/20166969.

Tadié, Jean-Yves. *Marcel Proust: Biographie I–II*. Paris : Gallimard, 1996.

—. *Marcel Proust: A Life*. Translated by Euan Cameron. New York: Viking, 2000.

Tausk, Petr. *A Short History of Press Photography*. Prague: International Organization of Journalists, 1988

Tennyson, Alfred. *Alfred Tennyson's Idylls of the King and Other Poems*. Illustrated by Julia Margaret Cameron. London, 1875.

Tytler, Graeme. *Physiognomy in the European Novel: Faces and Fortunes*. Princeton: Princeton University Press, 1982.

Walker, Jill. *Seeing Ourselves through Technology: How We Use Selfies, Blogs, and Wearable Devices to See and Shape Ourselves*. London: Palgrave Macmillan, 2014.

Williams, Raymond. "Structures of Feeling." In *Marxism and Literature*, 128–35. Oxford: Oxford University Press, 1977.

Wilson, Peter. "Leonard Woolf, the League of Nations, and the Peace between the Wars." *The Political Quarterly* 86, no. 4 (2015): 532–9.

Wirkner, Alfred. *Kafka und die Außenwelt: Quellenstudien zum "Amerika"-Fragment*. Stuttgart: Klett, 1976.

Wisor, Rebecca. "About Face: The 'Three Guineas' Photographs in Cultural Context." *Woolf Studies Annual* 21 (2015): 1–49.

Woolf, Virginia. "America, Which I Have Never Seen." In *The Essays of Virginia Woolf*, vol. 6, edited by Stuart N. Clarke, London: Chatto & Windus, 2011, 128–33.

—. "The Cinema." In *Selected Essays*, 172–6. Oxford: Oxford University Press, 2008.

—. "Modern Fiction." In *Selected Essays*, 6–12. Oxford World's Classics. Oxford: Oxford University Press, 2008.

—. *Mrs Dalloway*. London: Oxford University Press, 2000.

—. "The New Biography." In *Selected Essays*, 95–100. Oxford: Oxford University Press, 2008.

—. *Night and Day*. Oxford: Oxford University Press, 2009.

—. *Orlando: A Biography*. Oxford: Oxford University Press, 2008.

—. *Orlando: A Biography*. Edited by Suzanne Raitt and Ian Blyth. Cambridge: Cambridge University Press, 2018

—. "Three Guineas." In *A Room of One's Own & Three Guineas*, 115–365. London: Penguin Books, 2000.

—. *The Voyage Out*. Oxford: Oxford University Press, 2001.

Yacavone, Kathrin. "Barthes et Proust: La Recherche comme aventure photographique." *Fabula LHT*, no. 4 (2008). http://www.fabula.org/lht/4/yacavone.html

—. *Benjamin, Barthes and the Singularity of Photography*. New York: Continuum, 2012.

—. "Reading through Photography: Roland Barthes's Last Seminar 'Proust et la photographie.'" *French Forum* 34, no. 1 (2009): 97–112.

Zischler, Hanns. *Kafka Goes to the Movies*. Translated by Susan H. Gillespie. Chicago: University of Chicago Press, 2003.

Zuboff, Shoshana. *The Age of Surveillance Capitalism: The Fight for a Human Future at the New Frontier of Power*. New York: Public Affairs, 2019.